当代国外语言学与应用语言学文库（升级版）

二语语用学：理论与研究

Second Language Pragmatics: From Theory to Research

［英］Jonathan Culpeper

［美］Alison Mackey 著

［日］Naoko Taguchi

任伟 导读

外语教学与研究出版社
FOREIGN LANGUAGE TEACHING AND RESEARCH PRESS
北京 BEIJING

京权图字：01-2023-3184

图书在版编目（CIP）数据

二语语用学 ：理论与研究 = Second Language Pragmatics: From Theory to Research ：英文 ／（英）乔纳森·卡尔佩珀（Jonathan Culpeper），（美）艾莉森·麦基（Alison Mackey），（日）田口直子（Naoko Taguchi）著 ；任伟导读. -- 北京：外语教学与研究出版社，2023.8
（当代国外语言学与应用语言学文库 ：升级版）
ISBN 978-7-5213-4774-6

I. ①二… II. ①乔… ②艾… ③田… ④任… III. ①第二语言－语用学－研究－英文 IV. ①H003

中国国家版本馆 CIP 数据核字 (2023) 第 168377 号

出 版 人　王　芳
项目负责　姚　虹　李亚琦
责任编辑　都楠楠
责任校对　宋锦霞
装帧设计　李　高　颜　航
出版发行　外语教学与研究出版社
社　　址　北京市西三环北路 19 号（100089）
网　　址　https://www.fltrp.com
印　　刷　唐山市润丰印务有限公司
开　　本　650×980　1/16
印　　张　17.5
版　　次　2023 年 9 月第 1 版　2023 年 9 月第 1 次印刷
书　　号　ISBN 978-7-5213-4774-6
定　　价　43.00 元

如有图书采购需求，图书内容或印刷装订等问题，侵权、盗版书籍等线索，请拨打以下电话或关注官方服务号：
客服电话：400 898 7008
官方服务号：微信搜索并关注公众号"外研社官方服务号"
外研社购书网址：https://fltrp.tmall.com

物料号：347740001

记载人类文明
沟通世界文化
www.fltrp.com

当代国外语言学与应用语言学文库

（升级版）

学术委员会

（按姓氏拼音排列）

出版前言

"当代国外语言学与应用语言学文库"（以下简称"文库"）从2000年至今已出版近200个品种，深受语言学与应用语言学专业师生和研究者的欢迎，大家既把"文库"视为进入语言学与应用语言学百花园的引路人，又把"文库"视为知识更新的源泉，还把"文库"当成点亮科研之路的明灯。

为了追踪相关领域的研究进程，并满足广大读者的需求，外语教学与研究出版社从2020年开始启动了"文库"的更新升级工作，与牛津大学出版社、剑桥大学出版社、劳特利奇出版社等世界知名出版机构合作，推出"文库"（升级版）。

"文库"升级的原则如下：

1. 对原有经典图书，若无新版，则予以保留，并予以必要修订；若有新版，则以新版代替旧版，并请相关领域学者撰写新版中文导读。

2. 引进语言学与应用语言学领域的新锐力作，进一步拓展学科领域。

3. 用二维码代替CD-ROM，帮助读者更加快捷地获取内容。

"文库"（升级版）定位为一套大型的、开放性的系列丛书，希望它能对我国语言学教学与研究和外语教学与研究起到积极的推动作用。外语教学与研究出版社亦将继续努力，力争把国外最新、最具影响力的语言学与应用语言学著作奉献给广大读者。

外语教学与研究出版社

2021年8月

导　　读

任伟

　　《二语语用学：理论与研究》由三位不同领域的国际知名学者撰写：Jonathan Culpeper的研究兴趣为语用学，Alison Mackey的研究兴趣为二语研究方法，Naoko Taguchi的研究兴趣为二语语用。本书分为八章。除简介和结论两章外，主要分为三个部分，每个部分均按一章介绍理论、一章介绍数据收集方法的形式来编排。除正文外，每章均含有"重点记忆内容"和问题讨论；数据收集方法章节举例分析了相关的典型研究；第三章"二语语用产出中的数据收集方法"还列有后续活动；全书最后提供了术语词汇表，方便读者参考。以下为对本书主要内容的简要总结和讨论，如无特殊说明，所述内容和观点均出自本书，故不再一一给出引用来源。

1. 二语语用简介（第一章）

　　第一章首先在回顾Kasper & Schmidt（1996）以及Bardovi-Harlig（2010，2013）对二语语用界定的基础上，指出本书增加"学生如何理解意义，以及他们如何协商和共建意义"这一维度，认为理解、产出、互动对于二语语用同等重要。

语用学常被分为两个分支：社会语用学（sociopragmatics，强调语用的语境特征）和语言语用学（pragmalinguistics，强调语用的语言结构）（Leech，1983）。尽管二语语用的定义在发展，但是其基本研究内容没变，都是探究社会语境中二语学习者语言行为的本质。作者们用真实语料说明了语用学研究关注的是语境中使用交际资源所产生的意义，尤其是说话者隐含、听话者推断以及双方在互动中协商的意义。接着，本书介绍了二语语用关注的研究议题，包括交际能力、互动能力和跨文化语用，指出二语语用需要超越分析学习者在何种语境下使用何种语言形式的传统研究范式，应开展多方面的分析，包括学习者如何协商达成共识，如何使用不同资源和方法来展现语境适应能力等。

接着，本章回顾了二语语用发展历程，从时间上将二语语用研究分为四个阶段：20世纪80到90年代、20世纪90年代以后、21世纪以来，以及当今研究。

在第一阶段，二语语用主要采用跨语言对比研究，重点关注两个方面，即言语行为和礼貌。最具影响力的代表研究当属Blum-Kulka，House，& Kasper（1989）的跨文化言语行为对比研究项目（简称CCSARP）。该项目采用语篇补全任务（Discourse completion test，后来有些学者将其称作Discourse completion task，均简称DCT），对不同语言之间、学习者和母语者之间的请求和道歉言语行为进行了对比研究。CCSARP的研究方法和策略分析框架被后期研究广泛采纳。这一阶段的研究总体认为：语用能力很难准确定义，而衡量和对比不同二语学习者的语用能力则更加困难。

自20世纪90年代起，二语语用逐渐开始关注语用是否可以被教的问题；若可以被教，如何能够最好地评价语用能力？就语用教学而言，本章基于已开展的综述和元分析进行了归纳，包括Jeon & Kaya（2006）、Badjadi（2016）、Plonsky & Zhuang（2019）三篇元分析，以及Takahashi（2010）和Taguchi（2015）两篇系统性综述，总结了三个宏观趋势：1）教学效果因测试工具和语用目标而异；2）显性语用教学通常比隐性语用教学更有效；3）如果隐性教学既能使学生注意目标形式的作用，又能促进其进行深层次的加工，那么隐性语用教学可以和显性语用教学一样有效。以上综述和元分析都是基于2016年以前发表的成果，读者如对语用教学的新进展感兴趣，可以参见Ren，Li，& Lü（2022）的最新元分析成果。同时，在这一阶段，学者们开始呼吁要更多地采用长期跟踪研究的方法来研究语用发展，而不仅仅调查语用使用。这方面的代表当属Kasper & Schmidt（1996）和Kasper & Rose（2002）。在学者们的呼吁下，二语语用学自21世纪初以来涌现出一大批长期跟踪研究，研究方法也更加多样化。

21世纪以来，二语语用研究的一大特点是更加强调对二语习得理论的借鉴。本书很简要地介绍了五个理论：注意假说（Noticing hypothesis）、技能习得理论（Skill acquisition theory）、语言社会化理论（Language socialization theory）、动态系统理论（Dynamic system theory），以及互动理论（The interaction approach）。这些理论不仅可以帮助解释二语语用研究的实证发现，也可以更好地指导实验设计，建议读者们阅读相关文献。

当今研究部分强调了全球化、国际化和英语通用语对二语语用研究的影响。需要指出的是，目前有许多二语语用研究仅仅是在英语通用语框架下摒弃了用母语者语用作为标准来衡量学习者语用能力的做法，细致探究英语作为通用语交际中的语用策略的研究仍显不足，有兴趣的读者可以参见House（2013）、Ren（2018c）。

在本章的最后，作者们针对二语语用构念和研究方法、研究发展、个性化因素、语境因素等方面列出了近50条问题。这些问题非常具有启发性，值得读者们仔细阅读思考。大家不妨对照Kasper & Schmidt（1996）提出的14个问题，总结思考二语语用过去20多年的研究发展和今后值得继续探索的方向。

2. 语用产出（第二、三章）

第二章首先介绍了语用学主要探究语境中的意义构建。语用学经常被分为英美学派和欧洲大陆学派。英美学派将语用学视为语言学的分支，与语音学、句法学、语义学并列；欧洲大陆学派则将语用学看作语言研究的一个综观，研究语言学、社会学、心理学等各个层面。近些年来，学者们对这两个学派界限的处理越来越模糊，倾向于将这两个学派整合。Culpeper 和 Haugh 2014年出版的专著《语用学与英语》（*Pragmatics and the English Language*）就是一个例子。其实如果大家浏览一下语用学领域的期刊，比如*Journal of Pragmatics*，就可以看出这种融合的趋势。

前文讲到，Leech（1983）将语用研究分为语言语用和社会语用两个维度。语言语用是语用与句法的接口，关注语言现象的语用意义；社会语用是语用与社会学的接口，关注具体语境现象如何影响语用意义。二语语用主要探究语用能力，经常将语用能力按照这两个维度分为语言语用能力和社会语用能力。因此，尽管这两个维度有重合之处，但是理解这两个维度的内涵对二语语用研究十分重要。举例来说，如果你想请某人喝咖啡，你掌握了多少种语言形式来实现这一目的，即让对方知道你想请他喝咖啡，就属于你的语言语用能力。而你如何根据语境因素，包括你和对方的关系（比如，对方是你的老师还是你的朋友）、你们的熟悉程度、咖啡的价格、对方是否喜欢咖啡等等，选择当下最合适、有效的语言形式来实现你的交际意图，则属于你的社会语用能力。

言语行为是语用学的重要研究领域和支柱理论之一。本章在回顾言语行为理论的基础上指出，传统二语语用研究对言语行为的直接/间接分类与Searle（1979）的分类不同。二语语用对言语行为的研究大多遵循Blum-Kulka et al.（1989）在CCSARP项目中的分类和编码框架。Blum-Kulka & House（1989）曾解释说，在该框架中，间接性是对言外之意透明度的衡量。这不同于Searle（1979：31）对间接言语行为的定义："一个言外之意的实施间接地通过另一个言语行为的实施来实现。"本书指出，言外之意透明度很难操作，建议不如用语用显性度来表示。Culpeper & Haugh（2014：170）将语用显性度分为三个层面：言外之意的透明度、话语目标的透明度，以及语义内容的透明度。作者们举例分析了Blum-Kulka et al.（1989）

在CCSARP项目中的分析框架，并指出该框架存在的问题，包括：1）该框架适用于请求言语行为，对其他言语行为并不是很切合，例如拒绝。这个局限我在之前对拒绝言语行为的调查研究中深有体会（Ren，2013；任伟，2018）。2）某些策略分类的合理性，这也是很多二语语用学者都会对CCSARP的分类框架进行修正的原因（如，Economidou-Kogetsidis & Woodfield，2012）。

本章还介绍了礼貌研究，特别是Brown & Levinson（1987）的面子和礼貌理论。该框架中的三个语用变量，即社交距离、相对权势、干预程度，经常被用于设计场景，考查学生的社会语用能力。但其他语用变量并不在该理论框架中，例如权力和义务、第三方参与、正式程度、模态等。

第三章"二语语用产出中的数据收集方法"首先介绍了研究伦理。研究者需要得到参与者签署的知情同意书，需要通过所在高校或研究机构学术伦理委员会的审查，妥善处理数据及匿名事宜等。研究伦理确实是所有二语研究和语用研究都要注意的问题，尽管语言研究通常对参与者并没有危险。

本章介绍了三种收集二语语用产出的方法：语篇补全任务（DCT）、角色扮演、真实语料录音。DCT在早期二语语用研究中应用广泛，曾经是使用最多的数据收集方法。Blum-Kulka et al.（1989）是跨文化语用和二语语用领域里程碑式的研究，奠定了DCT设计和数据分析的研究基础，尤其在对请求和道歉言语行为的编码分类方面影响深远，是二语语用和跨文化语用研究的必读书目。Johnston，Kasper，& Ross（1998）对比了三种不同版本的DCT：无回答（no rejoinder）、偏爱的回答（preferred rejoinder）、非偏爱的回答（dispreferred rejoinder）。他们发现，是否有回答和回答的种类影响DCT收集到的语料，但是这些影响对不同言语行为不一样：抱怨受影响最小，而道歉受影响最大，请求受到的影响居中。因此，他们提醒：不同形式的DCT所收集的语料可能无法对比。注意，这里的偏爱/非偏爱并不是从对话双方的心理来看，而是由对话序列的结构特征决定，即后序回答是否和前序对话对应。比如，对于请求言语行为来说，接受请求就是偏爱的回答，而拒绝就是非偏爱的回答。对于会话中的偏爱/非偏爱，由于篇幅限制在此就不赘述，大家可以参考会话分析的书籍，例如Schegloff（2007）。Billmyer & Varghese（2000）就DCT背景介绍部分的长短是否影响收集的请求语料这一问题进行了对比研究，发现长背景介绍并不影响请求策略和内部修饰语的数量，但是却产出了更多数量的外部修饰语。

DCT具有许多优势，包括容易操控语境变量，方便收集，便于对比研究等。然而，它也有很多缺陷，例如DCT场景的真实性难以保证。受试对场景的熟悉程度会影响收集的语料。同时，语料的语言使用真实性也是DCT收集数据的另一个要考虑的问题。大量实证研究表明，DCT收集的语料和自然语料在语料长短、语义语步范围、重复和解释的数量等方面存在差异。考虑到以上缺陷，DCT经常被改编成不同形式。本书介绍了四种常见的改编形式：口语DCT；基于技术改进的DCT，包括多媒体语篇收集任务（Schauer，2009；Ren，2015）、计算机动画产出任务（Halenko，2021）；反转DCT，也叫学生产出的DCT；合作完成的DCT。本章还简要介绍了DCT和口述报告相结合带来的优势。

接着，本章介绍了角色扮演在二语语用中的使用。图3.3（第70页）列举了四种角色扮演的特征，即开放式、闭环式、自发式和结构式角色扮演，这对掌握不同类型角色扮演任务的优缺点很有帮助。传统上，受试被要求了解场景后以某个规定的身份进行对话。多数研究仅关注某些特定语用形式和策略的使用频率，而忽略会话中的互动特征。本章以近年来的一些实证研究为例，阐释了如何利用网络平台来收集角色扮演互动语料。和DCT一样，角色扮演相对容易管理，具有方便操控的优势。研究者可以通过控制权势、社交距离、干预程度等语用变量来考查它们如何影响受试的语言语用策略选择。相比DCT，角色扮演收集的数据更能反映自然交际中的语言使用。不过，因为参与者需要以某些假设的角色来完成任务，所以角色扮演收集的数据在互动方面仍然很受局限，它同时缺乏对话双方的真实关系和缺少现实交际后果。由于收集的数据需要转写，因此角色扮演比DCT更耗时。

所以，二语语用研究采用各种手段来努力收集真实交际语料，包括以录音、日记和现场记录的形式记录真实语言产出。然而，语料记录的准确程度、语料出现的频率、所收集的语料的可对比性等，约束着真实交际语料在研究中的应用。各种数据收集方法各有优缺点，研究者需要根据自己的研究目的和研究问题来衡量每种方法的优势和局限，选择最适合的研究方法。

3. 语用理解和语用意识（第四、五章）

第四章介绍了语用学的另一支柱理论——Grice的会话含义理论，并简要介绍了关联理论。Grice（1989）的合作原则和四个准则是会话含义理论的核心。Grice区分规约含义（conventional implicature）和会话含义（conversational implicature）。二者的区别在于规约含义并不依靠合作原则及其四个准则推导；而通过推导，可以理解说话人意图表达的会话含义。Grice总结了会话含义的特征，指出其具有可取消性、不可分离性、可推导性、非规约性和不确定性。他还区分了一般性会话含义（generalized conversational implicature）和特殊性会话含义（particularized conversational implicature）。前者指不需要特殊语境就能推导出来的含义，比如说从"我有些学生做二语语用"就能推导出"不是我所有的学生都做二语语用"；而后者一般需要更多的语境信息才能推导出所要表达的意图。

会话含义是二语语用理解研究的主要研究议题之一。比较早的研究有Bouton（1992）针对英语二语学习者对不同种类含义理解的调查。在这项研究中，一种被Bouton称为"教皇类含义"的对话被发现最难为学生习得。在这类对话中，回答通常为Is the Pope Catholic?（教皇是天主教的吗？）之类的表达，类似于常说的"太阳从东边出来吗？"等显而易见的含义。而间接言语行为是某些特定语言形式已经成为惯例（conventionalized）而引起的含义，比如Can you pass me the salt?（你能把盐递给我吗？）一类的问句。此类问句无论在英语还是汉语中都已经是人们请求别人递东西的惯例，听话者已经将其关联为请求。

元（meta-）是个比较时髦但又意义不明确的词。在语言学里，元一般指"关于"（about）。因此，元语用也就是关于语用的语用，通常指交际者对交际中的语用的自反意识（reflexive awareness），即人们对交际中自己和互动者使用的语用特征及其潜在意义的意识。显性的元语用表达包括对某些语用现象的谈论，例如"这个是请求吗？""别绕弯子""这不太礼貌吧"等等。隐性的元语用则关注说话者是否能够在元语用层面调控语言资源，比如索引词（indexicals）和语境化暗示（contextual cues）。在对话中使用"你"还是"您"就体现了对话语的元语用调控。

第五章介绍了调查语用理解和元语用意识的数据收集方法，主要包括选择题和元语用意识的调查方法。选择题是我们十分熟悉的考试题型。在二语语用中，选择题经常被用来考查学生对会话含义的理解。本章分析了Bouton（1992，1994）对于二语语用蕴含理解的研究。文中列举了相关性含义、教皇类含义、讽刺、间接批评、序列含义（方框5.1），并就如何用选择题来考查关联含义和间接批评进行了举例。Bouton的这两项研究不管是在用选择题研究语用含义方面，还是在考查语用理解能力方面，影响都很大，建议读者阅读原文。Roever（2005）将选择题问卷做成了网页版，便于发放。随着社交媒体的普及，利用网络和社交媒体发放问卷变得十分普遍。

选择题还可以用听力的形式来考查学生对会话的理解。借助电脑，研究者能够同时考查学生理解的准确度和速度，以探究不同惯例程度的会话含义对学生语用理解的影响。这方面研究做得最多的是Taguchi及其学生。本书指出，虽然Taguchi在一系列研究中用是否规约化（conventional）来区分间接拒绝和间接意见，但是严格来说，应该用是否符合惯例（conventionalized）来表达。Ren（2022b）也指出，二语语用和普通语用学在处理会话是否规约化的时候定义不一致，呼吁二语语用应在概念和术语使用上与普通语用学保持一致，促进二语语用研究成果在其他语用学分支领域的应用和影响。

对元语用意识的调查有多种方法，本章将其大致归为三类：1）元语用评估等级回复问卷（Scaled-response questionnaires for metapragmatic assessment）；2）元语用讨论、采访和口述报告；3）日记、日志和博客。元语用评估等级回复问卷在二语语用中经常使用，通常要求参与者对语境中的语用变量，比如社交距离、相对权势、语用现象的强度，或者某些表达的礼貌等级、合适程度等进行评分。需要注意的是，有些研究没有使用元语用意识，而是用语用意识来描述研究对象。等级打分任务并没有明确的正确答案，一般做法是将学生的打分和母语者的打分基准进行对比。学生的打分越接近母语者的基准，表明他们的语用知识越接近目标标准。

启发式元语用意识数据收集主要针对具体语境下的语用变量或语用特征，采用参与者自行讨论、采访和口述报告等形式。其中，口述报告被认为是这三种形式中最可靠和最常用的方法，虽然它也具有无法保证数据真实、全面的缺陷。本章采用Ren（2014）作为例子，阐述了口述报告可以提供参与者注意的语用变量、遇到的语用困难等信息。同时，为了提高口述报告数据的信度和效度，需要注意以下事项：在语用任务完成后立即开展口述报告任务；把参与者的语用任务录音或录像播放给他们以帮助回忆；对参与者进行口述报告培训；允许参与者自己选择汇报的语言（Ren，2014）。

此外，还可以采用日记、日志、博客等方法让参与者主动汇报学习过程中的反思。然而，这种汇报非常主观，而且对汇报者的语言和语用敏感度要求很高。现有研究中应用较广的主要是学者自己的日志记录。如果使用这几种方法则需要对参与者进行培训，但同时又要做到不暴露具体研究目的，以免造成参与者对数据过度记录。

4. 语用互动（第六、七章）

对语用互动的重视可以说是本书的亮点，体现了二语语用学关注语用互动的转向。互动能力自从被Kramsch（1986）提出以来，已逐渐成为二语习得领域的研究热点之一。学者们对互动能力构建了许多理论模型（例如，Galaczi & Taylor，2018）。简单来说，互动能力指人们"相互协调行动以成功参与互动的能力"（Ren，2018a：123），涵盖互动者在话语实践中使用互动资源和建立交互主观性的能力（Young，2011）。互动能力与语用能力关注的层面有诸多重合。有些学者认为互动能力包含语用能力（Young，2011）；有些学者认为语用学强调交际互动，因此语用能力包含互动能力（Ren，2018a）。语用能力的构念在二语语用学中是不断发展的。学者目前一致同意语用能力是多维度、多层面的（Taguchi，2019b；Ren，2022b），包括：1）通晓何种语境使用何种形式的语言和社会文化知识；2）依照语境的变化，灵活、顺应地使用知识的互动能力；3）在知情决策的基础上，决定是否使用特定知识的主观能动性（Taguchi，2019b：4）。

第六章首先回顾了语境对互动中意义构建的重要性。语境直接影响交际双方对话语的理解。语境不仅限于互动交际前存在的因素，而且是由交际双方共同构建，并直接影响语言使用的。比如，在师生交谈中，学生在权衡双方相对权势后选用"您"来称呼老师，老师为了降低学生的紧张感主动要求学生用"你"来称呼自己，师生双方共同改变交际中的语境和语言使用。又比如，在开国际学术会议时，大家常以"教授/博士 + 姓"来称呼首次见面者，以凸显尊重。但由于交际者都知道在国际学术会议上按照惯例也可以用名来称呼对方，在交谈过程中，为了拉近距离，交际者很自然地就会抛弃"教授/博士 + 姓"的叫法而直呼其名。

接着，本章介绍了共同行为（co-acts）和活动（activity）在互动中构建意义的作用。作者们指出，第二章回顾言语行为时更多地是从说话者一方将其看成独立的行为，但实际上言语行为及其他语言语用现象在语境中并不具有固定的意义，而是在所发生的话语和语境中逐渐显现其意义。因此，在分析语用现象时，应该将其置于语境之中，充分考虑其前后的共同行为。分析会话中的序列和共同行为可以从更深层次理解交谈参与者的语言使用。活动指有目的的行为或事件，类似于Hymes（1972）所用的话语事件（speech event）。活动类型则指具有文化特色的活动，对构建和解码互动意义起到重要作用。活动类型是动态的、基于习惯的、共同构建的，限制并引导交际双方的互动贡献。

最后，本章强调了多模态对分析二语语用能力的重要性，指出二语语用能力不仅包括正确使用词汇和语法，也包括在不同模态上都要合适，例如面对面交际中，既要听着自然，也要看着得体。将多模态资源纳入语用能力是当今二语语用研究的趋势。例如Ren（2022b：1）将语用能力定义为"在互动中有效、恰当地使用语言、符号和多模态资源来达到特定交际目的，以及理解上述使用的能力"。本章就多模态主要讲了韵律和图像两个方面。韵律可以包含丰富的语用信息，对交际起到十分重要的作用。特别是以汉语为目标语言的二语语用研究，由于不同声调对应不同汉字，韵律直接影响交际双方的理解。但是，二语语用对韵律的研究一直较少（Ren，2022b），这可能是由于缺少相关的系统分析方法（Romero-Trillo，2019）。读者可以参见现有相关研究（例如，Taguchi，Hirschi，& Kang，2022）。开展韵律研究可以借助Praat软件。图像是多模态分析的另一重要层面，ELAN软件为分析图像提供了便利。语用学及二语语用学已有一些研究对面部表情、手势等开展了图像分析。较早的研究包括Gass & Houck（1999）对拒绝交际的研究。近年来的多本二语语用和二语互动专著（例如，Salaberry & Kunitz，2019）以及语用学期刊上可以发现不少这方面的研究。

针对语用互动，第七章首先介绍了开放式角色扮演，并分析了它与封闭式角色扮演（见第三章）的不同。如作者们解释，封闭式角色扮演强调互动的结果，而开放式角色扮演可以更好地模仿真实互动，因为交际结果不是事先决定的。接着，本章以Gass 和 Houck 1999 年出版的专著《语际拒绝研究》（*Interlanguage Refusals*）为例，简要介绍了他们如何利用开放式角色扮演来探究语言层面的拒绝策略；此外，还分析了语言和非语言特征，话轮转换，以及交际策略。随着二语语用研究对互动的重视，应用会话分析（applied CA）被越来越多地用来研究句子层面之上的行为、意义和语境之间的关系，包括相邻配对、话轮、预扩展、会话顺序等（Al-Gahtani & Roever，2012；Youn，2015）。

纠正性反馈是二语习得和外语教学中的常见议题，但是在二语语用中研究却并不多。本章以Fukuya & Hill（2006）和Guo（2013）为例，说明了纠正性反馈及不同种类的纠正性反馈如何影响学生的请求策略。作者们指出，Fukuya和Hill仅考查了一种隐性反馈，Guo对比了重述（recast）和元语言提示，但这两项研究都只研究了请求言语行为。Lyster & Ranta（1997）把纠正性反馈分为六种，包括：明确纠正（explicit correction）、重述（recast）、请求澄清（clarification request）、元语言提示（metalinguistic clues）、引导（elicitation）和重复（repetition）。读者可以阅读该文，思考不同反馈形式对不同语用层面的影响。此外，反馈研究区分书面反馈和口头反馈，不同模态的反馈是否对二语语用影响不同，也是值得探索的议题。

其他收集真实或贴近真实语用互动数据的方法包括引发的对话、同盟者脚本技术（confederate scripting）、自然对话、电脑为媒介的交际和语料库方法。引发的对话在形式上与角色扮演相似，研究者邀请参与者就某些话题进行对话；但与角色扮演不同的是，参与者不需要去扮演设定的角色。因此，引发的对话比角色扮演更可能收集到接近真实互动的对话。但同时由于参与者按照自己的真实身份去对话，研究者无法像用角色扮演一样去探究一些他们感兴趣的语用变量。比如引发学生们就某个话题展开对话就无法研究相对权势对互动对话的影响。同盟者脚本技术在二语习得里已有应用，在二语语用研究中目前较少见到。其主要思路是研究者邀请一个研究助手，即"同盟者"，去和实验对象对话。该同盟者可以按研究者的设计去干预对话，比如固定使用某些句型，按计划说某些内容，甚至假扮人工智能去和实验者对话，而其他参与者并不知道"同盟者"的存在。作者们提醒大家在使用同盟者脚本技术收集语料时，不要让"同盟者"知道自己的真实研究目的，以免干扰其在实验中的表现。

自然对话比较好理解，就是让参与者将自己在生活中的某些对话录音保存。本章以Bell（2007）和Shively（2013）为例，介绍了自然对话语料对研究二语幽默的作用。需要注意的是，自然对话适合研究那些日常生活中发生频率较高的语用现象。对发生频率低的现象，自然对话很难收集到满足分析需求的数量，也较难探究语用变量对互动对话的影响。如Ren & Woodfield（2016）所讨论的，由于一些现象在自然对话中发生频率低，很难收集到研究所需的数量，很多时候研究者不得不采用媒体话语或其他方法来收集数据。Bardovi-Harlig & Hartford（2005）推荐利用机构话语来做语用研究，这样既能收集到真实发生的对话，又能对某些现象进行对比或跟踪。最后需要提醒大家的是，对自然对话的收集和研究更要注意研究伦理。

电脑为媒介的交际，或称网络交际，是宝贵的真实语料（Ren，2022b）。收集网络交际语料相对容易：它们真实发生，就在网上，这都为研究者收集数据提供了方便。而且，非口语的网络互动也不需要转写，大大提高了研究效率。网络交际提供了很多新的语言现象、新的研究视角，对一些传统语用学理论和发现带来了挑战（Ren，2018b）。例如，在面对面交际中，语境影响说话者的语用表现。然而，在网络交际中，很多时候说话者并不知道听众会是谁，也就是所谓的"语境坍塌"（context collapse）。网络交际和面对面交际的语用互动也有所不同。书中以González-Lloret（2016）为例展现了话轮的特点和表情符号在网络交际中的重要性。分析网络交际一定要考虑表情符号在交际中承载的意义，当然也要注意研究伦理。

最后，本章指出，语料库方法提供了新的范式和分析手段，有助于调查学习者在不同阶段的产出和追踪学习者的语用发展。作者们对语料库采用宽泛的界定，认为它不仅包括大规模语料库，也包括研究者针对具体研究语境自建的语料库。由于大多数语料库在建库时没有提供语用标注，现有基于语料库的语用研究大都就某些语用形式进行探索，例如语用标记（Aijmer，2019）、句末助词（Ren，2022a）等。对语料库语用学有兴趣的读者可以参见Landert, Dayter, Messerli, & Locher（2023），它既介绍了如何自建语料库进行语用学探索，又提供了利用语料库研究语用的例子。Aijmer & Rühlemann（2014）和Rühlemann（2019）这两本书也提供了研究思路和范例。国内对语料库语用研究的总结可参见李民、陈新仁（2019）。一些文献中提到的具有语用标注的语料库包括SPICE-Ireland语料库，它是ICE-Ireland语料库的子库，据说提供了语用和韵律信息，以及Sociopragmatic Corpus，它属于Corpus of English Dialogues 1560–1760。很遗憾这些语料库现在还没有对外开放。

第八章"结论"简要总结了书中提及的主要数据收集方法，并强调研究中可结合定量和定性研究的优点，采用混合研究方法。

总的来说，本书从语用产出、理解、互动三个方面介绍了语用学相关理论，并结合二语语用研究介绍了相应的数据收集方法。本书语言流畅，易读易懂，对重要概念和研究均提供了详细注释，并配有讨论问题，是了解二语语用所涉及的语用理论和数据收集方法的一本好书，建议对二语语用感兴趣的读者阅读。由于侧重不同，本书对二语语用的研究设计，二语习得领域的理论，二语语用已取得的研究成果和未来研究趋势，以及数据分析方法等，涉及较少。建议读者结合阅读Kasper & Rose（2002），Taguchi & Roever（2017），Taguchi（2019a），Ren（2022b）等二语语用书籍。

参考文献[1]：

Aijmer, K. (2019). 'Ooh whoops I'm sorry! Teenagers' use of English apology expressions. *Journal of Pragmatics, 142,* 258–269.

Aijmer, K., & Rühlemann, C. (Eds.). (2014). *Corpus Pragmatics: A Handbook.* Cambridge: Cambridge University Press.

Economidou-Kogetsidis, M., & Woodfield, H. (Eds.). (2012). *Interlanguage Request Modification.* Amsterdam: John Benjamins.

Galaczi, E., & Taylor, L. (2018). Interactional competence: Conceptualisations, operationalisations, and outstanding questions. *Language Assessment Quarterly, 15*(3), 219–236.

Halenko, N. (2021). *Teaching Pragmatics and Instructed Second Language*

---

(1) 在正文中出现的参考文献在此不再赘列。

Learning: Study Abroad and Technology-enhanced Teaching. London: Bloomsbury.

House, J. (2013). Developing pragmatic competence in English as a lingua franca: Using discourse markers to express (inter)subjectivity and connectivity. *Journal of Pragmatics, 59*, 57–67.

Kramsch, C. (1986). From language proficiency to interactional competence. *The Modern Language Journal, 70*(4), 366–372.

Landert, D., Dayter, D., Messerli, T. C., & Locher, M. A. (2023). *Corpus Pragmatics.* Cambridge: Cambridge University Press.

Lyster, R., & Ranta, L. (1997). Corrective feedback and learner uptake: Negotiation of form in communicative classrooms. *Studies in Second Language Acquisition, 19*, 37–66.

Ren, W. (2013). The effect of study abroad on the pragmatic development of the internal modification of refusals. *Pragmatics, 23*(4), 715–741.

Ren, W. (2015). *L2 Pragmatic Development in Study Abroad Contexts.* Bern: Peter Lang.

Ren, W. (2018a). Developing L2 pragmatic competence in study abroad contexts. In C. Sanz & A. Morales-Front (Eds.), *The Routledge Handbook of Study Abroad Research and Practice* (pp. 119–133). New York: Routledge.

Ren, W. (2018b). Exploring Chinese digital communication. *Discourse, Context and Media, 26*, 1–4.

Ren, W. (2018c). Pragmatic strategies to solve and preempt understanding problems in Chinese professionals' emails when using English as lingua franca communication. *International Journal of Bilingual Education and Bilingualism, 21*(8), 968–981.

Ren, W. (2022a). Effects of proficiency and gender on learners' use of the pragmatic marker 吧 *ba. Lingua, 277*, 1–13.

Ren, W. (2022b). *Second Language Pragmatics.* Cambridge: Cambridge University Press.

Ren, W., Li, S., & Lü, X. (2022). A meta-analysis of the effectiveness of second language pragmatics instruction. *Applied Linguistics*.

Ren, W., & Woodfield, H. (2016). Chinese females' date refusals in reality TV shows: Expressing involvement or independence? *Discourse, Context and Media, 13*, 89–97.

Romero-Trillo, J. (2019). Prosodic pragmatics and feedback in intercultural communication. *Journal of Pragmatics, 151*, 91–102.

Rühlemann, C. (2019). *Corpus Linguistics for Pragmatics: A Guide for Research*. London/New York: Routledge.

Salaberry, M. R., & Kunitz, S. (Eds.). (2019). *Teaching and Testing L2 Interactional Competence: Bridging Theory and Practice*. New York/London: Routledge.

Schauer, G. A. (2009). *Interlanguage Pragmatic Development: The Study Abroad Context*. London: Continuum.

Taguchi, N. (2019a). *The Routledge Handbook of Second Language Acquisition and Pragmatics*. New York/London: Routledge.

Taguchi, N. (2019b). Second language acquisition and pragmatics: An overview. In N. Taguchi (Ed.), *The Routledge Handbook of Second Language Acquisition and Pragmatics* (pp. 1–14). New York/London: Routledge.

Taguchi, N., Hirschi, K., & Kang, O. (2022). Longitudinal L2 development in the prosodic marking of pragmatic meaning: Prosodic changes in L2 speech acts and individual factors. *Studies in Second Language Acquisition, 44*(3), 843–858.

Takahashi, S. (2010). Assessing learnability in second language pragmatics. In A. Trosborg (Ed.), *Pragmatics across Languages and Cultures* (pp. 391–422). Berlin: De Gruyter Mouton.

李民，陈新仁. 2019. 语料库语用学研究的国际热点解析. 现代外语（1），122—133.

任伟. 2018. 汉语请求言语行为的变异语用学研究. 外国语（4），66—75.

Alison Mackey dedicates her work on this book to her mother, Deanna Mackey, of whom she thinks daily, and whenever Grice's maxims of quantity and relevance are mentioned.

CONTENTS

ILLUSTRATIONS

Figures

Tables

PREFACE AND ACKNOWLEDGEMENTS

This book was written by three authors in three different countries united by the relevant fact that they each bring a different perspective on the field of L2 pragmatics, and the irrelevant fact that they happen to be almost exactly the same age. This is what multidisciplinary collaboration should be: bringing together parts to make a greater whole. And the fact that we had fun and learned from each other along the way was an added bonus. We each have expertise and interest in different but overlapping areas. Jonathan's area is general pragmatics, Alison's is second language research methodology, and Naoko's is L2 pragmatics research. Jonathan is a Brit living in Britain, Alison is a Brit who is a long term resident of the US, and likewise, Naoko is Japanese and has lived in the US for many decades, so between us and our families, colleagues, and students, we have racked up many occasions of cross-cultural pragmatic failure, giving us an appreciation for L2 pragmatics that is both highly personal as well as academic.

We wrote this book hoping to reinvigorate the field of Second Language Pragmatics, moving it forward both theoretically and methodologically beyond frameworks (e.g., politeness theory) and methods (e.g., discourse completion tests) devised in the 1970s and 1980s. We do not reject those endeavors, but argue that current L2 pragmatics can fruitfully take on board more recent thinking from general pragmatics together with the most up to date methodological techniques, by which pragmatics of all types can be pursued in L2 contexts. We designed the book to be clear, accessible, and practical, as well as to be helpful for students, their instructors, and researchers alike.

As with any book, we have accumulated debts along the way. In particular, we would like to thank several research assistants at Georgetown University, who helped with various aspects of the book. These include the multi-talented

Lara Bryfonski, who, in addition to editing assistance, also provided many of the illustrations, Rachel Thorson Hernández, who brought tales of her experiences in Mexico and a keen editorial eye, Ashleigh Pipes, who had just returned from a multi-year stint in Turkey, Aysenur Sagdic, a Turkish Ph.D. student at Georgetown, and Margaret Borowczyk, whose editing skills are that rare combination of both careful and quick – they all worked extremely hard on the manuscript, resolving many of the issues that resulted from having authors from three different educational backgrounds, each with their own writing styles, as well as sharing their expertise and interest in the area, and in helping us with not just the text but also the glossary and the reference list. Their assistance was invaluable, and we appreciated their hard work and their humor, as well as their shared tales about L2 pragmatic development. We are grateful to Emily Culpeper, a budding new graphic designer, for the illustrations that she prepared, edited, tweaked, and tailored to our needs. We hope readers enjoy the illustrations and cartoons throughout the book. We also thank our editors at Routledge, who provided exactly what you want from editors, patience when it's needed and a push when it was not.

1

INTRODUCTION TO SECOND LANGUAGE PRAGMATICS

1.1 What is Second Language Pragmatics?

Second language pragmatics (henceforth L2 pragmatics) is a field of study that unites two broader disciplines, second language acquisition (SLA) and pragmatics. Kasper and Schmidt (1996) originally defined L2 pragmatics as the "study of the development and use of strategies for linguistic action by nonnative speakers" (p. 150). More recently, Bardovi-Harlig (2010) pointed to the connections between use and acquisition in L2 pragmatics, noting that pragmatics "bridges the gap between the system side of language and the use side, and relates both of them at the same time," and that it "brings the study of acquisition to this mix of structure and use" (p. 1). In other words, L2 pragmatics is the study of "how learners come to know how-to-say-what-to-whom-when" (Bardovi-Harlig, 2013, p. 68). In this book, we go a step further and add an important dimension to these definitions by arguing that it is equally important to study *how learners come to understand or comprehend meaning*, as well as how they negotiate and co-construct meaning. To this end, we view comprehension, production, and interaction as central to L2 pragmatics.

Pragmatics is often discussed in terms of two subareas: sociopragmatics (the contextual features of pragmatics) and pragmalinguistics (the linguistic structure of pragmatics) (Leech, 1983; Thomas, 1983). Conceiving pragmatics in terms of these two subareas has shaped the nature of L2 pragmatics, as we will see. Although the definitions of L2 pragmatics have evolved, the primary inquiry remains the same: What is the nature of L2 learners' language actions in a social context?

In the next few sections, we consider how this inquiry has led to various research agendas within L2 pragmatics. There are communicative competence, interactional competence, and intercultural pragmatics. Next, we examine the development of L2 pragmatics research over time.

> • L2 pragmatics investigates the developmental stages of L2 learners in learning pragmatics of their target language.
>
> • L2 pragmatics combines the fields of second language acquisition (SLA) and pragmatics.
>
> • Pragmatic competence is divided into two subcategories: sociopragmatics, which is concerned with the contextual features of pragmatics, and pragmalinguistics, which is concerned with the linguistic structure of pragmatics.
>
> Points to remember

We now turn to an example. A new Mandarin-speaking student has arrived at a UK university, and presents her advisor with a Chinese painting on a scroll by way of saying hello.

[1] British Professor: Wow! Really, you shouldn't have.
Chinese Student: Oh, sorry.
British Professor: No, I mean, it's lovely, thanks.

There is clearly no problem here with vocabulary or grammar. The problem lies with the interpretation of the words and grammar in context. In the context of gift giving in Britain, "you shouldn't have" is one of the conventional and formulaic ways of acknowledging and accepting gifts. Taken literally, it could be a statement that the gift giver ought not to have done something, an implied criticism. However, it is not intended literally. It is intended as a polite way to accept the gift. For example, it implies that the gift giver should not have gone to the trouble of giving the gift, and acknowledges that they did in fact go to trouble, and also professes the desire that they be trouble-free. However, if the gift giver does not understand that "you shouldn't have" does not literally mean that, but is rather conventional polite gift acceptance talk, an alternative interpretation is readily available, namely, that the gift should not have been given, and thus they have made a mistake. This may or may not have been the case here. The Mandarin-speaking student may well have understood that the British English-speaking professor was not literally telling her that she should not have brought a gift, but she may not have had the linguistic resources to say, "oh it's only something small" or "oh it was no trouble" or one of the other British English responses to "you shouldn't have." Instead, "sorry" covers a multitude of scenarios. But the professor assumes that his original acceptance utterance has been misunderstood (that the Chinese visitor took it literally), and attempts to clarify the meaning ("I mean"). Multiple ambiguities involved in exchanges like this are what constitutes the field of L2 pragmatics. L2 pragmatics investigates the speakers' meanings, especially their intended meaning (e.g., accepting the gift politely); the hearers' interpretations (e.g., here, that the speaker did not want the gift); conversational actions (e.g., performing an acceptance); routinized expressions that are conventionally associated with certain social contexts (e.g., "you shouldn't have"); social activities (e.g., gift giving); politeness (e.g., the maintenance or promotion of social harmony); and the negotiation of meanings between interactants (e.g., "I mean").

Such components are not working independently of each other. Some definitions of pragmatics already highlight the fact that speakers and hearers jointly construct meanings. LoCastro (2003), for example, defines pragmatics as "the study of speaker and hearer meaning created in their joint actions that include both linguistic and non-linguistic signals in the context of socioculturally organized activities" (p. 15). In Example [1], an acceptance of a gift only makes sense after a gift has been proffered, and the gift receiver's repair ("No, I mean, . . .") only makes sense after the Chinese visitor's apology ("Oh, sorry"). Their actions jointly create understandings in context. In a nutshell, the focus of pragmatics research is meanings that arise from the use of communicative resources in context, and in particular, the meanings implied by speakers, inferred by hearers, and negotiated between them in interaction.

Communicative Competence

The development of ideas and models of communicative competence have impacted and influenced the area of L2 pragmatics in terms of theoretical foundations and, hence, research methodology. The origins of the concept of communicative competence are typically traced to Dell Hymes. Hymes (1972b) proposed a two-sided conceptualization of language knowledge, with grammatical knowledge on one side and sociocultural knowledge on the other. Hymes claimed that these two types of knowledge jointly determine how one can use language appropriately and effectively in a social context. Building on Hymes's (1972b) framework, theoretical models of L2 communicative competence emerged (Bachman & Palmer, 1996, 2010; Canale & Swain, 1980). These models situated pragmatic competence among several interrelated components of language knowledge that enable learners to perform a communicative act in a social situation. Canale and Swain's (1980) model is one of the earliest lines of work in this area. Their model emphasizes that a successful communicative act involves an efficient integration of four sub-competencies: grammatical, sociolinguistic, discourse, and strategic. While grammatical competence involves the knowledge of linguistic systems (e.g., syntax, lexis), sociolinguistic competence refers to the knowledge of socially appropriate language use. Discourse competence is concerned with coherence and cohesion of a text. Strategic competence involves compensatory strategies that help prevent or manage communication problems.

Canale and Swain's model did not distinguish between sociolinguistic and pragmatic competence. Pragmatic competence was assumed to be part of sociolinguistic

> • *Communicative competence* includes both grammatical knowledge and knowledge about social situations and cultures. These two types of knowledge together enable speakers to decide how to use language appropriately and effectively in social contexts.
>
> **Points to remember**

competence, whereas subsequent research, for example, by Bachman (1990) and Bachman and Palmer (1996, 2010), developed a model that viewed pragmatic competence as a competence in its own right. Bachman's (1990) model has three sub-components: language competence, strategic competence, and psychophysiological mechanisms. Pragmatic competence in this model (subsumed under language competence) involves illocutionary competence (knowledge of conventions for performing language functions) and sociolinguistic competence (knowledge of social rules of appropriateness).

Bachman and Palmer's (1996, 2010) work divided pragmatic knowledge into two dimensions: functional and sociolinguistic knowledge. Functional knowledge enables us to interpret relationships between utterances and communicative functions (e.g., knowing a variety of forms that perform a speech act of refusal), while sociolinguistic knowledge enables us to create utterances that are appropriate in context (e.g., knowing which forms to use when refusing a friend's invitation to a party). Hence, Bachman and Palmer's (1996, 2010) work conceptualizes pragmatics within the dynamic relationship that exists among language, language users, and language use settings.

As elaborated in section 2.2, a key distinction between pragmalinguistics and sociopragmatics was introduced in foundational work by Leech (1983) and Thomas (1983), and later applied to L2 pragmatics by Kasper (1992b). Functional knowledge determines the range of linguistic resources available to perform language functions (pragmalinguistics), while sociolinguistic knowledge enables us to understand features of context and select the most appropriate linguistic resource in a given context (sociopragmatics). As Leech (1983) argues, pragmalinguistics is applied to the study of the more linguistic and grammatical end of pragmatics, while sociopragmatics is applied more toward the socio-cultural end. Hence, pragmalinguistics encompasses the organizational and functional knowledge in Bachman and Palmer's model, while sociopragmatics belongs to the domain of sociolinguistic knowledge.

Similar to these early models, more recent work by Celce-Murcia (2007) maintains a componential view of L2 communicative competence, but with a notable change: the explicit inclusion of interaction as the fundamental constituent of communicative competence. In her model, interactional abilities entail three components: action competence, conversation competence, and paralinguistic competence. Action competence involves knowledge of how to perform a communicative act in context, while conversational competence refers to knowledge of conversation

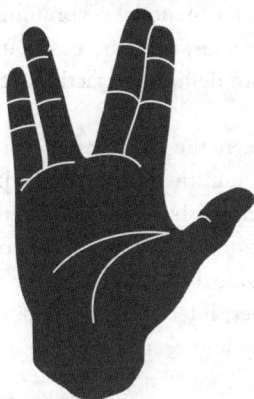

FIGURE 1.1 The Vulcan salute from *Star Trek*

mechanisms that help realize communicative acts such as turn-taking. Paralinguistic competence involves non-verbal language such as gestures (Figure 1.1). These three components together explain how learners co-construct a communicative act with their interlocutors during an interaction.

Interactional Competence

Interaction is also seen as central in a more recent, discourse-oriented model, known as interactional competence, which considers meaning as emerging from socio-semiotic systems (Hall, 1993, 1995; Hall, Hellermann, & Doehler, 2011; Young, 2008a, 2008b, 2011a, 2011b). Interactional competence deviates from the componential view of communicative competence by conceptualizing competence in a dynamic social interaction. This echoes Hymes' original framework on which early models by Canale and Swain and Bachman and Palmer were based. While these early models viewed language ability as a psycholinguistic trait that exists within individuals independent from a social context, interactional competence views language ability as fundamentally situated within a social context. Research on interactional competence emphasizes the importance of analyzing "socioculturally-conventionalized configurations of face-to-face interaction by which and within which group members communicate" (Hall, 1993, p. 146).

Points to remember

• *Interactional Competence* is the knowledge of various language abilities that are necessary for successful interactions in social contexts.

In the interactional competence model, a communicative act is co-constructed and negotiated among participants, and emerges from the sequential organization of talk. Young (2008a, 2008b) defines interactional competence as follows:

> [A] relationship between the participants' employment of linguistic and interactional resources and the contexts in which they are employed; the resources that interactional competence highlights are those of identity, language, and interaction . . . Interactional competence, however, is not the ability of an individual to employ those resources in any and every social interaction; rather, interactional competence is how those resources are employed mutually and reciprocally by all participants in a particular discursive practice.
>
> *(2008b, p. 101)*

In other words, interactional competence views language ability as locally situated and jointly constructed by all participants in discourse. Participants draw on a variety of resources in interaction, such as knowledge of register-specific linguistic forms, speech acts, turn-taking, and repair (Young, 2008a, 2008b). These resources are shared among participants in their process of joint meaning making.

Communicative competence as a theory, model, and paradigm has expanded our understanding of what it means to be pragmatically competent. The knowledge of the relationships among forms, functions, and contexts of use (i.e., pragmalinguistic and sociopragmatic knowledge) is a significant element in pragmatic knowledge, but suffices only as a partial explanation. Interactional competence is equally significant for pragmatic language use, which is situated in social interaction. During interaction, pragmatic knowledge is not stable or pre-determined; rather, it is emergent and contingent upon unfolding discourse because, depending on the interlocutors' reactions, speakers modify their ways of speaking, as well as the types of communicative functions they perform; these models together suggest a three-part definition of pragmatic competence: (1) knowledge of linguistic forms and their social functions; (2) sociocultural knowledge of appropriate language use in a situation; and (3) the ability to use these knowledge bases to co-construct a communicative act in a social interaction.

Intercultural Pragmatics

The evolution from "pragmatics-within-individuals" to "pragmatics-in-interaction-in-context" has led to pragmatic competence drawing not only from models of communicative competence, but also from the field of intercultural pragmatics, where communication among speakers of different first languages (L1s) is the focus (Kecskes, 2014). In intercultural encounters, communication is a dynamic process in which collaboration and negotiation constantly take place to reach the goal of mutual understanding among speakers of different cultural backgrounds.

In intercultural communication, participants' interactional competence is essential, because communication skills such as turn-taking, management of the direction of talk, and the use of paralinguistic cues directly affect the goal of mutual understanding.

> • Intercultural communication is a dynamic process that involves constant collaboration and negotiation in order to research understanding among speakers of different cultural backgrounds.
>
> **Points to remember**

Kecskes (2014) takes a socio-cognitive approach to intercultural pragmatics by combining a cognitive-philosophical perspective, which views intention as an *a priori* mental state of the speaker, with the sociocultural-interactional perspective, which views intention as a *post factum* phenomenon jointly constructed by the speaker and listener during interaction. In other words, speakers in intercultural settings may resort to their L1-based cultural repertoires, but these repertoires blend with emerging elements in a situation and develop into new, hybrid, multicultural norms such as translanguaging (Garcia, 2007; MacSwan, 2017). Hence, the focus of research in intercultural communication is often to understand how speakers from different cultures find common ground and co-construct norms of interaction unique to their communicative situations. Different standards of politeness, directness, and conventions are constantly negotiated in intercultural settings. Speakers develop their own discourse strategies and communicative styles while communicating in a shared language (Holmes, 2012; Koven, 2006; Rogerson-Revell, 2007).

By situating pragmatic competence within a framework of intercultural communication, we can see that L2 pragmatic behaviors can be best examined by analyzing what L2 learners actually do in an interaction. Hence, methods need to go beyond traditional practices of analyzing what linguistic forms learners use in what context. Instead, researchers need to present different aspects of analysis, including *how* learners negotiate toward mutual understanding and *how* they use a variety of materials and methods to uncover contextual adaptability.

1.2 Second Language Pragmatics: A Brief Historical Overview

From a historical perspective, definitions of pragmatics have gradually changed over time. An early definition of L2 pragmatics comes from seminal work by both Jenny Thomas in 1983, and Kasper and Dahl in 1991. Thomas (1983) introduces the terms "cross-cultural pragmatics" and "pragmatic competence" to refer to "the ability to use language effectively in order to achieve a specific purpose and to understand language in context" (p. 92). On the other hand, Kasper and Dahl (1991) use the term "interlanguage pragmatics" to refer to "nonnative speakers' (NNSs') comprehension and production of speech acts, and how their L2-related speech act knowledge is acquired" (p. 216). These initial definitions have expanded over time to reflect a broader understanding of pragmatic competence beyond just speech acts. Kasper and Rose (2002) situated L2 pragmatics within two investigative foci: L2 use and L2 acquisition. The former is concerned with how nonnative speakers comprehend and produce linguistic actions in a target language, while the latter focuses on how L2 learners develop pragmatic ability in a target language. The next few sections provide an overview of L2 pragmatics research and how it has developed over time.

The 1980s to 1990s: Comparative, Cross-sectional Research

In the 1980s and 1990s, cross-linguistic, comparative studies of L2 pragmatics dominated the field. Based on the assumption that different languages have different ways of conveying pragmatic meanings such as politeness and formality, a large body of work compared pragmatic language use across different L1s and L2s. Although in principle all aspects of pragmatics could be subject to cross-cultural comparisons, studies in this period primarily focused on two areas: speech acts and politeness.

This body of research drew heavily from speech act theory (Austin, 1962; Searle, 1969), which is concerned with the performative function of individual utterances, and politeness theory (Brown & Levinson, 1987), in which polite speech is compelled by a universal goal to achieve interpersonal harmony, primarily through the mitigation of face threats. Studies of L2 pragmatics at the time compared the range of linguistic forms used to perform speech acts across contextual parameters (e.g., interlocutors' power relationship, social distance, and degree of imposition) as well as across languages.

> **Points to remember**
>
> - Traditionally, two main areas of pragmatic inquiry have been speech acts and politeness. These are concerned with the function of individual utterances and how polite speech is compelled by a universal goal to achieve interpersonal harmony.

A landmark project in this vein was Blum-Kulka, House, and Kasper's (1989a) study. Their research compared requests and apologies across seven different languages using a discourse completion test (DCT), and its accompanying coding framework, as a uniform data collection instrument. They analyzed speech act patterns across languages, specifically looking at issues such as how many different types of speech act strategies exist in a single language, whether the strategies are direct or indirect, and how the requests and apologies vary across situations. They also collected data from L2 groups and analyzed similarities and differences between L2 patterns and those of native speakers. Their findings highlighted potential areas of pragmatic failure stemming from L1–L2 differences, as well as the nature of L1 transfer. The common DCT coding framework used to analyze speech act strategies in this study led to quite a few replication studies, providing further empirical descriptions of speech act patterns across cultures (e.g., ESL learners in the US, Hungarian EFL and Italian EFL learners [Bardovi-Harlig & Dörnyei, 1998]; Japanese, Chinese, South Korean, and Russian learners of English [Fukuya, Reeve, & Christianson, 1998]; Cantonese learners [Rose & Ng, 2001]).

Following this trend, in the same period, the comparative-descriptive practice of L2 pragmatics research expanded to include other factors, for example, L2 groups at different levels of proficiency, length of target language study, and duration residence in the country where the target language is spoken, among other things. The findings were quite varied. For example, some studies showed a positive relationship between proficiency or length of study and pragmatic competence, while others did not. The general conclusion was that pragmatic competence is difficult to define and even more difficult to measure and compare across L2 groups.

The 1990s and Beyond: Teaching and Assessment

After the comparative phase, research in the 1990s increasingly focused on whether pragmatics can be taught to language learners, and if so, how it might best be assessed. Diverting from the widespread trend at the time of researching the effects of instruction on grammar and vocabulary, a few researchers started to explore how instruction might promote sociocultural and sociolinguistic aspects of language use. Since then, dozens of instructional intervention studies of L2 pragmatics have been carried out, and more recently, researchers have conducted meta-analyses and research synthesis of this body of work. Jeon and Kaya (2006) carried out the first meta-analysis, which examined 34 instructional studies, Takahashi (2010) later examined 49 studies, and Taguchi (2015b) included 58 studies. The conclusions drawn from these overviews generally confirmed that pragmatics is teachable. Instructed groups, particularly those who received explicit metaprag-matic instruction—that is, information about the sociolinguistic "rules" of the target language or culture—tended to outperform their non-instructed counter-parts on a variety of measures. A notable trend that emerged from Taguchi's (2015b) research synthesis was the dominance of English as a target language. Of the 58 studies, 38 involved teaching English pragmatics. By comparison, lan-guages such as Japanese, German, French, Chinese, and Spanish were represented by between two and eight studies. Another commonality was the fact that most

L2 pragmatics studies used high-school or college students and ignored younger or older L2 populations. Other meta-analyses and synthesis reviews have been carried out by Badjadi (2016), and Plonsky and Zhuang (forthcoming).

These overviews also show that the scope of pragmatic targets being researched is skewed. Most L2 pragmatics research has focused on speech acts, with requests being the most popular. Studies not focusing on speech acts have involved address forms, discourse organizational skills (such as small talk), or interactional devices (including discourse markers such as *well* and *I mean,* and hedging devices such as *It might be* and *I wonder if*). The development of formulaic language has also been investigated extensively under various names such as routines, formulae, situation-bound utterances, and conventional expressions. Another trend that has emerged in recent reviews is the use of technology in teaching pragmatics. Teachers are increasingly making use of tools such as blogging, video conferencing, computer-mediated communication (CMC), and virtual gaming to teach L2 pragmatics. From the large body of research on instructed pragmatics, some general themes have emerged.

General themes that have emerged in relation to teaching L2 pragmatics (see, for example, Taguchi, 2015b, pp.35–36):

1. The effects of instruction vary depending on the assessment tasks and pragmatic targets. Pragmatic targets that are structurally simple (such as routines like greetings, goodbyes, service encounters, etc.) and pragmatic rules that are systematic are generally learned more easily. Evidence of learning is stronger for assessment tasks that are less cognitively demanding and more similar to treatment tasks.

2. Explicit teaching is generally more effective than implicit teaching, particularly when it involves direct metapragmatic information followed by production practice.

3. Implicit teaching can be as effective as explicit teaching if it promotes both noticing of the function of the target form as well as deeper-level processing of the forms. Effective teaching is closely related to the quality of processing depth. Learners who receive direct metapragmatic information, or learners who are guided to deduce pragmatic rules, seem to be able to process the input at a deeper level.

> **Points to remember**
>
> - Previous research in L2 pragmatics has shown that explicit teaching (especially direct metapragmatic information) is generally more effective than implicit teaching.
> - The effects of the treatment in instructional pragmatics studies change based on the pragmatic target and assessment tool being used.

Corresponding to the advancement in instructional studies, a wide variety of materials and activities have been created to teach and assess L2 pragmatics. Over a dozen teachers' guides, websites, and resource books illustrate how L2 pragmatic input can be incorporated into instructional tasks (e.g., Houck & Tatsuki, 2011; Ishihara & Cohen, 2010; Martínez-Flor & Usó-Juan, 2006). Cohen and Ishihara (2013) also outlined several tips for materials development. Researchers have suggested that the best practices in materials design include those designed to raise learners' awareness of pragmatic language use, to engage learners in pragmatically focused communication, and to guide learners toward independent discovery and understanding of pragmatic rules. Recently, Cohen and colleagues have initiated a Wiki-based repository called *wlpragmatics* (wlpragmatics.pbworks.com) to which L2 pragmatic researchers and instructors can upload their lesson plans for teaching pragmatics in the classroom.

During the same period that the teaching of L2 pragmatics became a focus, there was a similar expansion in research on how L2 pragmatic knowledge could best be assessed (Bardovi-Harlig & Shin, 2014; Hudson, Detmer, & Brown, 1995; Liu, 2007; Roever, 2005; Roever, Fraser & Elder, 2014). Many of the traditional concerns from the field of L2 testing were incorporated, such as careful operationalization of terms and taking account of an assessment's validity and reliability. Hudson et al. (1995) initiated this trend by presenting a multimethod approach to the assessment of L2 pragmatics. They showed how different measures, such as role plays and DCTs like the one popularized by Blum-Kulka et al. (1989a), can be triangulated to evaluate speech acts of requests, apologies, and refusals. Today, the range of methods for collecting and assessing language samples includes written and spoken DCTs, role plays, self-assessment surveys, interviews, think-aloud protocols, and multiple-choice tests, among others. Roever (2005) was one of the first to utilize technology to assess L2 pragmatics, implementing a web-based test for assessing speech acts (e.g., requests, refusals), implicature (nonliteral meaning), and routines (e.g., greetings, service encounter exchanges).

> **Points to remember**
>
> - *Speech acts* are language that performs some kind of action (e.g., refusals, requests, promises).
> - *Implicature* denotes the difference between speaker's meanings and the literal meaning of words. For example, "There's a bear behind you!" is a literal statement of fact, but carries the speaker's intended meaning: "you should get out of the way!"
> - *Routines* are expressions that are to some degree conventional and systematic according to a particular context. Examples are greetings (phone calls "Hello this is Anne speaking"), service encounters ("Can I have one order of pancakes?"), and so on.

Analyses of learners' performance on these assessment measures have led to a better understanding of the stages learners go through in developing L2 pragmatic competence. This research has also led to insights about curricula decisions and materials development. More recently, the testing of L2 pragmatics has shifted from assessing knowledge of isolated speech acts (requests, compliments), to including comprehension of implicature and recognition of routine formulae, and finally interaction abilities and participation in extended discourse (Roever, 2011).

The 1990s and Beyond: Longitudinal Research

At around the same time that the teaching and assessment of L2 pragmatics started to receive attention, the field also began supplementing the traditional practice of cross-sectional investigation by expanding research to longitudinal studies, in which time, as Figure 1.2 makes clear, is crucial: observations of the phenomena under investigation are made at periodic intervals for an extended period of time. Longitudinal designs are particularly useful for studying pragmatics because the acquisition of L2 pragmatic competence is a long-term process. It involves the development of abilities to manage a complex interplay between language, language users, and contexts of interaction. To become pragmatically competent, learners need not only linguistic resources but also the ability to evaluate layers of contextual information, select from the appropriate resources, and then use them effectively. Given this complexity, longitudinal lenses, which allow researchers to track learners over time, can provide fuller insights into the process as well as the product of learners' changing pragmatic abilities.

FIGURE 1.2 The 1990s and beyond: Longitudinal research

Early research in L2 pragmatics mainly focused on pragmatic use, not pragmatic development. This was noted in Kasper and Schmidt's (1996) seminal paper, which stated the following:

> Unlike other areas of second language study, which are primarily concerned with acquisitional patterns of interlanguage knowledge over time, the great majority of studies in ILP has not been developmental. Rather, focus is given to the ways NNS' pragmalinguistic and sociopragmatic knowledge differs from that of native speakers (NSs) and among learners with different linguistic and cultural backgrounds. To date, ILP has thus been primarily a study of second language use rather than second language acquisition.
>
> *(p. 150)*

This observation was repeated by subsequent researchers (e.g., Bardovi-Harlig, 1999, 2010; Kasper & Rose, 1999, 2002), who underscored the need for more longitudinal studies. Although their call did not immediately lead to a substantial expansion of longitudinal studies, the number of studies with a developmental focus gradually increased over time. Only nine longitudinal studies were included in Kasper and Rose's (1999) early review, but the number increased to about a dozen in Bardovi-Harlig's (2010) work. More recently, Taguchi's (2010) review located 21 longitudinal studies. This trend illustrates the growing interest in a longitudinal perspective on L2 pragmatics.

Longitudinal studies have documented changing patterns of development for a variety of pragmatic targets, ranging from the traditional constructs of speech acts, implicature, and routines, to interactional features that facilitate learners' participation in a communicative act such as acknowledgement and alignment expressions. Several generalizations can be made about the pace and pattern of L2 pragmatic development. Research in the area of *pragmatic comprehension* suggests that learners typically progress from a stage where meaning is marked via conventional linguistic cues or discourse patterns, to a stage where meaning does not involve those cues and thus requires extensive inferencing (e.g., Bouton, 1992; Taguchi, 2005, 2007). In the area of *pragmatic production*, learners usually show an initial tendency to stick to one-to-one correspondence between form and function, often symbolized by the overgeneralization of a few pragmalinguistic forms over a range of functions or the use of routine formulae (e.g., Hassall, 2006; Ohta, 2001; Salsbury & Bardovi-Harlig, 2000; Shively, 2011). Learners gradually expand their pragmalinguistic repertoire by adopting a new form-function association into their systems. This process is typically slow, but feedback and modeling from community members can facilitate the process (as was the case in Hassall [2006], who found that explicit pragmatic knowledge of leave-taking in social conversations was acquired after repeated noticing of the form and practice in informal interactions. His study showed that informal, out-of-class practice and observation can be effective for pragmatic learning). However, it is also worth mentioning that some longitudinal studies showed that mere exposure does not always lead to acquisition of certain pragmatic targets such as Pope Q implicature as in the case for Bouton (1994) and certain aspects of institutional discourse during advising sessions in Bardovi-Harlig and Hartford's (1993) studies. Based on these acquisitional studies, it can be observed that pragmatic comprehension and production in an additional language may show different patterns of development.

Longitudinal research has also shown developmental variation across pragmatic targets. Some aspects of pragmatics seem to be associated with a faster developmental pace than others. For instance, learners' use of pragmalinguistic forms (including hedges and lexical and syntactic mitigations, like *somewhat,* or *maybe,* or phrases like *I'm not an expert but . . .*) tend to take a longer time to develop than semantic strategies and tactics used to organize a speech act (such as engaging in small talk to build solidarity or using expressions of consideration) (e.g., Félix-Brasdefer & Hasler-Barker, 2015; Ren, 2012; Schauer, 2007; for a review, see Li, 2016). Diverse methodologies have been used to elicit data in longitudinal research, ranging from ethnographic studies that involve observation of naturalistic phenomenon to descriptive-quantitative and experimental studies that use construct-eliciting instruments.

Of the 21 longitudinal studies in Taguchi's (2010) review, 16 were conducted in a second language (SL) context where the target language is spoken, while the rest took place in a foreign language (FL) environment. The opposite pattern was seen in reviews of instructional intervention research, where more studies were conducted in a FL rather than SL context. This lopsided pattern raises the question of whether naturalistic pragmatic development might best be observed in a SL context where sociocultural input and practice are readily available. Lacking such input, learners in a FL context might benefit more from direct teaching of pragmatics.

The 2000s and Beyond: The Application of SLA Theories to L2 Pragmatics Research and Teaching

The first two decades of this century have seen important developments in both instructional and longitudinal research on L2 pragmatics. This work has centered on two related questions: What mechanisms drive pragmatic development? How are learners pushed from their current state to a higher level of pragmatic competence? To address these questions, longitudinal studies have investigated changes in learners' pragmatic systems in naturalistic contexts, with the goal of revealing factors – both individual and contextual – that contribute to development. These questions are also addressed via instructional studies that conceptualize teaching as the factor that most directly leads to pragmatic development. Instructional studies typically control for individual characteristics and contextual factors so that researchers can attribute the observed development (or non-development) to instruction.

>
> • Instructional research and longitudinal research (research conducted over a period of time as opposed to "one shot" research) in L2 pragmatics is designed to answer questions such as: What mechanisms drive pragmatic development? How are learners pushed from their current state to a higher level of pragmatic competence?
> • Pragmatic knowledge shows developmental variations based on the target pragmatic construct (e.g., speech acts, routines, implicature) and knowledge or modality type (i.e., comprehension, production).

Whether longitudinal, instructional, or cross-sectional, grounding L2 pragmatics research in SLA theory is fundamental. SLA theories are needed as a foundation for tracing change in longitudinal research or developing instructional methods. Kasper and Rose (2002) criticized L2 pragmatics studies for not explicitly situating themselves within a theoretical framework and argued that "theoretical positions have been appealed to as post hoc explanations of findings rather than serving as the basis for the design and conduct of the study in question" (p. 13).

Responding to this criticism, the last decade has seen an increasing diversity in SLA theory in general as illustrated in various textbook introductions to SLA theories and research programs. Mainstream theoretical foundations for L2 pragmatics research include:

Noticing hypothesis
Skill acquisition theories
Language socialization theory
Dynamic systems theory
The interaction approach

Sample illustrations of a range of theoretical paradigms in L2 pragmatics research are as follows (for further information, see Taguchi & Roever, 2017).

The Noticing Hypothesis

The *noticing hypothesis* (Schmidt, 1993, 2001) has been important in SLA literature since the 1990s. It posits that L2 learners' attention to linguistic form is a necessary condition for development. In other words, learners must demonstrate some level of awareness about the relationships between language form and meaning in different situations. Schmidt contends that input leads to acquisition only if learners notice the input. This theoretical claim has been tested in a number of studies of L2 pragmatics, both instructional and longitudinal (e.g., Belz & Kinginger, 2003; Fordyce, 2014; Hassall, 2006).

Language Socialization Theory

Language socialization theory has been used in L2 pragmatics research since the 1990s (e.g., Kanagy, 1999). Language socialization views learning as a process in which novices become competent members in a society through interaction with expert members in that society (Schieffelin & Ochs, 1986). During this process, language is both the means and end of the socialization process: Novices are socialized *through* the use of language, and they are socialized *to use* language. The learning-through-participation framework has been documented in a number of recent studies (e.g., Cook, 2008; Diao, 2014; McMeekin, 2014; Shively, 2011). For instance, Diao (2014) analyzed conversations among learners of Chinese and their Chinese roommates. Her data revealed instances of peer socialization in the gendered practices associated with Chinese sentence final particles.

Dynamic Systems Theory

Dynamic systems theory (Larsen-Freeman & Cameron, 2008; De Bot, Lowie, & Verspoor, 2007) attempts to account for the often messy, noisy, and/or chaotic patterns found in L2 output. In dynamic systems theory, many factors interact simultaneously and over time leading to developmental patterns that are not always linear or predictable from looking at just one or two variables. Taguchi's (2012) study conducted in an immersion setting revealed intricate interactions between context and individual characteristics shaping pragmatic development.

In sum, there are strong and important connections between SLA theories and the field of L2 pragmatics. Despite different epistemologies and assumptions, most theories of how second languages are learned are similar in that they all aim to explain how pragmatic knowledge becomes consolidated (Taguchi & Roever, 2017). While the noticing hypothesis emphasizes attention as a primary state, interaction approaches highlight the role of corrective feedback and attention in the process of L2 pragmatic development. Skill acquisition theories view repeated practice as a force for the consolidation of pragmatic knowledge. Collaborative dialogue and sociocultural theory consider verbalization a means for externalizing understanding of pragmatics, which in turn facilitates internalization of pragmatic knowledge. In the language socialization paradigm, pragmatic knowledge becomes consolidated through participation in routine social activities with competent members. Critically, these different theories − which sometimes entail different research methodologies − have jointly enriched our understanding of L2 pragmatic development. We return to this point in Chapter 8.

> • There are strong and important connections between SLA theories and approaches, and the field of L2 pragmatics.
> • Various SLA theories from socially to more cognitively oriented theories guide L2 pragmatics research by providing us a multiple framework that helps explain the development of the L2 pragmatic system.
>
> *Points to remember*

L2 Pragmatics Research Today

L2 pragmatics is an exciting research area that is undergoing some significant changes. A re-conceptualization of L2 pragmatic competence is taking place. The traditional view was that L2 pragmatic competence is a trait within individual learners. However, the field is increasingly adopting the position that pragmatics is a socially constructed phenomenon situated in a context. Parallel to this shift, current analytical frameworks and procedures have changed their focus from "pragmatics-within-individuals" to "pragmatics-in-interaction-in-context" by drawing on concepts like interactional competence (Young, 2008a, 2008b, 2011a, 2011b), discursive pragmatics (Kasper, 2006), and methods of conversation analysis (Sacks, Schegloff, & Jefferson, 1974).

> • Traditional views in L2 pragmatic competence posit that L2 competence is a trait within individual learners.
> • L2 pragmatics researchers today has adopted the positions that pragmatics is cognitively and socially constructed and situated in contexts.
>
> *Points to remember*

Globalization, Internationalization, and L2 Pragmatics Research

Another change currently underway is the influence of globalization and internationalization on L2 pragmatics. With international trends toward multilingualism and multiculturalism, SLA researchers are increasingly beginning to reconsider our traditional assumptions about language and language use. The stability of nation-states, the existence of codified norms of language, and the presence of clear boundaries between native and foreign languages are changing (Kramsch, 2014, p. 296; Tarone, 2013). Concomitantly, there is growing interest in the areas of intercultural pragmatics (Kecskes, 2014; Spencer-Oatey & Franklin, 2009), pragmatics in *lingua franca* communication (House, 2010), multilingual pragmatic competence (Alcón-Soler, 2013), and heritage learner pragmatics (e.g., Park, 2006; Pinto & Raschio, 2008) (see Taguchi & Roever, 2017, for a review).

Pragmatics in English as Lingua Franca

The influence of globalization has transformed traditional practices of L2 pragmatics research in a number of important ways. For instance, pragmatics research in English as a *lingua franca* (ELF) is extending beyond the traditional notions of politeness and appropriateness to incorporate a wider domain of pragmatics strategies for analysis, including negotiation of meaning, interactional management, creative idiomaticity, and the use of multilingual resources (Cogo & House, 2017). This shift suggests that ELF pragmatics research is focusing on how L2 speakers co-construct mutual understanding while coping with communication difficulties.

ELF research has also led us to question the use of native speaker norms in assessing L2 pragmatic competence. A generalization is emerging in the ELF literature, as in other areas of applied linguistics, that some people use English not to identify with native English speakers, but to achieve mutual understanding with other speakers (Jenkins, 2015; Seidlhofer, 2011). Because ELF speakers focus on mutual intelligibility over native speaker-like correctness, native speaker norms do not necessarily serve as a reference point (Seidlhofer, 2011). It is also common to find variation among native speakers in terms of what "sounds right" and what does not; therefore, speakers may have divergent opinions about the same situation or context. Multilinguals often bring their other languages' pragmatic norms into play, which can change how they comprehend and produce language.

Researchers in L2 pragmatics have been significantly influenced by the wider discussion on native speaker norms, as they evaluate what counts as socially appropriate language use. For instance, appropriateness can be conceptualized according to local norms rather than idealized native speaker norms. We can evaluate what communicative needs are shared among L2 speakers, what resources they possess, and what goals they orient to in their local context. This type of needs analyses helps us capture norms respective to the local community, and those norms in turn can serve as criteria for assessing learners' success in an intercultural exchange. The necessity to consider the local community's and learners' needs is also echoed in Brown's (2014) article on world Englishes and testing. Seidlhofer (2011) claims that appropriateness in ELF refers to the "legitimate appropriation of the English language by its majority expanding circle users, together with whatever diversity and hybridity suited their own purposes rather than the purposes of inner circle speakers" (p. 149). The notion of "legitimate appropriation" is useful for L2 pragmatics researchers as they review appropriateness from the local community viewpoint.

As research topics and agendas have shifted over time, methods used to investigate those topics have also shifted. Exciting developments in methodology and instrumentation have taken place, expanding our options in terms of research methods and driving our findings further. Let's now turn to research questions.

1.3 What Research Questions are Asked in Second Language Pragmatics?

Research in L2 pragmatics has expanded rapidly as seen in the steep increase in the scope and number of empirical studies produced in the last few decades, together with new books, journals, and conferences. A large, diverse body of international literature has expanded the focus of L2 pragmatics analysis far beyond Kasper and Dahl's (1991) original presentation of L2 pragmatics as "comprehension and production of speech acts" and "L2 related speech act knowledge" (p. 216). Although speech act studies continue to be carried out, other characteristics of pragmatic competence such as the ability to perform communicative functions in a given situation, knowledge of socially appropriate language use, and the ability to interact in a sociocultural activity have been adopted to operationalize pragmatic constructs.

In line with the evolution in focus in the field of L2 pragmatics, new tasks and methods for data collection and analysis have been developed. L2 pragmatics research now focuses not only on linguistic but also on discourse-level and interactional units. Some traditional and recent units of analysis in L2 pragmatics research include speech acts, implicature, humor, routine formulae, honorifics and speech styles (e.g., polite and plain forms), address terms, rules of institutional talk (e.g., service encounters, academic advising), politeness strategies, communication strategies, interactional devices (e.g., response tokens, discourse markers), and mechanisms of conversation (e.g., turn-taking, sequential relevancy, and preference organizations) amongst many others. This list is in no way exhaustive, as the body of research continues to expand by exploring different ways to define, operationalize, teach, treat, and assess pragmatic competence.

L2 pragmatics studies to date have employed descriptive, quasi-experimental, survey-based, qualitative, and quantitative methods to address a variety of research questions. These questions can be roughly organized into four areas of investigation: (1) constructs and methodology; (2) development; (3) individual factors; and (4) contextual factors. Construct and methodology based questions relate to the definition, operationalization, and measurement of pragmatic competence. Developmental questions are concerned with L2 learners' changing pragmatic abilities across time. The individual and contextual questions explore how individual characteristics and contextual factors influence L2 pragmatic development. Although we present these questions in separate categories, it should be noted that they are neither mutually exclusive nor exhaustive.

Questions About What L2 Pragmatics is and How it is Studied

- What are the defining characteristics of pragmatic competence? What does it mean to be pragmatically competent in a second language?
- How are communicative competence, pragmatic competence, and interactional competence related and how are they different?

- How can we operationalize sociolinguistic and pragmalinguistic competence? Are they separable? If not, what are the best ways to investigate these competences separately?
- How did previous pragmatics studies operationalize pragmatic competence? What pragmatic constructs did they investigate?
- What are the differences and similarities between cross-cultural pragmatics and interlanguage pragmatics research? How can one inform the other branch?
- What measurements and tasks can be used to illuminate L2 learners' developing pragmatic competence? Do the measures and tasks have construct validity? Are the measures reliable? Are the interpretations about pragmatic competence drawn from those measures generalizable?
- How are pragmatic constructs operationalized in L2 pragmatics studies? To what extent do they match with studies' definitions of pragmatics?
- Given the fact that most studies use DCTs to measure learners' pragmatic ability, to what extent are they reflective of the definition of L2 pragmatic competence and language learners' target language use domain? How can DCTs be improved?
- Does modality (e.g., speaking versus listening versus writing) affect pragmatic performance? Are pragmatic comprehension and production related to each other? Does the ability to comprehend pragmatic meaning develop in parallel with the ability to convey meaning appropriately, or does one precede the other?
- Is the demonstration of pragmatic knowledge (e.g., effective use of a speech act) different from the efficient processing of pragmatic knowledge? How are they related? Do they generate distinct information about learners' pragmatic competence?
- Based on the ongoing discussion about the nature of language knowledge in the field of SLA, what can you say about explicit/implicit pragmatic knowledge? What types of knowledge does L2 pragmatics research investigate? How are these different types of pragmatic knowledge assessed? Can explicit pragmatic knowledge become implicit with practice?
- Do L1-L2 similarities and differences in linguistic forms, social conventions, and cultural norms lead to positive or negative pragmatic transfer? Does the transfer affect patterns of pragmatic performance and rates of pragmatic development?
- Is pragmatic competence constrained by learners' grammatical knowledge and general language proficiency? Do learners at different proficiency levels exhibit different pragmatic performances, and if so, what are those differences?
- What are the characteristics of advanced pragmatic competence in a second or additional language?
- How can pragmatic language use be documented in intercultural communication?

- To what extent do traditional assessment practices apply to the context of intercultural communication in which participants do not operate on native speakers' norms?
- What is the extent of variation in pragmatic performance among native speakers?
- In the current globalized society, if there are no uniform native speaker standards, or if the standards are not valid or relevant in evaluating L2 pragmatic abilities, what are alternative approaches to assessing pragmatic competence? By what criteria should appropriateness be determined and evaluated?
- How does L2 pragmatics research contribute to the field of applied linguistics? What are some of the key findings of the L2 pragmatic research that are important for the field in general?

Questions About L2 Pragmatics and L2 Development

- Is there a common order of development within specific pragmatic constructs, in other words, do learners progress through set stages? Is there a common developmental trajectory among participants for all languages?
- How do mainstream SLA theories, hypotheses, and frameworks inform and explain pragmatic development?
- What are the differences and similarities between L1 and L2 pragmatic development?
- Do learners exhibit meaningful gains in pragmatic competence, outside grammatical, lexical, and phonological competence? How does a gain in pragmatic competence compare with that of other areas of language competence?
- How do pragmalinguistic and sociopragmatic dimensions unfold during the course of pragmatic development?
- Do learners demonstrate an even pace in development across pragmatic features and functions, or do some features and functions develop more quickly than others?
- Do the knowledge and processing aspects of pragmatic competence unfold in parallel, or does one lag behind the other?
- Does pragmatic competence develop naturally with input, or does development require instruction, feedback, and modeling?
- What kinds of feedback promote pragmatic development the best? Is implicit or explicit pragmatic feedback better?
- Is a full (advanced) mastery of L2 pragmatic competence possible?
- How long is long enough for learners to develop functional-level pragmatic competence?
- What are the optimal number of data points and their spacing to capture a change in pragmatic competence?

Questions About Learners as Individuals

- What sort of individual variations exist in pragmatic development? What are the sources of those variations (e.g., proficiency, personality, creativity, motivation, attitudes, intercultural sensitivity, and cognitive factors)?
- Do the nature and domains of social contact explain variations in pragmatic change among individual learners? Do learners have equal access to opportunities for pragmatic practice, or do individual characteristics (e.g., gender) affect access to opportunities?
- Do learners' dynamic identities, subjectivity, and agency promote or constrain their access to opportunity, affecting individual trajectories of pragmatic development?
- What is the role of learners' resistance to learning L2 pragmatic norms in their L2 pragmatic competence?
- Given the unique properties of pragmatic competence, is there a specific set of individual characteristics that uniquely affect pragmatics learning? What individual characteristics can differentiate between successful and less successful learners of pragmatics?
- Is there a traits-constructs interaction in L2 pragmatics? For instance, do individual traits such as motivation and attitudes (which fluctuate) differentially affect learners' comprehension and production of pragmatic functions? How?

Questions About the Context of Learning Languages

- To what extent do the exposure to target language input and learners' amount of social contact with target language speakers assist pragmatic development?
- What types of learning resources and experiences are available in context, and how do they shape developmental trajectories of individual learners?
- What are the differences between SL and FL contexts in terms of providing opportunities for learning L2 pragmatics?
- Does an instructional setting that does not focus on L2 pragmatics afford enough sociocultural opportunities to lead to increased pragmatic abilities?
- How effective are study abroad contexts for L2 pragmatics learning? What aspects of pragmatic competence do learners develop while abroad? What resources and opportunities in a study abroad setting facilitate pragmatic development?
- Is pragmatics teachable? What instructional methods lead to robust pragmatic knowledge and learning? Is explicit teaching more effective than implicit methods? What are the characteristics of effective instruction?
- What opportunities for pragmatic practice are available in less-studied contexts, such as international workplaces and heritage language learning environments?

- What is known about pragmatic acquisition in less commonly taught languages? Do research findings on such languages corroborate research conducted in frequently studied languages?
- Can we speak of "universal" pragmatic norms across languages regardless of context? Or do contextual factors influence pragmatic norms?
- What are the recent developments in technology-supported contexts for pragmatics learning? How can technology best be leveraged as a solution to existing barriers to pragmatics research, teaching, and assessment?
- Given the undeniable impact of technology in daily conversations, what are the similarities and differences between face-to-face communication and CMC in terms of their pragmatic expectations? What about traditional pragmatic instruction and computer-mediated instruction? Which one is more helpful?
- How do contextual affordances and individual learner characteristics interact with each other and jointly shape developmental trajectories in L2 pragmatics?

Accumulated research findings have, either individually or collectively, provided some answers to these empirical questions, but these have, inevitably, led to more questions. Many of the studies that exist need to be replicated and extended to research with different populations before we can be confident of the results (Porte, forthcoming). We will discuss some of these studies in the rest of this book, as we focus on methods of data collection.

Discussion Questions

1. Communicative competence includes both grammatical knowledge and knowledge about social situations and culture. Imagine you are a language learner working on a group project on travel in a university English class. What kinds of grammatical knowledge will be necessary to successfully complete the project? What kinds of cultural or social knowledge will be important? What are the consequences of breakdowns in communicative competence in this setting?
2. Some of what we know about L2 pragmatic development focuses on only a few forms such as speech acts, with requests being the most popular. Why do you think this is the case? What areas of pragmatic development seem most important for L2 learners? Least important? Brainstorm some other speech acts that could be important for learners' pragmatic competence.
3. International trends in multilingualism and globalization compel researchers to reconsider traditional assumptions about language and language use. Take the case of border communities where there are no clear boundaries between a native and foreign language, and *lingua franca* are common. What kinds of problems or new research questions in L2 pragmatics do these contexts

generate? Why might these issues be important to researchers in the field of L2 pragmatics?

4. Review the list of research questions above and choose one that relates to an area that interests you. What aspects of this question are in need of more research or replication? Are there any gaps in the research on L2 pragmatics that need to be addressed? See if you can add one or two research questions in your area to the list.

2
LANGUAGE PRODUCTION: CONCEPTUAL BACKGROUND

Introduction

In this chapter, we focus on foundational theories and concepts in general pragmatics, viewing pragmatics as a branch of linguistics. Our particular aim here is to look at what has been influential in L2 pragmatics.

2.1 Pragmatics

Although the field of modern pragmatics is often said to have developed as a field in the 1970s, 1983 was a special year when several key works were published. These included Stephen Levinson's *Pragmatics* and Geoffrey Leech's *Principles of Pragmatics*. However, while these books were, and are, extremely influential, a surprising but common theme is that their definitions of pragmatics are somewhat tortured or missing. For example, Levinson spends pages attempting to define the area and simply defines pragmatics as "the study of language use" (Levinson, 1983, p. 5), while Leech (1983) largely ducks the issue. Pragmatics researchers today usually point to definitions revolving around statements such as "meanings in context" or "what you really mean by what you say or don't say." To repeat an often-used example of a pragmatic phenomenon, someone saying "it's cold," while in the context of a window being open (see Figure 2.1), and even perhaps looking meaningfully at the person closest to the window, might intend the meaning of a polite request to please close the window.

But when we consider meaning in context more carefully, what kind of meanings and contexts are we talking about? In corpus linguistics, researchers use computers to analyze language in large, usually systematically collected, amounts of authentic language data in electronic form (i.e., corpora). In their studies

FIGURE 2.1 "It's cold"

(e.g., Biber, Conrad, & Cortes, 2004; Garcia, 2007; Staples, 2015), corpus research-ers typically view word meanings as meanings shaped by their local contexts or collocational contexts, that is, their co-occurrence with other words. This is a very narrow approach to context, one that is focused on co-text. Pragmatics does encompass co-text, including the broader co-text that makes up an interaction, but in addition, importantly, it encompasses the situational context (both the setting of the interaction, such as a lecture theatre, and the activity constructed within it, such as a lecture), the cultural context (the taken-for-granted understandings that members of certain social groups bring to bear in interactions), and the cognitive context (the knowledge that people bring to bear in interactions). Regarding meanings, recollect our definition of pragmatics in Chapter 1. Pragmatics revolves around meanings that are implied, inferred, and negotiated. Below, we will think more about how to define the meaning of words by considering:

(a) a detailed pragmatic analysis;
(b) the perspectives other researchers have taken on the subject; and
(c) what researchers tend to include in their studies.

Meaning in Context

[1] [*In a countryside area in the UK, traveling in a car, past a field with cows in it.*]

   1. *Jonathan:* They're lying down . . . means it's going to rain.
   2. *Emily:* Well, what if it doesn't.
   3. *Natalie:* They'd be lying.

(Culpeper, Katamba, Kerswill, Wodak, & McEnery, 2009, p. 202)

The first word of the interaction, the pronoun *they,* could not be understood without the situational context. It has a deictic function, inviting the hearers to pick out the cows from the context. When we see *they* again in line (3), it is not only identifying something in the situational context but creating a cohesive link with the mention of *they* earlier in the talk. The focal point of this interaction is the word *lying*. Because it has two senses, either telling untruths or the opposite of standing/sitting, we can see that simple decoding does not work – how do we know which sense, or indeed whether both senses, should be understood? In fact, the lexical context strongly restricts the choice: the spatial proposition *down* clearly works with the second of these senses (the opposite of standing/sitting). Furthermore, this meaning is consistent with the cultural context of the UK in which there is folklore about cows lying down on the ground signifying rain. The sense of the word *well* in (2) is also indeterminate. Here it has nothing to do with being healthy. But what does it actually mean? To understand this, one needs to take on board its interactional context, the adjoining speech acts: it is used to signal a qualification to or disagreement with what has just been asserted in line (1). *What if it doesn't* is a WH-question that not only serves as an act eliciting information, but also implies that there is a possibility that it might not rain. This implication is a humorous challenge. All the participants in this interaction already share the knowledge that it is folklore and that folklore is not a truth: there is no real guarantee that cows lying down means that it will rain. So why imply what we already know? The implication conveyed by the question (falsely) treats line (1) as if it were an assertion about some kind of truth with (philosophical) consequences if it does not rain. This is not an impolite challenge; more of a humorous tease. The utterance in line (3) is produced as an answer to the question in line (2). Moreover, this answer exploits the earlier ambiguous potential of the word *lying* in the assertion of line (1). This exploitation generates humor, partly because the ambiguity was not that obvious in line (1) and line (3) exposes it.

The key point about the previous example is that to fully understand the meaning, you cannot simply decode the word meanings. Instead, meanings are generated and understood in context, and, moreover, those meanings partly create that context as it develops over the course of the interaction. Language is indeterminate: meanings are not simply matched to language forms on a one-to-one basis. Pragmatics accepts the existence of indeterminacy – unlike formal syntactic and semantics theories – and offers principled ways in which indeterminacy can be handled.

> **Points to remember**
> • Language is indeterminate: meanings are not simply matched to language forms on a one-to-one basis. To fully understand the meaning of an utterance, you cannot simply decode the word meanings. Instead, meanings are generated and understood in context.

Two Views of Pragmatics

Where particular controversy arises, however, is the scope of pragmatics. Two particular views have emerged in the literature. One, in some respects the more traditional view, sees pragmatics as a component in a theory of language, adding to the usual phonetics, phonology, morphology, grammar/syntax, and semantics. An early proponent of this view is Charles Morris. Morris, in his *Foundations of the Theory of Signs* (Morris, 1938, pp. 6–7), argues for the following three-way distinction:

- Syntax (or syntactics) – mono relationship (relationships between linguistic signs)
- Semantics – dyadic relationship (relationships between linguistic signs and the things in the world that they designate)
- Pragmatics – triadic relationship (relationships between linguistic signs, things they designate, and their users/interpreters)

Pragmatics, then, can be seen as the area of linguistics that adds context. This view of pragmatics is often referred to as the *Anglo-American view of pragmatics*. A particular characteristic of this view is its more micro concerns. The topics illustrated by our example above, which would typically be discussed within this view, include reference, deixis, speech acts, implications, implicatures, and inferences.

In contrast, a broad view of pragmatics moves beyond pragmatics as a component of linguistics. In the broad view, pragmatics becomes the superordinate field with linguistics as one discipline within it, along with sociology, psychology, and so on. This is generally known as the *Continental European view of pragmatics*. As Verschueren (1999, p. 7) puts it, pragmatics is a "general cognitive, social, and cultural perspective on linguistic phenomena in relation to their usage in forms of behavior." So for him, pragmatics is not located in linguistics, but is a "general cognitive, social, and cultural perspective." A particular characteristic of this view is its more macro concerns. The topics illustrated by our example above, which would typically be discussed within this view, include the dynamics of inter-action, the construction and understanding of humor and teasing, and the role of culture. Scholars pursuing this view of pragmatics would not avoid issues to do with, for example, speech acts or implications/implicatures, but they would typically discuss them in the broader context of the data in which they were being used. Some topics, politeness being a case in point, are covered in both views, but in rather different ways. As illustrated in Figure 2.2, in the Anglo-American view, politeness might be broken down into the specific speech acts that contribute to the politeness, while the Continental European view would discuss how cultural factors influence the appropriateness of certain features. In the Anglo-American view, the focus is more on micro linguistic structures; in the Continental European view, the focus is more on macro socio-cultural aspects.

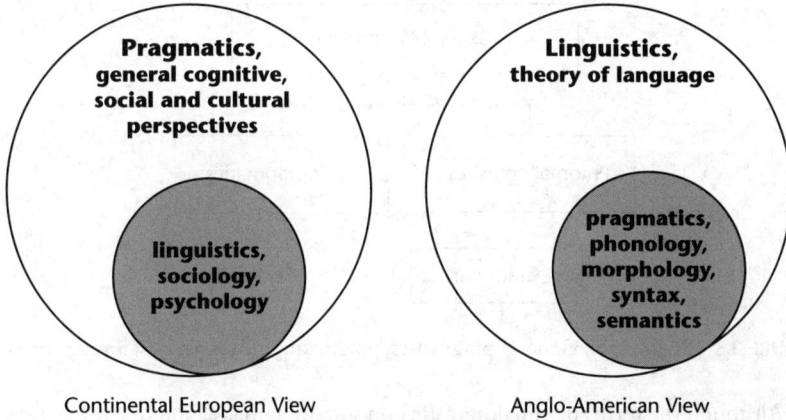

| Continental European View | Anglo-American View |

FIGURE 2.2 The Continental European and Anglo–American view of pragmatics

We believe that thinking about this distinction between the Anglo-American and Continental European views of pragmatics as a dichotomy is overly simplistic. Over the last few years especially, there have been moves to synthesize Anglo-American ideas with Continental European, with Culpeper and Haugh's (2014) book, *Pragmatics and the English Language,* being an example.

> • The traditionally *Anglo-American view of pragmatics* defines pragmatics as the area of linguistics that adds context.
> • The traditionally *Continental European view of pragmatics* takes a broad view of pragmatics as a superordinate field with linguistics as one discipline within it, along with sociology, psychology, and other disciplines.
> • Scholars have been working recently toward a more synthesized approach.

2.2 General Pragmatics, Pragmalinguistics, and Sociopragmatics

Pragmatics, according to Leech (1983), can be approached by making the following three distinctions:

General pragmatics: "the general conditions of the communicative use of language" (p. 10);

Sociopragmatics: "more specific 'local' conditions on language use" (p. 10); and

Pragmalinguistics: "the particular resources which a given language provides for conveying particular illocutions" (p. 11; "illocutions" are a central part of speech acts).

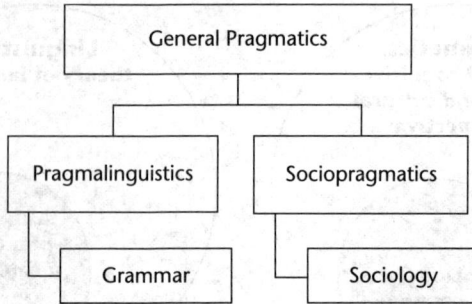

FIGURE 2.3 Pragmatics: General pragmatics, pragmalinguistics, and sociopragmatics

Although the terms pragmalinguistic and sociopragmatic, and to a lesser extent the theories behind them, slightly predate their work (see Marmaridou, 2011), it is Leech (1983) and Thomas (1981, 1983) who established these terms and their meaning. Leech (1983) attributes the formulation of the pragmalinguistic/ sociopragmatic distinction to Thomas (1981, 1983), but it is Leech who published a view of pragmatics incorporating them. A diagram displaying the relationships between these areas is shown in Figure 2.3.

In a nutshell, *general pragmatics* captures relatively universal pragmatic principles and mechanisms. *Pragmalinguistics* captures linguistic phenomena that are imbued with pragmatic meanings, and *sociopragmatics* captures the specific contextual phenomena that shape pragmatic meanings on a particular occasion of use. It is important to note that pragmalinguistics and sociopragmatics are not considered subcategories of general pragmatics, but complementary areas of study within pragmatics as a whole.

One thing we should note at this early stage is a critique of definitions of pragmalinguistics and sociopragmatics – they either lean toward the perspective of the speaker or do not make it clear which participant it applies to. This is particularly obvious in Leech's definition of pragmalinguistics, which is, essentially, about the resources available to speakers for conveying intentional meanings. Hearers are less often considered, and there is no sense that some meanings are worked out jointly between speakers and hearers – which is particularly important to L2 pragmatics.

As we briefly noted in Chapter 1, the pragmalinguistic/sociopragmatic distinction is particularly useful and well known to researchers working in the areas of cross-cultural pragmatics and L2 pragmatics. This evolved from Thomas's important (1983) work on the notion of "pragmatic failure." As she notes:

[P]ragmalinguistic failure is basically a *linguistic* problem, caused by differences in the linguistic encoding of pragmatic force, sociopragmatic failure stems from cross-culturally different perceptions of what constitutes appropriate linguistic behaviour.

(Thomas, 1983, p. 99)

Four brief examples illustrate this:

[2] [*Draft work by a Japanese student.*]

It is principle of conversation.

[3] [*Conversation with an Italian in English.*]

Jonathan: It's sad it turned out that way.
Italian friend: In fact.

[4] [*The film director Paul Spurrier describes his experiences of making the first Thai language film, "P" ever shot by a Westerner.*]

So I worked closely with a Thai translator to try to get authenticity, and used a Thai crew. Even so, I made mistakes. In one scene, a character greets someone by saying "How are you?" I watched the scene recently and realized that in fact Thai people don't greet each other in this way. They are far more likely to ask "Have you eaten rice yet?"

(Spurrier, 2005, https://screenanarchy.com/2005/04/
paul-spurrier-talks-thailand-ghosts-and-p.html)

[5]   *Example of pragmatic failure from the TV show* The Big Bang Theory

Raj: Hold on, Sheldon, is there ketchup on that table?
Sheldon: [looks at the table] Yes, there is. Here's a fun fact, ketchup started as a general term for sauce, typically made of mushrooms or fish brine with herbs and spices. Popular early main ingredients included: blueberry, anchovies, oyster, kidney bean, and grape.
Raj: No, that's okay. I'll get it.

Example [2] has little to do with pragmatics. It simply contains a grammatical error: the lack of a definite or indefinite article (i.e., "it is a/the principle of conversation"). The error is probably due to the fact that Japanese lacks grammatical articles. Example [3] is an example of pragmalinguistic failure. Italian *infatti* resembles English *in fact* in form and has a similar history, both coming from the same roots. However, it is a false friend. English *in fact* implies, unlike the Italian expression, that a qualification to what has just been said will follow. But in [3], *in fact* is all that is said – there is, oddly, no following qualification. A more target-like expression would have been *indeed*. Example [4] is an example of sociopragmatic failure. The issue lies not in the expression "How are you?" but the context in which it is appropriate for it to be used, and that does not include, according to the director, the Thai cultural context. Example [5] is another example of sociopragmatic failure, but this time very much on the part of the hearer, Sheldon.

In saying what they already know (they can see the ketchup on that table), Raj flouts the maxim of quantity (part of H.P. Grice's Cooperative Principle accounting for implied meanings; discussed in Chapter 4), and in so doing implies a request to pass the ketchup. Sheldon fails to work out the implied meaning (implicature). Sheldon's character often pragmatically fails in this way, something that partly characterizes him as a "nerd" and also provides amusement for the audience.

> **Points to remember**
>
> - Pragmalinguistic failure is an issue with *linguistic* features, caused by differences in the linguistic encoding of pragmatic force.
> - Sociopragmatic failure stems from cross-culturally different perceptions of what constitutes appropriate linguistic behavior.

While the pragmalinguistic/sociopragmatic distinction is clearly helpful for the analysis of intercultural interactions of all kinds, it is not entirely unproblematic. They are not discreet categories, but rather two ends of a continuum (cf. Thomas, 1983), as we illustrate below.

Politeness

When it comes to politeness phenomena, separating pragmalinguistic failure from sociopragmatic failure becomes particularly tricky. For example, did someone use an inadequately polite expression in an L2 encounter because it has a different politeness value for them in their L1 (thus pragmalinguistic failure), or is it that what they were asking for in that particular social context requires less politeness (thus sociopragmatic failure)? Or both? For example, in [6] below from the TV show *Friends* we see pragmatic failure being parodied. But is it pragmalinguistic or sociopragmatic, or both?

[6] [*Phoebe calls a friend for information in the TV show* Friends.]
 [Phone rings]

 British Housekeeper: The Waltham residence.
 Phoebe: Oh yes, is this Emily's parents' house?
 Housekeeper: This is the housekeeper speaking. And by the way, that is not the way one addresses a person on the telephone. First one identifies oneself and then asks for the person with whom one wishes to speak.
 Phoebe: What are you saying?
 Housekeeper: Now, let us try that again shall we? [Hangs up]
 Phoebe: No! Oh! Oh my god! [Calls again]

Housekeeper: The Waltham residence.

Phoebe: [British accent] Hello, um this is Phoebe Buffet. I was wondering please, if it's not too much trouble please, might I speak with Miss Emily Waltham please?

Housekeeper: Miss Waltham is at the rehearsal dinner and it is not polite to make fun of people. Good bye.

Does Phoebe's first utterance ("is this Emily's parents' house?") carry an acceptable level of politeness in opening a phone call in a North America context? Or is it that that context requires less politeness in North America? Or a combination of these things? As can be seen, pragmatic failure can stem from several sources.

Leech (2014) suggests that the pragmalinguistic/sociopragmatic distinction is a matter of different orientations, one being more linguistic and the other more socio-cultural. Marmaridou (2011) suggests that the issue is focusing on one while placing the other in the background. It is certainly not straightforward to draw a line between them, and this has important consequences for methods in L2 pragmatics. As Marmaridou (2011, pp. 93–94) points out "it is difficult to devise a test that would assess pragmalinguistic knowledge to the exclusion of pragmatic knowledge, or the reverse." We will return to this issue in Chapter 3.

2.3 Speech Act Theory

The language philosopher, J. L. (John Langshaw) Austin, is probably the single most important figure in the rise of modern pragmatics. The title of his book, *How to do Things with Words* (Austin, 1962), encapsulates the revolution he sparked. His theory of speech act has been widely used and is still being used by many researchers from linguists to sociologists to philosophers. Up until its publication, approaches to meaning in linguistics and philosophy were dominated by truth conditions: utterances could be described in terms of whether the state of affairs they reported were true or false. Austin argued that utterances involve much more than this – they "do things." Thus, utterances assert, request, complement, refuse, warn, advise, threaten, apologize, and so on. The theory of doing things with words is the theory of speech acts.

Austin introduced a number of distinctions that are important for understanding the kind of pragmatics that informs L2 pragmatics. One is that speech acts vary in terms of explicitness. Initially, Austin focused on "performative verbs," verbs that name the action they perform, as in the following examples:

[7] I name this ship the QEII.
I apologize for the interruption.
I promise I'll be there tomorrow.
I sentence you to life imprisonment.

FIGURE 2.4 "I sentence you to life imprisonment"

All these utterances achieve an action, but only if the circumstances are appropriate. For example, if a member of the audience in the courtroom said, "I sentence you to life imprisonment," nothing would be done, because that audience member is not empowered to do the action. A judge bringing down a gavel on a block, as in Figure 2.4, symbolizes the power of the court in enacting the words of the judge. Appropriate circumstances became known as "felicity conditions" and apply to all speech acts. The idea that the context must be appropriate for a speech act to be felicitous (successfully performed) is a thread that weaves through much pragmatics. The examples in [5] are explicit ways of performing particular speech acts. But note that there are implicit ways of achieving the same speech acts. Compare "I promise I'll be there tomorrow" with "I'll be there tomorrow." Both can be understood as a speech act of promising, given appropriate circumstances (i.e., felicity conditions).

> **Points to remember**
> - The idea that underpins doing things with words is the theory of speech acts. Speech acts are utterances that assert, request, complement, refuse, warn, advise, threaten, apologize, and so on.
> - Appropriate circumstances are known as felicity conditions and apply to all speech acts. For a speech act to be felicitous it must be successfully performed and that means that the context must be appropriate.

Austin proposed that utterances can be viewed in terms of three different acts (Table 2.1). Although speech act theory encompasses all three aspects, in subsequent work, the notion of a speech act is virtually synonymous with illocutionary act (or "illocutionary force"). John R. Searle, a student of Austin's, did much to develop Austin's work, especially illocutionary acts. In the remainder of this section, we will outline his formalization of felicity conditions and his development

TABLE 2.1 Types of act: Locutionary, illocutionary, and perlocutionary

Type of act	Austin's definition	Clarification	Example "Someone opened my letter"
Locutionary	"the act *of* saying something" (Austin, 1975, p. 94; our emphasis)	The production of an expression with sense and reference	Someone opened my letter
Illocutionary	"the performance of an act *in* saying something" (Austin, 1975, p. 99)	The act the expression performs, such as asserting, requesting, apologizing, and sentencing	Tell me who opened the letter (i.e., a request); this is not acceptable to me (i.e., a complaint)
Perlocutionary	"what we bring about or achieve *by* saying something" (Austin, 1975, p. 109)	The effects on the participants' feelings, thoughts and actions that were brought about by the expression	Stating who opened the letter; inducing fear of consequences

of a taxonomy of speech act types, while in the following section we will consider indirect speech acts.

Searle (1969) went one step further than Austin's idea of felicity conditions. He approached them as "constitutive rules," like the rules that constitute a game of tennis, as opposed to "regulative rules" that, for example, regulate traffic. Here are Searle's felicity conditions for a speech act of promising (adapted from Searle [1969], with clarifications from Culpeper and Haugh [2014], and using our own examples) (Table 2.2).

Theoretically, other speech acts can be devised by tweaking these felicity conditions or "rules." Thus, to get from a promise to a threat, we just need to change the first preparatory condition to "H does not want S to perform A." In practice, however, naturally-occurring data is complex and indeterminate. Indeterminacies, as we noted earlier, are a part of what pragmatics needs to accommodate. Speech acts are no exception to this. Commands can easily blur into advice or even warnings and vice versa. Also, as we will see in upcoming chapters, speech acts often work in the context of other speech acts, drawing some of their meaning from the way in which they are sequenced. Searle's theory has nothing to say about that. We should also note that Searle aligns speech act theory much more closely with what the speaker is doing (rather than what the listener is interpreting) than Austin did. Table 2.2 illustrates the central role played by the speaker and especially the association with speaker intentions. In fact, while Austin (1975) associated speech acts with social conventions, in the hands of Searle, speech acts encapsulate speaker intentions.

TABLE 2.2 Felicity conditions for promising

Felicity condition	Clarification	Exemplification: promising	Example "I'll be at the party tomorrow"
Propositional content	What the utterance is about (what the utterance predicates)	Future A (act) of S (the speaker)	The presence of the speaker at the party tomorrow
Preparatory	Real-world pre-requisites (the interlocutors' beliefs about ability to perform the act, the act's costs or benefits, its norms of occurrence, etc.)	1. H (the hearer) wants S to perform A 2. It is not obvious that S will do A in the normal course of events	1. The hearer wants the speaker to come to party 2. The speaker does not habitually go to the party
Sincerity	The beliefs, feelings, and intentions of the speaker	S intends to do A	The speaker intends to attend the party tomorrow
Essential	What is needed for the act to be performed (i.e., the mutual recognition that the speaker intends an utterance to count as a certain act)	Counts as an undertaking by S of an obligation to do A	The speaker is obligated to attend the party tomorrow

Various schemes for classifying different types of speech act have been proposed, including one by Austin (1975). However, Searle's (1969, 1985) classification remains the most influential. The reason why such classifications are relevant to L2 pragmatics is that studies in L2 pragmatics are often designed to capture some of the variety in different types of speech act. Studying requests and apologies is a favorite topic of many masters and Ph.D. theses. For example, a search in ProQuest Dissertations & Theses Global for "apologies" between 2010 and 2017 produced 23,182 results!

The illocutionary point of requests is transactional, a matter of getting things done, whereas for apologies it is interpersonal, a matter of maintaining social relations. Searle (1969, 1985) proposed a number of features underpinning speech act variation. However, perhaps the most important feature is "direction of fit," the way in which the words of an utterance orientate to the world. An assertion, for example, fits words to a state of affairs in the world. Table 2.3 displays the five speech act categories that constitute Searle's taxonomy.

Regarding direction of fit, one tricky area is that of expressive speech acts, like thanks, which do not seem to be a matter of orienting words to the world

TABLE 2.3 A classification of speech acts based on Searle (1969, 1985) (incorporating Peccei's [1999] world distinctions)

Speech act type	Direction of fit	Responsibility
Representatives (assertatives) (e.g., stating, describing, affirming)	The words fit the "outside" world	Speaker
Expressives (apologizing, thanking, congratulating)	The words fit the "psychological" world	Speaker
Commissives (promising, threatening, offering)	The world will fit the words	Speaker
Declarations (e.g., naming, sentencing, baptizing)	The words change the world	Speaker
Directives (requesting, commanding, suggesting)	The world will fit the words	Hearer

> **Points to remember**
> • One important feature underpinning speech act variation proposed by Searle (1969, 1985) is "direction of fit," or the way in which the words of an utterance orientate to the world.

or vice versa. Table 2.3 adopts Peccei's (1999) idea of distinguishing the inner psychological world from the outside physical world. Thus, *thank you* fits the speaker's psychological state of indebtedness. Table 2.3 also indicates who is responsible for making that direction of fit relationship happen.

An important issue impacting the choice of methods in L2 pragmatics speech act research is how frequently particular speech acts occur. Very little research has addressed this issue. Kallen and Kirk (2012) attempt to provide a solid empirical answer. They added 54,612 speech act annotations to the Irish component of the International Corpus of English (626,597 words in total), thereby creating SPICE-Ireland (Systems of Pragmatic annotation for the spoken component of ICE-Ireland). The frequencies of occurrence (per 1,000 words) are as follows: representative, *"He affirmed that all was well"* (57); directives, *"Can you give me a hand?"* (16); expressives, *"Thank you for your help"* (2); commissives, *"I promise I'll be at the party"* (1); and declarations, *"I now pronounce you married under the laws of Massachusetts"* (0). The large frequency of occurrence of representatives, relatively speaking, would suggest that they are a good candidate for research. However, little research has been done on speech acts of this type, whether in

L2 pragmatics or more broadly. Perhaps the reason for this is that representatives are not considered especially important for the achievement of task-based goals (as requests are, for example) or social goals (as apologies are, for example). Directives are fairly common, and this is where we find requests. Then we have expressives, where apologies are located. But by this point, the frequency of occurrence figure has significantly dropped. An implication of this is that if we want to investigate apologies in naturally-occurring data, we may need to collect a huge quantity of data in order to find an adequate number of apologies. In other words, we need to elicit apologies.

However, we must caution that these numbers do not take the context of the utterances into account. Expressives, for example, are more frequent in telephone conversations, parliamentary debates, face-to-face conversations, and business transactions (Kallen & Kirk, 2012). So, targeting specific contextual varieties of language may increase the potential for analyzing more instances of a particular speech act in less language data overall.

2.4 Directness and Speech Act Realization

In the previous section, we observed how there are different degrees of explicitness with which a particular speech act can be realized (a performative verb is not needed to realize a particular speech act). One way of looking at this is in terms of directness. Scholars in L2 pragmatics have devoted much attention to analyzing the directness levels of learners' speech act expressions. A reason for this is that the acceptable level of directness for pursuing a particular speech act in a particular context varies from culture to culture, and getting it wrong can have social consequences. This was famously investigated by Gumperz (1982) in his study of Indian and Pakistani workers in London, who were discriminated against by British workers, for example, because of their falling intonation on commissives such as "Would you like some gravy?"

This has also been the claim of a variety of "self-help" books for understanding other cultures such as Jean-Benoit Nadeau and Julie Barlow's *Sixty Million Frenchmen Can't Be Wrong* (Nadeau & Barlow, 2003), which claims that it is rude to ask a French person their name or job upon first meeting. The same can be true for British people, who often recoil very slightly when a North American person approaches them with a big smile and an outstretched hand, giving their name and their occupation at a first meeting, as explained by Fox (2004) in her successful and readable popular audience book, *Watching the English: The Hidden Rules of English Behavior.* Fox is a sociologist not a linguist, but it is interesting to take a linguist's perspective on her book, which contains many examples of what we would call second *dialect* pragmatics, which we could analyze from a speech act perspective (for dialect pragmatics in general, or what is more usually referred to as variational pragmatics, see Schneider & Barron, 2008).

Indirect Speech Acts

One of Searle's most notable contributions was to describe indirect speech acts, which he defined as "cases in which one illocutionary act is performed indirectly by way of performing another" (1975, p. 60). Thus, to use Searle's own often-quoted example, "Can you pass me the salt?" is indirectly a request performed by means of performing a question. Similarly, "This could do with a little more salt" is indirectly a request performed by means of performing an assertion. In contrast, "Pass me the salt" performs a request directly. The first two indirect cases mismatch canonical expectations associated with the syntax: the first is an interrogative, but does not ultimately perform a question, and the second is a declarative, but does not ultimately perform an assertion. This provides the three principal levels of directness, as laid out in Table 2.4 for the speech act of request.

In Searle's account, the notion of "conventional" does not simply refer to regular ways of doing particular speech acts. Instead, he proposed that conventionally indirect speech acts have a systematic relationship with the direct speech act's felicity conditions. *Can you pass me the salt* orientates to the preparatory condition of the speaker having the ability to perform the act denoted in the request (it would be odd to make this particular request to somebody sitting well out of reach of the salt).

Whilst there is little agreement in general pragmatics as a whole on the status of (in)direct speech acts or how indirect speech acts work (see Aijmer, 1996, pp. 126–128, for a brief overview), and some have even proposed that a scale of directness be dispensed with altogether (Wierzbicka, 1991/2003), in L2 pragmatics investigating the (in)directness of speech acts is very popular. Many such studies have deployed in full or in part the more detailed (in)directness classification devised by Blum-Kulka, House, and Kasper (1989a) as part of the well-known *Cross-cultural Speech Act Realization Project* (CCSARP). They identified nine (in)directness strategy types for the speech act of request based on the empirical data collected via DCT. Those strategies are given in brief below (full details can be found in Blum-Kulka et al. [1989a], and the CCSARP coding manual in Blum-Kulka, House, and Kasper [1989b]):

TABLE 2.4 Principal levels of directness: Requests

Sentence type	Example	Speech act	Directness level
Imperative	Pass me the salt	Request	Direct
Interrogative	Can you pass me the salt?	Request	Conventionally indirect
Declarative	This could do with a little salt	Request	Non-conventionally indirect (i.e., a hint)

Direct

1. Mood derivable (e.g., Pass me the salt)
2. Performatives (e.g., I ask you to pass me the salt)
3. Hedged performatives (e.g., Might I ask you to pass me the salt?)
4. Obligation statements (e.g., You must pass me the salt)
5. Want statements (e.g., I want you to pass me the salt)

Conventionally indirect

6. Suggestory formulae (e.g., Why don't you pass me the salt?)
7. Query preparatory (e.g., Can you pass me the salt?)

Non-conventionally indirect (hints)

8. Strong hints (e.g., This could do with a little salt)
9. Mild hints (e.g., This is a little bland)

The CCSARP allowed for investigations of speech acts to compare across languages as well as to establish similarities and differences between speakers' realizations of speech acts (e.g., requests). Researchers have modified this scheme to suit their questions, often adding specific categories to accommodate their data. For English data, a striking absence, for instance, is that "let's-requests" (e.g., *Let's see it*) are not actually accommodated within the scheme, despite being fairly frequent in English. However, there are serious issues that go beyond such tinkering, but which are rarely discussed in L2 pragmatics studies. Chief amongst these concerns is exactly what is meant by directness. Blum-Kulka's work does not have the sense that Searle intended. If that were so, "obligation *statements*" (e.g., *you must go now*) and "want *statements*" (e.g., *I want you to go now*) would be considered indirect, as they are assertions (statements) performing the job of requests. Similarly, "hedged performatives" (e.g., "might I ask you to pass me the salt?") typically involve questions indirectly performing requests. Even "performatives" (e.g., "I ask you to pass me the salt") can be seen as assertions indirectly performing requests. Blum-Kulka and House (1989, p. 133) clarify that they intend indirectness as "a measure of illocutionary transparency." However, this is not in accordance with Searle's proposal that indirect speech acts are performed by referencing the relevant felicity condition, despite the fact that there is experimental evidence in support of it (Holtgraves, 2005).

Pragmatic Explicitness

Moreover, "illocutionary transparency" is difficult to operationalize because of its complexity. Culpeper and Haugh (2014, p. 170), preferring the label "pragmatic explicitness," suggest that there are three key aspects. One concerns the transparency of the illocutionary point, and this is Searle's idea of (in)directness (i.e., a [mis]match between sentence-type and speech act). Compare *Be quiet!* with *Could you be quiet?* Another concerns the transparency of the target. Compare *Be quiet!* with *You be quiet!* where the latter is considered more explicit. The third concerns the transparency of the semantic content. Compare *Be quiet!* with *Be like a mouse!*

Blum-Kulka and her colleagues also propose a model for how requests are structured, a proposal that has influenced much L2 pragmatics research. They posited three major structural categories for, in particular, requests: "head act," "alerter," and "support move" (Blum-Kulka et al., 1989a). In the next example (square brackets distinguish the categories) we see this more clearly:

[8]   [Tom], [could you let us know the salient points and your views on the Max Hastings column?] [That would be interesting.]
(Melissa, 2004, www.boris-johnson.com/archives/2004/12/
christmas_and_n.html)

The head act is the middle segment, the "minimal unit which can realise a request" (Blum-Kulka et al., 1989a). If the other elements of the request were removed, it would still have the potential to be understood as a request. Note that the (in)directness categories outlined above all refer to head acts. At the beginning, *Tom* is an alerter, "whose function it is to alert the hearer's attention to the ensuing speech act" (Blum-Kulka et al., 1989b, CCSARP coding manual, p. 277). Finally, *That would be interesting* is a support move, a segment that can occur before or after the head act and functions to mitigate or aggravate the request (Blum-Kulka et al., 1989b, CCSARP coding manual, p. 287). Here, the specific support move is a grounder, giving grounds as to why the target should perform the action. In addition, Blum-Kulka and colleagues allow for the internal modification of head acts. For example, the word *just* could be added as a minimizer to the head act, giving "Could you just let us know the salient points?".

Problems with L2 Speech Acts Analysis

In our view, a close look at this model for speech act analysis reveals significant problems, most of which relate to its categorical approach to analyzing the structure of speech acts. These problems are not exclusive to L2 pragmatics, but the model is dominant in L2 pragmatics and quite often used uncritically. For example:

• The three structural categories work fairly well for requests, but less well for other speech acts (e.g., refusals).
• Alerters do much more than the label suggests. In English, they often consist of a name, for instance, and the choice of name can convey important social

information that may influence the way the request is formulated. For example, the name *Tom* in the previous example suggests a degree of familiarity.

• Apparent support moves can do the job of the entire request without there being a head act to support. For example, a requestive support move such as "Do you need those?" could be followed by the response "You can have them" (i.e., the responder understood the support move as the request itself).

• Many requests in naturally-occurring data are elliptical, not fitting any of the categories suggested. For example, "Jonathan," in an appropriate context, could be a request for help.

The final two bullet points above are in tune with the broader arguments we will make in Chapter 6. There we will argue that speech acts are not created or understood as one-sentence units in isolation, but rely on the context in which they occur, including the context of interaction.

2.5 Politeness

Moving on from our introduction to the classic pragmatic frameworks, we turn to other models that have been influential in L2 pragmatics research. Initial research on politeness is usually attributed to Lakoff (1973), Leech (1983), and Brown and Levinson (1987). Not surprisingly, these models lean on the classic pragmatic theories of their time, notably, speech act theory, and conversational implicature (Grice, 1975/1989), which we will discuss in Chapter 4. There is no single agreed definition of politeness shared by these or any other politeness theories. In fact, what exactly it is has been fiercely debated. Nevertheless, some trends can be identified. Researchers of the classic models articulate what might be described as the pragmatic view of politeness. Thomas nicely summarizes this view like this:

> All that is really being claimed is that people employ certain strategies (including the 50+ strategies described by Leech, Brown and Levinson, and others) for reasons of expediency – experience has taught us that particular strategies are likely to succeed in given circumstances, so we use them.
>
> (Thomas, 1995, p. 179)

Here it is a matter of "people," understood as speakers or writers, pursuing "strategies," that is, plans to achieve certain illocutionary goals. This view does not focus on the hearer or the communication between the speaker and hearer. There is, however, a competing view, and one that is well-established. The social-cultural view of politeness emphasizes the social context. More specifically, the emphasis is on either (or more often both) social norms or the constructions of participants – the notions that participants use to understand each other rather than the notions researchers use to understand participants. For example, small

FIGURE 2.5 Social-cultural norms of politeness

Image: Lara Bryfonski.

children in some cultures are taught to always accompany requests with politeness markers such as "please" and "thank you" (see Figure 2.5).

This view of politeness is neatly summed up by Fraser (1990):

> Briefly stated, [the social-cultural view] assumes that each society has a particular set of social norms consisting of more or less explicit rules that prescribe a certain behavior, a state of affairs, or a way of thinking in context. A positive evaluation (politeness) arises when an action is in congruence with the norm, a negative evaluation (impoliteness = rudeness) when action is to the contrary.
>
> *(p. 220)*

In the remainder of this section, we will introduce the leading model of politeness in pragmatics, which has also proved popular in L2 pragmatics.

Brown and Levinson's Model of Politeness

Without doubt, the most cited and most applied politeness model is that of Brown and Levinson (1987). Their model did result in some serious criticisms (e.g., Mao, 1994). However, Locher and Watts (2005), two scholars who have been in the vanguard of criticisms of classic politeness approaches, write:

> The Brown and Levinson theory . . . provides a breadth of insights into human behavior which no other theory has yet offered and it has served as a touchstone for researchers who felt the need to go beyond it . . . It is clearly in a class of its own in terms of its comprehensiveness, operationalizability, thoroughness and level of argumentation.
>
> *(pp. 9–10)*

No wonder it has proved popular in empirical studies, including in L2 pragmatics. However, our view is that Brown and Levinson's model is often applied in an overly mechanical, unthinking way. Critical awareness of its weaknesses is needed for research to progress. We will explain what we mean by some of those weaknesses here, some in the following section, and some in later chapters.

Brown and Levinson's model (1987) involves the following components: face, facework and acts that threaten face, sociological variables influencing face threat, and five general ways (or "superstrategies") of counterbalancing face threat with (at least some) specific linguistic strategies. The notion of face relates to one's public image, reputation, and self-esteem. The loss of face often results in humiliation or embarrassment, a fact that hints at the emotional sensitivity of face. Goffman's (1967) definition of face is frequently cited:

> [T]he positive social value a person effectively claims for himself by the line others assume he has taken during a particular contact. Face is an image of self-delineated in terms of approved social attributes.
>
> *(p. 5)*

This is partially echoed in Brown and Levinson's (1987) scheme, which consists of two related components of face. "Positive face" is defined, echoing Goffman, as follows: "the want of every member that his wants be desirable to at least some others . . . in particular, it includes the desire to be ratified, understood, approved of, liked or admired" (p. 62). "Negative face," which has no obvious echo in Goffman, is defined as "the want of every competent adult member that his actions be unimpeded by others" (p. 62). Note: the terms positive and negative do not refer to good and bad evaluations. Face is couched in terms of psychological "wants," and they also assume these to be universal: "every member wants to claim for himself" (p. 61). With Goffman, as can be seen in the above quotation, it is not just the positive values that you yourself want, but what you can claim about yourself from what *others* assume about you. When you lose face, you feel negatively about how you are seen in other people's eyes. This important social interdependence has been stripped out of Brown and Levinson's definition. Also, the general focus on the individual seems to ignore cases where the positive attributes apply to a group of people (e.g., a winning team), or where an imposition on yourself is not the main concern, but rather it is how you stand in relation to a group (e.g., whether you are afforded the respect associated with your position in the team). Interestingly, researchers have argued that Brown and Levinson's emphasis on individualism is a reflection of Anglo-Saxon culture, and not at a universal feature of language (e.g., Gu, 1990; Matsumoto, 1988; Nwoye, 1992; Wierzbicka, 1991/2003).

> **Points to remember**
> - Positive face is defined as the need to be desirable, ratified, understood, approved of, liked, or admired by others. Negative face is defined as the desire to be unimpeded by others.

Facework, according to Goffman (1967), is made up of "the actions taken by a person to make whatever he is doing consistent with face" (p. 12). Any action that impinges to some degree upon a person's face (typically, orders, insults, criticisms) is a face-threatening act (hereafter, FTA). Brown and Levinson conceive FTAs in terms of speech acts (cf. 1987), and so the limitations and problems attending speech act theory, as outlined in Sections 2.3 and 2.4, also attend this politeness model. Facework can be designed to maintain or support face by counteracting threats, or potential threats, to face. This kind of facework is often referred to as redressive facework, since it involves the redress of a FTA, and Brown and Levinson's discussion of politeness is confined to redressive facework. This has implications. Unexpected, out of the blue compliments, for example, are not, strictly speaking, accommodated by this politeness model, because a compliment is not redressing anything. Brown and Levinson (1987) claim that politeness can be distinguished according to the type of face addressed, including whether it is positive or negative. Thus, requests are typically oriented to negative face (they impose on one's freedom of action) and criticisms to positive face (they detract from the positive values one lays claim to).

Tannen (1984) and Tannen (2005) extended the concepts of negative and positive face to what she termed "conversational style" with certain linguistic elements characterizing the culturally relative value of different interactive goals. For example, "high-involvement" speakers demonstrated rapport during conversation with rapid turn-taking and fast rates of speech, which "high considerateness" speakers found face-threatening as they preferred slower rates of speech and longer pauses between turns. Tannen's work demonstrates how a variety of linguistic elements work in unison to preserve positive or negative face in interactions and vary by individuals.

Brown and Levinson (1987) argue that an assessment of the amount of face threat of a particular act involves three sociological variables: power, social distance, and what they call "rank" (degree of imposition). We will discuss these in the following section. Brown and Levinson proposed five superstrategies (general orientations to face) that are systematically related to the degree of face threat. A rational actor – a "Model Person" (Brown & Levinson, 1987) – will select an appropriate superstrategy to counterbalance the expected face threat. The individual superstrategies are briefly outlined below (the first superstrategy is associated with the lowest face threat, and the last with the most).

(1) *Bald on record*: The FTA is performed "in the most direct, clear, unambiguous and concise way possible" (Brown & Levinson, 1987, p. 69); in other words, in accordance with Grice's Maxims (1975). No attempt is made to acknowledge the hearer's face wants. This strategy is typically used in emergency situations (e.g., shouting "Get out" when a house is on fire), when the face threat is very small (e.g., "Come in" said in response to a knock at the door), and when the speaker has great power over the hearer (e.g., "Go to your room!" said by a parent to a child) (Figure 2.6).

(2) *Positive politeness*: The use of strategies designed to redress the addressee's positive face wants. The speaker indicates that in general they want to maintain some of the hearer's positive face wants, by, for example, treating the hearer as a member of the same group or by expressing liking for the hearer's personality. Output strategies include the use of in-group identity markers, presupposing common ground, expressing interest in the hearer, joking, and being optimistic (e.g., saying "Hey buddy, can I have your pen?"). The sphere of relevant redress is not restricted to the imposition incurred in the FTA itself. The idea is that the general appreciation of the hearer's wants will serve to counterbalance the specific imposition. It is a sugaring of the pill technique.

(3) *Negative politeness*: The use of strategies designed to redress the addressee's negative face wants (Figure 2.7). The speaker indicates respect for the hearer's face wants and the wish not to interfere with the hearer's freedom of action. Negative politeness is avoidance-based and is characterized by:

> self-effacement, formality and restraint, with attention to very restricted aspects of H's self-image, centering on his want to be unimpeded. Face-threatening acts are redressed with apologies for interfering or transgressing, with linguistic and non-linguistic deference, with hedges on the illocutionary force of the act, with impersonalizing mechanisms (such as passives) that distance S and H from the act, and with other softening mechanisms that give the addressee an "out," a face-saving line of escape permitting him to feel that his response is not coerced.
>
> *(Brown & Levinson, 1987, p. 70)*

In contrast with positive politeness, negative politeness focuses on the redress of a particular face threat caused by an act. It is a softening of the blow technique (e.g., "I'm so sorry to bother you, but could I possibly ask if I could borrow a pen?").

(4) *Off-record*: The FTA is performed in such a way that "there is more than one unambiguously attributable intention so that the actor cannot be held to have committed himself to one particular intent" (Brown & Levinson, 1987, p. 69). In other words, it is performed by means of an implicature (Grice, 1975/1989). For example, "I'm thirsty," said with the goal of getting a cup of tea, flouts the

FIGURE 2.6 Face-threatening act in power imbalance

Image: Lara Bryfonski.

FIGURE 2.7 Negative politeness

Image: Lara Bryfonski.

Maxim of Relation (Grice, 1975/1989). In a suitable context, the hearer may be able to infer that the speaker is asking for a cup of tea, but, if challenged, the speaker could always deny this.

(5) *Withhold the FTA:* The speaker actively refrains from performing the FTA.

A number of researchers have challenged the ordering of these strategies, their mutual exclusivity, or the fact that they are placed on a single dimension. Blum-Kulka (1985), for example, suggests that off-record strategies could be less polite than negative politeness strategies in some circumstances, since it is impolite to require a superior to calculate the force of an off-record request. Baxter (1984) suggests that positive politeness may presuppose negative politeness and should therefore occupy a higher position in the hierarchy. Craig, Tracy, and Spisak (1986), for example, claim that it is possible for a strategy to involve both negative and positive politeness; they are not mutually exclusive. In fact, as Craig et al. (1986, p. 446) point out, "certain verbal hedges (negative politeness strategy 2; 'I wonder whether' or 'I was wondering') also appear to count as conventional indirectness (negative politeness strategy 1)." Several researchers (e.g., Craig et al., 1986; Lim & Bowers, 1991; Scollon & Scollon, 1981; Tracy, 1990) argue that because positive and negative politeness are different in type, they cannot be ranked unidimensionally.

Beyond Brown and Levinson's Politeness Model

In general, it is difficult to assess the evidence, since it is not clear what the underlying politeness dimension linked to the superstrategies actually is. Problems seem to multiply when we consider the specific output strategies for positive and negative politeness superstrategies. Shimanoff (1977) notes that sometimes they are defined functionally (e.g., "Be pessimistic") and sometimes linguistically (e.g., "Question, hedge"). Also, the output strategies can perform other functions aside from polite face redress. For example, they can be used, as Brown and Levinson admit, as a social "accelerator" or "brake."

We think the most serious problem with Brown and Levinson's model is how it has been applied in subsequent work. The tendency has been to treat the strategies as straightforward evidence of politeness, which led to simple quantitative methods based on the assumption that the more strategies of politeness there are the more politeness there is. Intuitively, this might seem a reasonable assumption, and, in fact, there is some support for it in Brown and Levinson (1987): "In general, the more effort S expends in face maintaining linguistic behaviour, the more S communicates his sincere desire that H's face wants be satisfied" (p. 93). Elsewhere, however, Brown and Levinson (1987) explicitly contradict this approach: "politeness is implicated by the semantic structure of the whole utterance, not communicated by 'markers' or 'mitigators' in a simple signalling fashion which can be quantified" (p. 22). Politeness is not just determined by a particular strategy; it is determined by a particular strategy in a particular context and the participants' assessment of the whole. Sarcasm, for example, has the formal strategy trappings of politeness, but in context, is not taken to be polite. Cross-cultural interpretations of politeness also lend insight to these strategies. For example, Americans are accustomed to hearing music while on "hold" on the telephone, and this happens in the UK too, but perhaps more frequently a message plays: "sorry to keep you waiting," "your call is important," "we'll be with you shortly." This replaying litany of apologies can irritate North American listeners, while listening to ongoing music without regular interruptions for an apology can annoy UK listeners. All this does not preclude quantitative approaches, but it does preclude simplistic quantitative approaches. It would be justified, for example, to count politeness strategies *plus* an interpretation that in context that strategy is doing politeness.

2.6 Social Variables and Context

Next, we discuss the classic social variables that have been studied within pragmatics, and more often than not within politeness studies. We will briefly point out some problems with treating context in this way.

Both Leech (1983) and Brown and Levinson (1987) took a very similar approach to social variables, and a large number of subsequent studies followed suit. They drew on the seminal work of Brown and Gilman (1960), which argues for the importance of the variables of social distance and power. To these Brown and Levinson added a third variable, absolute ranking. All three are summarized as follows:

1. *Distance (D)* is a symmetric social dimension of similarity/difference between the speaker and the hearer. It is often based on the frequency of interaction. The reciprocal giving and receiving of positive face is symptomatic of social closeness.
2. *Relative Power (P)* of the hearer over the speaker is an asymmetric social dimension. It is the degree to which a participant can impose his/her own plans and self-evaluation. Deference is symptomatic of a great power differential.
3. *Absolute Ranking (R)* refers to the ordering of impositions according to the degree to which they impinge upon an interactant's face wants in a particular culture and situation. Negative face impositions can be ranked according to the expenditure (a) of services (including the provision of time) and (b) of goods (including non-material goods like information, as well as the expression of regard and other face payments). Positive face impositions can be ranked according to the amount of "pain" suffered by the other, based on the discrepancy between the other's self-image and that presented in the FTA.

(Brown & Levinson, 1987, pp. 74–78)

These variables can, according to Brown and Levinson (1987), feed into a computation about how face-threatening an act is likely to be and thus how much politeness is needed to counter-balance it (see Figure 2.8). For example, asking a new colleague for a cup of tea is more face-threatening than asking a long-standing colleague (the distance variable); asking one's employer for a cup of tea is more face-threatening than asking a colleague (the power variable); and asking for a glass of vintage port is more face-threatening than asking for a glass of water (the ranking variable). Brown and Levinson argue that these three variables subsume all other factors that can influence an assessment of face threat.

Computing social variables in this way was methodologically popular in the dominant sociolinguistics paradigm at that time, with its emphasis on quantification, as promoted by Labov and his colleagues. Numerous researchers, including in L2 pragmatics, began administering questionnaires or Discourse Completion Tests (explained in Chapter 3) to quantify the kind of politeness strategies used by people of different relative power, social distance, and so on (Spencer-Oatey [1996] provides many references).

However, this model has significant problems. Chief amongst these is that researchers understood and/or operationalized power and social distance in widely varying ways, as demonstrated by Spencer-Oatey (1996). Furthermore, these variables sometimes subsumed other factors. Baxter (1984), for example, showed that affect (operationalized as whether there is liking or disliking between participants) was getting muddled up with social distance. In fact affect is generally understood to be independent from social distance, and interrelated with gender and other situational factors such as power dynamics. Brown and Levinson (1987) conceded that they "underplay the influence of other factors" (p. 12) in determining the seriousness of face threats. For example, the rights and obligations, the presence of a third party, formality, or mood may be important in addition to power, social distance, and rank.

FIGURE 2.8 Avoiding a face-threat

Image: Lara Bryfonski.

In terms of combinations of variables, Brown and Levinson assume that the effects of power, distance, and rank on the perceived degree of face threat are independent of each other and additive. In other words, each variable would have the same effect regardless of the other variables. This understanding is implicit in their formula for the calculation of face threat. Importantly though, empirical evidence suggests that the combination of these variables is not simple. For example, Holtgraves and Yang (1990) found a relationship between power and distance such that when the speaker and hearer differed in power, distance had little effect.

Ultimately, reducing context to a handful of social variables cannot reflect the complexity of real-world interactive events. The sheer complexity of context is daunting, encompassing not only aspects of the world relevant to communication, but also their cognitive representation, their emergence in dynamic discourse, different participant perspectives on them and their negotiation in discourse, and so on. We will return to these issues in subsequent chapters.

2.7 Conclusions

In this chapter, we have outlined the scope of pragmatics, and shown how it involves much more than speech acts, despite the centrality that speech acts have had in L2 pragmatics. We have described pragmalinguistics and sociopragmatics, how they relate to pragmatics, and how they are difficult to separate, theoretically and methodologically, which we will discuss later in this book. We have also made the point that many of these constructs are inherently biased toward the speaker. Speech acts, despite Austin's (1962, 1975) emphasis on conventions, morphed into vehicles for speakers' intentions (e.g., a request encapsulates the speaker's intention to have the hearer do something), and speech acts are involved in all the other sections of this chapter. We focused on indirect speech acts, noting how the framework that seems to have almost ubiquitous use in L2 pragmatics, namely, that of Blum-Kulka and colleagues, actually departs significantly from Searle's (1969) original definition of indirect speech acts, and has a number of clear limitations in its ability to account for

> **Points to remember**
> - Frameworks used in L2 pragmatics research (e.g., Blum-Kulka et al., 1989a) depart from Searle's original definition of indirect speech acts, and have a number of distinct limitations in their ability to account for what happens in naturally-occurring data. However, these frameworks and data analysis methods are still popular due to the push to replicate and compare with other studies.

what might happen in naturally-occurring data. The fact that it is still popular is likely due to the push to replicate and compare with other studies, as well as the fact that not all of the L2 pragmatics literature is up to date in terms of findings in general pragmatics. We finished by discussing contextual areas, that of politeness and social variables, but we noted how even with more of a focus on context, there are many factors at play in understanding how context and politeness are related.

Discussion Questions

1.   Describe the locutionary, illocutionary, and perlocutionary forces present in the speech act illustrated in this image.

> I promise to pick you up from the station!

2.   This chapter has demonstrated differences in context, generating differences in the ways we use language to interact. Collect greetings from three different sources: emails, phone calls, and text messages. What differences between them exist? Which context includes the most use of positive face? Negative face?
3.   Requests are one type of speech act described in this chapter. However, there are many ways in which requests are realized in authentic conversation. These might vary by direct vs. indirectness ("Come over!" vs. "Are you up to anything today?") or by context (spoken vs. written). Keep a running list of requests you see or hear and compare and contrast them based on these dimensions (directness and context). How do they vary in these contexts?
4.   Speech acts and face-threatening acts vary across cultures. Have you ever had an experience in another culture that has frustrated you? Have any of the pragmatic features discussed in this chapter shed new light on your experience? Talk to friends who are from different cultures and see if they share or have different experiences to yours.

3

DATA ELICITATION METHODS IN L2 PRAGMATIC PRODUCTION

Introduction

In this chapter, following an introduction to ethical concerns, we look at research tools for eliciting and examining an L2 learner's ability to produce meaning. A range of tasks has commonly been used to examine learners' linguistic resources when performing a communicative act. Those tasks have often used the unit of speech acts to operationalize a communicative act. We describe three types of data collection tools commonly used in L2 pragmatics production research: (1) discourse completion tasks; (2) role plays; and (3) recording of authentic data. We also explain how current research is using cutting edge new findings and techniques to extend the scope of the more traditional methods.

3.1 Data Collection: Ethical and IRB Concerns

Those wanting to collect data on L2 pragmatics, like many in the social sciences, often have questions about why ethical approval from their institutions, including informed consent from participants, is necessary to collect data, particularly since language research usually poses minimal to no risks and often provides added benefits, such as practice in producing and understanding language. Several books address these questions and a full discussion can be found in Mackey and Gass (2015, Chapter 2) and a critique in Schnieder's (2015) book, *The Censor's Hand: The Misregulation of Human-Subject Research*, which argues against the current climate of regulation. Many institutions require that faculty and students undergo human subjects training, and that before collecting data, they make an application to an Institutional Review Board (IRB) or ethics panel, for approval to carry out research. These boards or committees typically provide an application form (most often online) that solicits the information necessary for review. There is usually a short introduction or abstract requiring an overview of the study's objectives, population, design, and potential results of interest. In the Background section, framework information is provided along with a review of the relevant literature. Study Design and Methods sections ask how participants will be chosen and how any treatment is to be administered. In a Human Participants section, the researcher usually provides information about any strategies or procedures for recruitment (including advertising, if applicable), a description of the potential benefits that may reasonably be expected from the research, an explanation of the potential risks (physical, psychological, social, legal, or other), their likelihood, and what steps the researcher will take to minimize those risks, and a description of the consent procedures to be followed. While time consuming to fill in, protocols can be useful, as pointed out in Mackey and Gass (2015), in that they can be used to provide a "roadmap" for researchers. A detailed protocol "helps the researcher to anticipate problems in advance while also acting as a checklist for the many variables and factors the researcher needs to consider and balance while carrying out the procedure" (see also Gass & Mackey, 2000, p. 57).

Thus, even if researchers feel constrained by the requirements to make applications to IRBs, human subjects committees, or ethics boards, they should feel encouraged that the preparation of a protocol can be a helpful step in thinking through and planning out the steps involved in the research and importantly, it provides legal confidence for researchers that their peers and colleagues have looked over their research plans, and found them to be sound and not prejudicial in any way to the needs and interests of the language users they plan to study. Ensuring that our participants are adequately informed about research and their rights as participants fosters confidence between the research community and the public.

There are, of course, issues that L2 pragmatics researchers need to grapple with. For example, in a study of the effect of second language instruction on speech acts, there might be a control group that does not receive equal instructional time to experimental groups. Should learners be informed that they could be assigned to a group that, theoretically, could benefit less than a treatment group? Should learners receive compensatory instruction after the study? If intact classes are used and group assignment is made on this basis, should learners be informed about this method of assignment – even if it leads them to ask questions or wish to change classes? What about when we want to collect data on how L2 learners respond to complaints, but we do not want them to know we are collecting data in case it influences how they respond?

Filling out detailed protocols prompts us to think through these issues. We describe a study that had to grapple with ethical issues later in this chapter (see Box 3.6). Confidentiality of data is also an issue of particular concern in L2 pragmatics research, where misunderstandings often occur (sometimes prompted by researchers). We advise making it clear from the beginning, in the consent forms, that all information will remain confidential and anonymous *wherever possible*, and to explain the various steps that will be taken to protect the learners' anonymity (e.g., using numbers instead of names to refer to participants, not revealing identifying information, and discussing the location of records and who will have access to them). In particularly sensitive situations, such as those involving refugees, second language researchers might even volunteer to check with the participants before using any potentially identifying information in transcripts, data, reports, papers, or presentations, even when numbers are assigned instead of names. Some review boards or committees might even ask where the data are to be stored and with whom they are to be shared. For example, the use of learner corpora is growing in the field of second language research, and many corpora are freely available over the Internet. As noted in Mackey and Gass (2015), corpora can be an excellent way to avoid duplication of effort in the extremely time-consuming practice of data elicitation, collection, and transcription. However, this practice of sharing data may occasionally lead researchers to forget that sharing transcripts or data from their research has to be covered under the informed consent documents the learners signed. In summary, then, it is important to understand and comply with ethical and IRB requirements before embarking on a research project, and it may be helpful to try to view the inevitable forms and assurances as beneficial to researchers, as well as participants, in clarifying goals and putting the needs of learners in a primary position.

3.2 Discourse Completion Tasks

Standard Written Discourse Completion Tasks

Discourse completion tasks (DCTs), originally developed by Blum-Kulka (1982) to examine speech acts of native and non-native Hebrew speakers, have been used extensively in studies of L2 speech act production (for a review, see Kasper, 2008; Kasper & Rose, 2002; Taguchi & Roever, 2017). A typical DCT involves a learner being presented with a brief situational scenario describing the setting, followed by a dialogue that has at least one open-slot turn to be completed by participants with a targeted speech act utterance. The situational description usually includes information on setting, interlocutor relationships, social distance, and the goal(s) of the interaction. Participants are asked to imagine (put themselves into) the situation and produce the response as if they were performing the role indicated in the description.

The research we described in Chapter 2, namely, Blum-Kulka, House, and Kasper's (1989a) Cross-Cultural Speech Act Realization Project (CCSARP), was one of the earliest empirical investigations of L2 speech using DCTs. The goal of their project was to examine the variations in speech act strategies across different situations and languages. See below for example DCT items used in this project.

(a)   DCT: Request elicitation

Ann missed a lecture yesterday and would like to borrow Judith's notes.
Ann: _____
Judith: Sure, but let me have this back before the lecture next week.

(b)   DCT: Apology elicitation

A student has borrowed a book from her teacher, which she promised to return today. When meeting her teacher, however, she realizes she forgot to bring it along.

Teacher: Miriam, I hope you brought the book I lent you.
Miriam: _____

(Blum-Kulka et al., 1989a, p. 14)

Item (a) was constructed to elicit a request and (b) to elicit an apology. Situations in these items vary along the dimensions of social power and distance. Item (a) involves a situation where interlocutors are in an equal power relationship and their social distance is narrow, while in (b), the hearer has power over the speaker and their social distance is wide. Box 3.1 provides a summary of this study.

BOX 3.1   Blum-Kulka, S., House, J., & Kasper, G. (1989a). *Cross-cultural Pragmatics: Requests and Apologies*. Norwood, NJ: Ablex.

Purpose: To investigate similarities and differences in linguistic realizations of requests and apologies across different languages, across different situation types, and between native and non-native speakers.

Participants: 1088 native speakers of English (Americans, Australians, and British), Canadian French, Danish, German, and Hebrew; 858 non-native speakers of English, German, and Hebrew.

Instrument: A written DCT consisting of 16 items that elicit requests and apologies in a range of situations of different social dominance and distance.

Data analysis: Speech act expressions were categorized based on a coding framework that specified speech act strategies according to different levels of directness. For instance, request strategies were classified into three categories: direct requests (e.g., Please speak up), conventional indirect requests (e.g., Could you speak up?), and non-conventional indirect requests (e.g., I can't hear you). In addition to these main strategies, syntactic/lexical downgraders (e.g., use of hedges) and upgraders (e.g., use of intensifiers), as well as supportive moves (e.g., getting a pre-commitment by saying "Can you do me a favor?") were analyzed.

Findings: Different speech act strategies emerged across different languages, situation types, and participant groups. Non-native speakers were more verbose than native speakers in request-making using long explanations and justifications for a request. Non-native speakers opted for higher levels of directness in request and used fewer syntactic downgraders. Non-native speakers avoided transferring L1-specific linguistic expressions.

Since this landmark project, different variations of DCTs have emerged in the field. Several studies examined the effect of a rejoinder (turn coming after the target speech act) and the length of situational descriptions in selection of speech act strategies. Johnston, Kasper, and Ross (1998) analyzed speech acts elicited through three DCT versions: one with no rejoinder, preferred rejoinder, and dispreferred rejoinder. The examples below illustrate this:

1. Complaint – No rejoinder

   You were in a hurry to leave on a trip, and you asked your roommate to mail an express letter for you. When you get back a few days later, the letter is still lying on the table.

   You: _____

2. Request – Preferred rejoinder

   You are giving a dinner party for 12 people, but you don't have a bowl big enough for the salad. You go to your neighbor's house to see if she has one.

   You: _____
   Your neighbor: Yes, I'll just get it for you.

3. Apology – Dispreferred rejoinder

   At an office party, you had a bit too much to drink and were rude to one of your colleagues. The next day, you call her up to check that she wasn't offended.

   You: _____
   Your colleague: Well, it's a long time since I was insulted like that. You
       should be ashamed of yourself.

   (Johnston, Kasper, and Ross, 1998, pp. 163–164)

Analysis of speech act strategies by native and non-native participants revealed that the presence and type of rejoinder affected response patterns, but the effect differed across speech acts. Complaints were affected the least, while apologies were affected the most, with requests holding an intermediate position. In apology situations, participants displayed strong sensitivity to rejoinder type in their choice of apology strategies. When the rejoinder was dispreferred in nature, participants tended to take responsibility and downgrade responsibility more often than situations with a positive or no rejoinder. The authors cautioned that data from different DCT formats may not be comparable, calling for validation studies comparing different DCT types.

In another early study, Billmyer and Varghese (2000) compared short versus content-enriched DCT scenarios on native and non-native speakers' request realizations. The short version included a one- to three-line description (Version 1), while the enriched version included an extended description stretching over eight lines with specific details (Version 2).

Version 1 Situation

You missed a class and need to borrow a friend's notes. What would you say?
You: _____

Version 2 Situation

You are at the end of a history class and you are sitting next to Tom Yates. You missed last week's class and need to borrow his notes. He has been in the same program as you for one year and you see him socially about once a month in a group. You will also be taking classes together in the future. He is a good note taker and one of the best students in the class. You have borrowed his notes twice before the same class and the last time you borrowed he was reluctant to give them up. In two weeks, you both have the final exam for your class. What would you say?
(Billmyer & Varghese, 2000, pp. 548–549)

The researchers found that the longer version did not affect the main request strategy or amount of internal modifications, but did elicit a significantly greater amount of external modifications. Hence, similar to the findings in Johnston et al. (1998), this study also suggests that the type of DCT can affect the quantity and quality of the data. Because situational descriptions are condensed into a few lines, participants may have difficulty with developing a mental construction of an imagined situation, leading to fewer external moves used in a short DCT description.

Advantages of DCTs

DCTs have enjoyed unparalleled popularity since the beginning of L2 pragmatics research for several reasons. First, DCTs allow a manipulation of contextual factors (i.e., power, social distance, and rank of imposition), so researchers are able to examine how these factors affect language use in terms of level of directness and formality. Because the contextual variables are controlled, DCTs make it possible to compare speech act expressions across cultures. Results of the CCSARP project (Blum-Kulka et al., 1989a) indeed revealed great variations in how people from different cultures perform the same speech acts. These cross-cultural variations can also provide a yardstick to examine transfer of L1-based speech act strategies to L2. Data may show how L2 speech act patterns are similar to, or different from, native speaker patterns. The systematic approach used to develop a situational scenario also helps explore a connection between pragmalinguistics and sociopragmatics (form-context associations). Finally, by taking a survey format, DCTs offer quick and convenient ways to collect a large amount of data in one setting. DCTs are particularly useful for speech acts that do not occur very often in naturalistic conversation because, as O'Keeffe, Clancy, and Adolphs (2011, p. 23) observe, "without this methodology, it would have been difficult if not impossible to conduct such research because some speech acts are very difficult to obtain in any other way." Finally, the uniform format of DCTs also serves as a useful model for future replication studies.

A large number of studies have used DCTs for cross-cultural comparisons of speech act strategies, as well as for examinations of L2 pragmatic development. In Bardovi-Harlig's (2010) review, 40% of pragmatic production studies used DCTs. Similarly, in Taguchi's (2015b) research synthesis of instructional intervention studies, 25 out of 58 studies, or 43%, used DCTs as a measure of learning outcome of pragmatic knowledge.

Challenges Associated with DCTs

Despite this popularity, DCTs have also been criticized. Researchers have questioned the authenticity of the situational prompts used in DCTs by noting that participants may not be familiar with certain situations. This mismatch between the researcher and participant's perceptions was documented in a classic study by Eisenstein and Bodman (1993). The authors collected naturally-occurring tokens of "thank you" in American English. From these tokens, they selected situations for a DCT, which was administered to non-native English speakers. The authors found that some participants had no previous experience with some of the situations in the DCTs because of their social roles (e.g., people with no working experience). These findings indicate that participants' lack of familiarity with aspects of the DCTs may affect data.

As well as the authenticity of situations, the authenticity of language use has been another area of concern with DCT-elicited data. Several studies have revealed discrepancies between DCT-elicited and naturalistic data in terms of the length of responses, range of semantic moves, and number of repetitions and elaborations (e.g., Beebe & Cummings, 1996; Economidou-Kogetsidis, 2013;

Golato, 2003; Hartford & Bardovi-Harlig, 1992; Turnbull, 2001; Yuan, 2001). For instance, in Golato's (2003) study of German compliments, the compliment response, *danke* (thank you), which occurred over 12% in the DCT responses, never appeared in the naturalistic data. Similarly, Hartford and Bardovi-Harlig (1992) compared naturalistic data on the speech act of rejections in academic advising sessions with data collected from a DCT. The DCT elicited a narrow range of semantic formula because some formulae in naturalistic data (e.g., indefinite responses and condition statements) never appeared in the DCT-elicited rejections.

Perhaps the most serious limitation of DCT-elicited data is the lack of features specific to spoken interactions. Because DCTs elicit a one- or two-turn (usually) written response, language elicited through DCTs does not represent typical conversational features such as turn-taking, sequential organization of talk, speaker-hearer collaboration, features of speech (e.g., hesitation, repetition), and non-verbal features (Kasper, 2008). This leads to construct underrepresentation in assessing pragmatic ability in pragmatics studies that used DCTs. The one-directional format of DCTs does not represent real-life situations where speech acts are often co-constructed.

In her review of the pragmatic studies, Bardovi-Harlig (2010) argued that the production studies that employed DCTs did not meet the "desired goals of pragmatics research involving the study of language use, interaction, and speaker effects on interlocutors" (p. 242) because they failed to present authentic, consequential language use. Hence, although DCTs may address locution and illocution of a speech act, they do not assess perlocutionary effect of the act, that is, real-life consequences of one's pragmatic behavior in imagined contexts. In addition, standard DCTs do not address the online, immediate nature of spoken production because they allow for planning when producing expressions in writing, or what Bardovi-Harlig (2015) calls "written-for-oral tasks." Cohen and Shively (2007) also define DCTs as an "indirect means for assessing spoken language in the form of a written production measure" (p.196). The advantages and disadvantages of DCTs have surfaced in the literature time after time. They are common in the limitations sections of a number of studies and dissertations.

We should keep in mind these advantages and disadvantages as we move to the next section, which surveys different formats of DCTs that emerged after Blum-Kulka's (1982) early version. These newer formats have been developed in response to some of the criticisms of DCTs and have the aim of improving the validity of the instrument. Here, we will present four variants of DCTs: (1) spoken DCTs; (2) technology-enhanced DCTs; (3) reversed DCTs; and (4) collaborative DCTs.

Spoken DCTs

Although DCTs have taken a predominately written survey format, several studies have used a spoken DCT (e.g., Bardovi-Harlig & Bastos, 2011; Hudson, Detmer,

& Brown, 1995; Li, 2012; Li & Taguchi, 2014; Roever, Wang, & Brophy, 2014; Taguchi, 2011a, 2012; Taguchi, Xiao, & Li, 2016; Yamashita, 1996). Some of these studies were assessment-oriented, comparing different test measures for validity and reliability (Hudson et al., 1995; Yamashita, 1996). In these studies, knowledge of speech acts elicited using a spoken DCT was compared with knowledge elicited from a written DCT, multiple-choice DCT, role play, and self-assessment. These studies focused on the functionality of different measures by calculating reliability estimates of individual measures and building validity arguments.

Other studies pursued an SLA-focused investigation by using a spoken DCT to tap into both knowledge and processing aspects of pragmatic competence. Kasper (2001) argues that pragmatic competence involves dual dimensions: pragmatic knowledge and gaining automatic control over processing the knowledge in real time. Following this claim, several studies have examined the fluency aspect of pragmatic production in addition to accuracy and appropriateness of production. A spoken DCT is useful in this regard because it can elicit features of spoken discourse that characterize oral fluency (e.g., speech rates, pause length, response time). These temporal measures provide complementary criteria to speech act analyses, going beyond usual analyses of accuracy, appropriateness, and types of speech act strategies used.

Response times, typically meaning the measurement of pauses and responses in milliseconds, have been used widely in psycholinguistics research. Response time data have been argued to provide an indirect reflection on ease or difficulty in processing the stimuli, as well as the relative amount of linguistic, cognitive, and affective resources required for processing. Shorter response times have been shown to be obtained with conventional implicatures such as indirect refusals (see Chapter 5). In contrast, non-conventional implicatures such as indirect opinions require more extensive processing of linguistic and contextual cues to deliver or derive meaning. Lacking conventional features that link form with meaning, non-conventional speech acts and implicature requires both bottom-up processing of linguistic information and top-down processing of contextual cues, leading to longer response times.

Holtgraves's (2007) study analyzed response times in online activation of speech acts (Box 3.2). Native and non-native English speakers read 24 utterances. In the experimental items, the target utterance was followed by the speech act verb naming the utterance (e.g., the speech act verb "compliment" following the utterance "I like your coat."). In the control items, the target utterance was followed by a non-speech act verb. Participants were asked to judge whether the letter string that appeared after the target utterance was a real word. Native speakers showed faster response times in speech act utterances than in control utterances, while non-native speakers showed similar response times for both utterance types.

BOX 3.2 Holtgraves, T. (2007). Second language learners and speech act comprehension. *Language Learning, 57*: 595–610.

Purpose: To investigate whether or not the comprehension of implicit speech acts by non-native speakers entails online activation of illocutionary force.

Participants: Eighteen native speakers of English and 16 non-native speakers of English at an American university. The non-native speakers had been speaking English for an average of 9.18 years.

Instrument: A set of two-to-six-sentence scenarios describing a situation between two people, followed by a remark or remarks said by those people and a probe naming the speech act. The last remark either performed a specific speech act or did not (control). There were 24 speech act scenarios and 24 control scenarios. Participants were presented with the scenarios and asked to judge if the probes were or were not. See the example item.

> Jenny and Emily had been close friends since grade school. Now they were rooming together at college. Emily tended to be very forgetful.
> Today, Jenny was sure Emily *didn't remember* (had forgotten) her dentist appointment.
>
> Jenny: *Don't forget* (I'll bet you forgot) to go to your dentist appointment today.
> Probe: Remind.

Findings: L1 participants were able to activate illocutionary force online, and were therefore faster at judging the target words following speech act utterances than following the control utterances. Speech act activation did not occur online for L2 participants. Unlike the native speakers, their performance on the lexical decision task was independent of whether or not the given scenario did or did not perform a speech act; they were no faster judging the targets when they followed speech act utterances.

Other than speech acts, recent studies have used a spoken DCT to assess production of routines (e.g., Bardovi-Harlig & Bastos, 2011; Taguchi, Li, & Xiao, 2013). The spoken modality is critical for routines and formulaic expressions.

Because routines are fixed or semi-fixed syntactic strings that are stored in mind as a holistic unit and tied to a specific situation (e.g., Bardovi-Harlig, 2012; Wood, 2006; Wray, 2002), fluent retrieval and production of routines are indicators of L2 formulaic competence. A spoken DCT might help reveal whether formulae are indeed stored and produced as one chunk without pause or hesitation.

Technology-enhanced DCTs

Advancements in technology have broadened the options for data collection and analysis methods. A computer-delivered spoken DCT is one example. Another type of technology-promoted innovation is seen in the use of DCTs with audio-visual enhancement, which are also known as multimedia elicitation tasks (METs). Schauer (2007) provided an early study. She developed a computer-based MET, which included 16 scenarios eliciting requests. The study examined whether L2 learners of English varied the use of external modifications corresponding to the different interlocutor status and the degree of the request's imposition. The MET consisted of a series of slides. The first slide introduced a brief situational description (e.g., asking a professor for directions). After ten seconds, the introductory slide switched to the scenario slide, which displayed a picture illustrating the situation (as shown in Figure 3.1) and an audio description of the situation. The audio description ended with the cue, "You say," which prompted participants to start speaking.

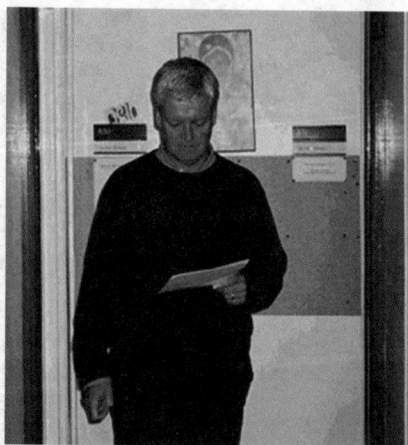

FIGURE 3.1 Multimedia elicitation task slide

Scenario

> *You are in the corridor of your department. Your next seminar is taking place in the Trent Building, but you don't know where the Trent Building is. One of your professors, Professor Jones, is walking down the corridor toward you. You ask him for directions to the Trent Building.*
>
> *You say:* _____
>
> *(Schauer, 2007, p. 203)*

More recently, Halenko (2013) developed a 12-item Computer-Animated Production Task (CAPT) to simulate more real-world contexts in eliciting speech acts of apology and request. She used Xtranormal (www.nawmal.com), an internet-based animated movie site, to develop animated scenarios for virtual role plays. These role plays were presented in PowerPoint format as a spoken DCT. Using Xtranormal, researchers can transform text-based scripts to movies using animation technologies. This process is user-friendly since settings and characters are pre-designed, and researchers can simply add their own to existing scenarios by importing visuals and voice recordings. See Figure 3.2 for a sample scenario.

Scenario

> *The library is closing but you want to book a study room for tomorrow. You do not know the library assistant.*
> You say?
>
> *(Halenko, 2013, pp. 286–290)*

FIGURE 3.2 Computer-animated production task

In this task, participants view a PowerPoint presentation of scenarios and engage in a single-turn interaction with animated characters in each scenario. In each scenario, the animated character begins the conversation with a brief prompt (e.g., The neighbors reported that you had a loud party last night). Participants are asked to provide a subsequent oral response.

In Halenko's (2013) study, 45 undergraduate Chinese students of L2 English completed both a CAPT and a traditional written DCT. Three native speaker raters assessed speech acts on a five-point rating scale. Interestingly, mean scores were slightly higher, although not statistically, in the CAPT than in the written DCT. The difference between the scores could be due to the visual cues (e.g., gestures, facial expressions) that came with the computer animation in the CAPT, which could help and cue the participants in their performance. A post-study questionnaire revealed the students' overwhelming preference toward the CAPT. The CAPT was perceived as more authentic, fun, and useful than the DCT. These data indicate that the CAPT can be a viable alternative, which can partially overcome some of the shortcomings of a traditional DCT (lack of audio-visual input, limited authenticity, and neglected spoken features).

Winke and Teng's (2010) study also used a technology-enhanced DCT assessing speech acts in L2 Chinese. Instead of providing written scenarios, participants watched video clips of vignettes on a computer. At various sections during each vignette, the video stopped and prompted participants to produce target speech acts. Finally, there are also studies (Kuha, 1999; Yang & Zapata-Rivera, 2009) that utilize computer-assisted interactive DCTs (IDCTs). For the speech act of complaints, Kuha (1999) found that the IDCT afforded longer outcomes with more variation compared with the outcomes by the traditional DCT. Focusing on request making, Yang and Zapata-Rivera (2009) used an assessment tool named "A Game of Persuasion," which enables test takers to interact with an animated professor in various academic contexts through three-turn written dialogues. IDCTs are promising as they not only simulate real-life like contexts but also allow learners to engage in interaction that is sequential.

Reversed DCTs

Most DCTs have used researcher-generated situational scenarios and asked L2 learners to supply their responses in an imagined situation. However, other DCTs have reversed this direction by asking learners to develop DCT scenarios based on their needs and experiences (i.e., reversed DCTs, or student-generated DCTs, which is a more intuitive name) (McLean, 2005; Takamiya & Ishihara, 2013), or by having learners construct a scenario based on the given pragmalinguistic forms (Kanik, 2013).

McLean (2005) reported on a classroom activity in which his ESL students in Canada were asked to think about speech act situations that they had experienced in their real lives. He described this activity as highly engaging and interactive, generating great metapragmatic discussion among students and enhancing their pragmatic awareness. He reported that students were motivated to share their experiences and let the instructor know the types of speech acts that they found difficult to perform (e.g., presenting information to a doctor and responding to interview questions). See below for a sample student-generated DCT item.

Scenario

> *Your phone is out of order and you need to make an emergency long distance call to your family back home. You want to ask your neighbor if you can use his or her telephone.*
>
> What would you say? : _____
>
> *(McLean, 2005, p. 156)*

These self-oriented DCT scenarios are helpful in eliciting speech acts that are relevant to participants' experiences, which challenges one of the criticisms toward DCTs described in the previous section – participants' lack of familiarity with scenarios affecting the resulting data. By asking students about scenarios that they have actually experienced, researchers can build an authentic base of tasks for use in eliciting pragmalinguistic expressions based on the learners' needs.

Another example of student-generated DCTs is found in Kanik's (2013) study. Traditional DCTs present a situation and ask participants to supply expressions appropriate for the situation. This approach helps researchers examine participants' pragmalinguistic repertoire and make inferences about their sociopragmatic knowledge. Kanik's instrument reverses this direction by providing participants with pragmalinguistic forms first and then having them come up with a situation in which the forms may occur. The focus of this instrument is on sociopragmatics rather than on pragmalinguistics. The author contends that the reversed DCT can provide access to participants' understanding of social variables (e.g., power, distance), as well as their understanding of pragmalinguistic forms associated with a situation. This is illustrated in the following sample item.

> *Write a situation in which the below statement could be uttered. Also, provide information regarding setting, who the speaker is, who the listener is, and what is asked.*
>
> *Speech act*: I know you came from another city, but to reach a final decision about you, I need to see you again next week.
>
> *Situation:* _____
> *Setting:* _____
> *Speaker:* _____
> *Hearer:* _____
> *Request:* _____
>
> *(Kanik, 2013, p. 89)*

As illustrated above, in the student-generated DCT, the aspect of *production* in focus is the production of sociopragmatic knowledge – knowledge of context, speaker-hearer relationship, and topic of interaction. Participants need to recognize the illocutionary force (i.e., requesting) behind the speech act utterances. Then, the utterances need to be associated with contextual parameters. In the sample item above, the context involves a situation in which the speaker has power over the hearer, the distance between the interlocutors is large, and the imposition of the speech act is high. Kanik's study compared these sociopragmatic factors across 12 learners of L2 Turkish. Data yielded useful information on how participants interpreted the speech act utterance and the sociopragmatic dimensions associated with the utterance.

The student-generated DCTs help researchers explore potential explanations for pragmatic failure. When participants are not able to produce target expressions in a traditional DCT, their responses to the reversed DCT can reveal sources of the problem – whether it is due to participants' misinterpretations of DCT situations, or to their lack of pragmalinguistic resources in repertoire.

Collaborative DCTs

Previous sections have presented a DCT as an individual task. Here, we discuss a DCT task in which participants collaboratively construct a dialogue based on a scenario. Taguchi and Kim (2016) call it a drama script construction task. See Box 3.3 for the description of this study. This task is different from free DCTs used in Barron (2003), in which participants compose both interlocutors' turns individually. Rather, participants construct both sides of a conversation collaboratively via oral interaction.

Taguchi and Kim's study (2016) explored the extent to which learners negotiated and co-constructed knowledge of pragmalinguistic forms and sociopragmatic factors through collaborative dialogue. Collaborative dialogue is about language being used as a cognitive tool that mediates the process of thinking (Swain, 2006). When verbalization is guided strategically through a collaborative task, it is considered to precipitate a deeper-level understanding of the forms. In this study, the DCT task implemented as a collaborative (rather than individual) task generated rich metapragmatic discussion around speech act strategies, which led to the collaborative group's superior knowledge of the request speech act in the immediate post-test. These findings suggest promising benefits of using interactive, collaborative DCTs – DCTs as an instrument tapping into co-constructed metapragmatic knowledge.

DCTs with Verbal Reports

In order to increase the reliability of DCTs that are used in pragmatics research, several studies (Beltrán-Palanques, 2013; Robinson, 1992; Woodfield, 2008, 2010)

BOX 3.3 Taguchi, N., & Kim, Y. (2016). Collaborative dialogue in learning pragmatics: Pragmatic-related episodes as an opportunity for learning request-making. *Applied Linguistics, 37,* 416–437.

Purpose: To investigate the effects of collaborative dialogue in learning the speech act of request by comparing a group who constructed a DCT-based dialogue in pair and a group who constructed the same dialogue alone via think-aloud.

Participants: Seventy-four junior high school South Korean students of English were divided into three groups. The "collaborative group" received explicit metapragmatic information on requests followed by a dialogue construction task in pair. The "individual group" received the same information but completed the same task individually. The control group did not receive instruction.

Instrument/task: The collaborative and individual groups completed a dialogue construction task. They received scenarios with pictures of main characters and created a dialogue involving a request. The collaborative group created a dialogue in pair, while the individual group created a dialogue alone. Both groups vocalized their thoughts during the task in Korean, either collaboratively or individually, depending on their treatment condition. See the sample task scenario.

> Scenario: Look at the picture which displays a TV scene. Jeonghyun is a student representative at Yongshin middle school. Many students complain about old computers in the computer lab. In this scene, you will see Jeonghyun visiting the principal's office to discuss this issue. Jeonghyun makes a request to the school principal politely on whether old computers can be replaced by new computers next year.

Data analysis: During task interaction, data were audio-recorded and analyzed for the frequency of pragmatic-related episodes (PRE). PREs were defined as any part of language production where learners talk about the pragmalinguistic forms they are producing and the sociopragmatic factors they are attending to (e.g., setting, interlocutor relationship), question their pragmatic language use, or correct themselves or others (based on Swain & Lapkin's [1998] definition of language-related episode). In addition, instructional effect was measured by a written DCT. Target request head acts were scored, and request modifications were analyzed for frequency.

Results: The collaborative group outperformed the individual group on the production of the request head act at immediate post-test. No group difference was found in request modifications. Analysis of during-task interaction and think-aloud data showed that the collaborative group produced the target head act more successfully than the individual group, but no group difference was found in the use of modifications.

implemented DCTs alongside verbal reports, retrospectively, concurrently, or utilizing both protocols. In his review of the data collection methods used in speech act studies, Felix–Brasdefer (2010) also pointed out that using verbal reports together with DCTs can address some of the problems that come with DCTs. For instance, in addition to written DCTs, Robinson (1992) used concurrent think–alouds and retrospective verbal reports to collect data on the speech act of refusals. Verbal protocols can provide rich data on learner–internal processes and their thought processes, which can complement data by DCTs and help researchers accurately interpret the results of DCTs.

Points to remember

- DCTs are often used to elicit speech acts such as requests, apologies, and refusals.
- DCTs allow for manipulation of contextual factors, such as power, social distance, and degree of imposition, and make it possible to compare speech act expressions across cultures.
- DCTs do not allow for elicitation of typical conversational features such as turn-taking, sequential organization of talk, speaker-hearer collaboration, features of speech (e.g., hesitation, repetition), and non-verbal features.
- DCTs can be spoken or written, and they can make use of audio-visual enhancement, animation, and audio and video clips.
- DCTs can be researcher generated or student generated, and they can be resolved individually or collaboratively.
- Concurrent and retrospective verbal reports can be used with DCTs in order to gain an understanding of learner's cognitive processes and thoughts.

3.3 Role Plays

Role Playing in L2 Pragmatics Research

Role playing has been defined as "participation in simulated social situations that are intended to throw light on the role/rule contexts governing 'real' life social

Open	Closed	Spontaneous	Structured
Played out by two or more individuals in response to a given situation	Essentially oral DCTs	Give participants more freedom in terms of language production	Tend to focus specific problem-solving and communication skills
Reflect natural data more closely than closed role plays (e.g., no predetermined outcomes)	Usually involve one learner and a native speaker interlocutor	Allow for greater variety of speech acts and discourse functions	Often involve scripts
Allow for elicitation of a variety of speech acts	Commonly used to elicit speech acts such as requests, apologies, and suggestions	Give learners more insight into their own behavior and linguistic choices	Obviously a role play and may feel artificial to learners
	May not reflect naturally-occurring language		Also-called "formal" role playing

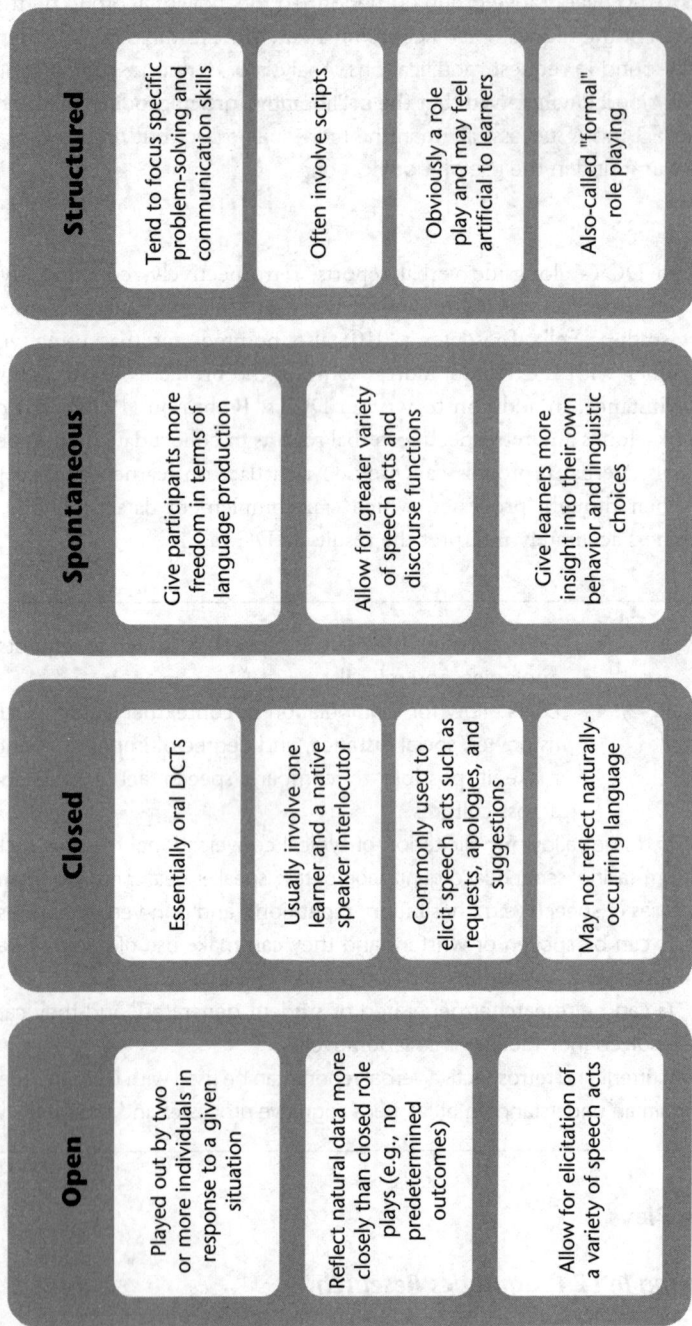

FIGURE 3.3 Types of role play

episodes" (Cohen & Manion, 1994, p. 252). Role plays involve interactions played out by two or more people in response to certain situations. Role plays can be categorized according to the locus of control. Kipper (1988) distinguishes between spontaneous and mimetic-replication role plays. In the former, participants maintain their own identities, while in the latter, participants assume different identities by following a visually presented model. Another categorization comes from the extent of interaction elicited in role plays. Kasper and Dahl (1991) distinguish between closed and open role plays. In closed role plays, participants act out the set situational description by responding to the interlocutor's standardized initiation. In contrast, open role plays specify the initial situation including each character's role and setting, but there are no outcomes of interaction given in the situation. Because the end result of the communicative act is not predetermined, open role plays are likely to elicit a longer exchange over multiple turns and discourse phases (Kasper & Rose, 2002). Figure 3.3 summarizes types of role play.

Turnbull (2001) carried out a study showing the application of role play to pragmatics research. The study (see Box 3.4), which looked at refusals given to interlocutors of differing statuses, made a case for using role play instead of DCTs in order to elicit refusals similar to those occurring in natural data.

BOX 3.4   Turnbull, W. (2001). An appraisal of pragmatic elicitation techniques for the social psychological study of talk: The case of request refusals. *Pragmatics, 11*, 31–61.

Purpose: To assess the relative appropriateness of various pragmatic elicitation techniques.

Hypothesis: More work to save face will occur in refusing a request made by someone of high status.

Method: Turnbull manipulated requester status through oral and written discourse completion tests (DCTs), role plays, and an experimental elicitation technique. In the role play, participants engaged in open role plays with the researcher. They were asked to imagine themselves in a given situation involving a request and respond naturally. Turnbull compared the types of refusals the participants gave to refusals found in naturally-occurring data.

Results: The results showed that the refusals given in DCTs were not representative of natural language. The refusals elicited through the role plays, however, were found to be similar to naturally-occurring refusals. Turnbull proposed that the best pragmatic elicitation techniques allow speakers to talk freely, without being aware that aspects of their speech are being investigated.

Traditional Role Plays

A number of early studies used role plays as outcome measures in instructional interventions (Félix-Brasdefer, 2008; Liddicoat & Crozet, 2001; Martínez-Flor, 2008; Nguyen, 2013; Takimoto, 2009), while others used them as part of assessment battery (Ishihara, 2009; Sasaki, 1998; Yamashita, 1996). Still others used role plays to gain information about pragmatic competence and development (Cheng, 2011; Félix-Brasdefer, 2007; Taguchi, 2006; Trosborg, 1995). In a typical role play, participants read the scenario and act out the scenario with an assigned interlocutor (a native speaker or peer learner). Role plays are recorded and analyzed for target pragmatic features occurring during role plays.

Role plays can elicit a complete two-way interaction, rather than a one-directional monologue as in DCTs. However, most previous studies did not analyze role-play data for interactional features. Instead, they presented quantitative analyses such as frequency counts of specific pragmalinguistic forms and strategies, or ratings of role-play performance based on scoring rubrics. To illustrate, Félix-Brasdefer's (2007) cross-sectional study compared role-play performance across three L2 Spanish groups of different proficiency (beginning, intermediate, and advanced; N=50). Participants role played seven request-making situations in pairs. The data were coded for request strategies (e.g., request head act type, internal/external modifications). Frequency counts of these strategies were compared across groups. See the following role play excerpt from the intermediate group.

Situation: Asking a roommate to clean the bathroom

Female 1: 1 *Tengo una problema*
"I have a problem"
Female 2: 2 *qué*
"what"

Female 1: 3 *mis padres, ah van a visitor en el fin de semana,*
"my parents, ah, are going to visit over the weekend"
4 *pero no puedo limpiar el baño.*
"but I can't clean the bathroom"
Female 2: 5 *pero es tu semana*
"but it's your week"

Female 1: 6 *sí yo sé, pero si tú hiciera aquí,*
"yes, I know, but if you do (lit. would do) it now"
7 *yo voy a limpiar para el fin de semana próxima*
"I will clean for the next weekend"
Female 2: 8 *sí.*
"yes."

(Félix-Brasdefer's, 2007, pp. 273–274)

Results showed that the intermediate and advanced groups used the conventional indirect strategies about 60% to 80% of the time, while the beginning group used the direct strategies over 80% of the time. These differences were statistically significant. In terms of external strategies, intermediate and advanced groups used the "preparator" strategy twice as often (Line 1 in the excerpt). The "promise of reward" strategy, as shown in the excerpt, also appeared, although the frequency was small and similar across proficiency levels (11–16%).

Although the frequency data allows for a statistical comparison across groups and thus provides valuable developmental insights, this type of analysis does not account for interaction. Specifically, it does not reveal why the "promise for reward" strategy appeared in this particular interaction. In Lines 3 and 4, the speaker provides a justification for her request, but the request is indirectly rejected by her interlocutor, who argues that she is not due for cleaning this week. Facing this argumentative stance, the speaker probably opts for the "promise for reward" as a strategy to appeal to the hearer. Because the appearance of this strategy is conditioned by the previous turn, the strategy should be analyzed within the sequential organization of talk, rather than as isolated from discourse. In other words, in a role play task that intends to simulate a real-life interaction, the resulting data needs to be analyzed with interactional perspectives in mind by attending to turn-taking, sequence, and other features of interaction (e.g., overlap, body language, intonation). We come back to role play-based interactions in Chapter 7 when we discuss the conversation analytic perspective to role play data.

Recent Developments in Role Plays

Although role plays usually involve audio or video-recording of face-to-face interactions, more recent studies have used online virtual spaces as platforms for role-play interactions. Using *Second Life*, Vilar-Beltran and Melchor-Couto (2013) created the Hobbit Village consisting of six huts, each featuring a refusal scenario (e.g., refusing a friend's invitation to a party). L2 learners of Spanish were organized in dyads. They created their own avatars and performed a role play via text-based chat. Data showed that the learners in an upper-level course produced more pre- and post-refusal strategies than those in a lower-level course. Proficiency effect was also found in the extent of elaboration in refusal. The upper-level students produced more turns and delayed the refusal head acts by using various external modifications (e.g., request for information, apologies). In addition, these students' refusal expressions showed a clear influence of digital literacy: they used emoticons to mitigate their refusals and letter repetitions to show insistence (e.g., *vengaaaaaaa* meaning "come on").

Because the body of research on using a virtual world is still limited, this study offers considerable potential in terms of how technology can transform a traditional method of data collection into a novel technique with enriched context. In a traditional role play, contextual information is condensed in a short, written scenario. Learners are asked to read the scenario and take up the imagined identities to act out the scenario. Hence, the context that learners operate in is limited to their mental construction of an imagined situation. In contrast, a virtual environment can provide a context-rich, authentic environment for communicative activities. Rich graphics and animation offer an immersive space in which learners can create and perform their own identities. Through interaction with built-in avatars, learners can simulate participant roles and perform pragmatic acts in diverse social settings. Because of these features, a virtual role play is more likely to reflect a real-life performance than a face-to-face role play in a laboratory setting. More recently, Taguchi, Li, and Tang (2017) implemented a virtual role play by using video-based interactions in a game-based environment that was designed to teach formulaic expressions to L2 Chinese learners.

Another innovation in role play is found in Cheng's (2011) naturalistic role play used to examine the speech act of compliment. Different from a traditional role play, a naturalistic role play ensures that participants are unaware of the research focus. In Cheng's study, L2 English learners performed a series of communicative acts specified in a situational scenario (greeting, giving directions, asking for and offering help, and describing a place or procedure). However, these communicative acts were not the target areas. Instead, the focus was on how learners respond to compliments coming from their interlocutors during a role play. While learners were not informed that they would receive compliments, interlocutors were explicitly instructed to give compliments to learners in designated parts of the role play. See Box 3.5 for the study summary and task directions to the interlocutor. As shown in the box, supplied compliments focusing on specific areas (e.g., ability, appearance) were inserted in the role-play directions.

BOX 3.5 Cheng, D. (2011). New insights on compliment responses: A comparison between native English speakers and Chinese L2 speakers. *Journal of Pragmatics, 43*, 2204–2214.

Purposes: To compare L2 English learners' compliment responses to those produced by native English speakers and to examine reasons of the compliment response types used by learners.

Participants: Fifteen native English speakers, 15 Chinese EFL learners, and 15 Chinese ESL learners.

Data collection materials: Naturalistic role play and retrospective interview incorporating stimulated recall. See below for abbreviated instructions given to role-play interlocutors.

Role-play scenario: It's now around 4 pm and you are leaving school. You want to stop by a bookstore and have heard that there is one named "Barnes & Noble" not far from school, but you do not know where it is. You are passing by the library and see your new classmate. You approach him/her to say some greetings. You two talk while walking together. The talk should include but may not be limited to the following points:

___ Start the conversation by greeting your friend and asking him/her about his/her classes. When it is most natural during the talk, compliment on his/her writing skills by referring to his/her essay published in the school newspaper.
___ Ask for directions to get to the Barnes & Noble shop by bike/by car.
___ Ask what time the bookstore is closed today.
___ Accept his/her company of riding the car/bike together to the bookstore. When it is most natural during the talk, compliment on his/her car/bike. You should pick a specific feature of the car/bike to give your compliment.
___ While you are both riding on the road, please talk about each other's hometown (e.g., compare the weather/food/population).
___ Before leaving the bookstore, invite your new friend to a dinner party held in your apartment next week. Your party will start at 6:00 pm next Friday.

Data analysis: Learners' compliment responses were categorized into three macro strategies (i.e., accept, evade, and combination) and 11 micro strategies (e.g., returning the compliment, credit-shifting). Retrospective interviews were analyzed for major themes reflecting the rationale for participants to adopt specific compliment response strategies.

Results: Acceptance was the most preferred response strategy by all three groups. It was used most frequently by the EFL group, followed by the ESL learners, and then by the native English speakers. The same trend was found for the use of evasions, while a reverse pattern was found for the use of the combination strategy. In terms of the choice of compliment response strategies, participants reported a number of explanations: saying "thank you" to play safe; transfer of L1 cultural norms; explicit instruction; and showing alignment with the interlocutor. Data also showed that participants were unaware of compliment responses as the focus of the study.

Cheng used interviews that involved *stimulated recall*, an introspective data-gathering technique that can yield insights into a learner's thought processes during a linguistic task, although it is collected after the task (Gass & Mackey, 2016).

In the study described in Box 3.5, Cheng played the parts of the role plays containing compliments and responses back to the participants in a stimulated recall protocol and asked them what they were thinking when responding to the compliments. Cheng reported that when the research focus, that is, compliment responses, was revealed to the participants, they were surprised about being assessed on an area that they were unaware of, indicating that the target pragmatic act was elicited in a semi-naturalistic manner. In other words, the task was able to yield data on impromptu responses to compliments, which were embedded naturally in the course of a role play.

Another recent innovation can be seen in Sydorenko's (2015) study, which constructed computer-delivered structured tasks (CASTs) to elicit request-making strategies in L2 English. The CASTs involved four request scenarios consisting of varying contextual factors. These scenarios were incorporated into the CASTs, which were created using the *Conversations Program* developed by the Center for Language Education and Research at Michigan State University. Learners watched a series of video-recorded scenarios. The computer stopped the video in pre-planned places and asked learners to provide a response to the interlocutor appearing in the video. See Figure 3.4 for the screen shot when the prompt is presented (p. 340).

Using this scenario, participants practiced both the student and instructor role individually by interacting with the computer. Data were analyzed for the use of

You are a student. Ask your instructor if you can change the topic of your paper. The paper is due soon. You realize (= you know) that you do not have a lot of time to work on the new topic. However, you have good reasons for changing the topic of your paper. Try to get permission from your instructor to change the topic. **Be polite.**

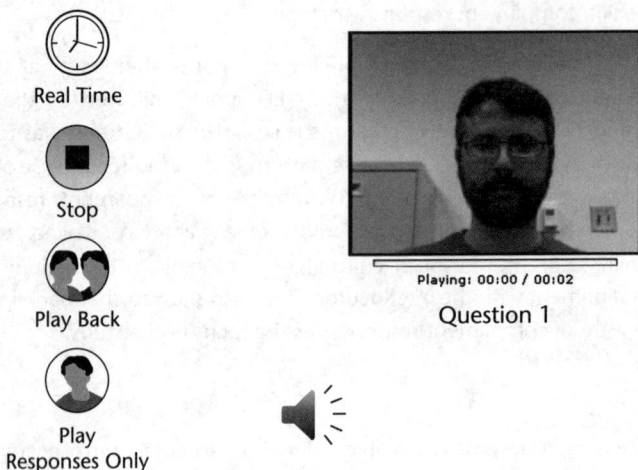

FIGURE 3.4 Created computer-delivered structured tasks

request strategies (e.g., bi-clausal request forms). The study showed that the group who practiced requests with the CAST produced more target-like forms than the traditional face-to-face role plays with peers, because the pre-programmed expressions in the CAST served as models for learners to emulate during role play. The CAST was not adaptive to learners' responses and thus the CAST prompts sometime did not logically match learners' previous responses. However, the author claimed that such discrepancies were minimized by having learners rehearse each scenario several times and conducting extensive pilot-testing.

Role plays have an advantage because they can elicit the target pragmatic features at a relatively high frequency. Like DCTs, role plays are relatively easy to administer and thus have the benefits of convenience and practicality. Because researchers can manipulate and control situational variables, they can examine how contextual elements (e.g., power, social distance, and degree of imposition) may affect participants' choice of pragmalinguistic strategies. Role plays have an advantage over traditional, one-turn DCTs because they can better simulate real-life communicative encounters. Because role plays can elicit two-way communication, researchers can examine how learners perform a pragmatic act through interactions.

Empirical studies indeed revealed that role-play data exhibits different features from DCTs (e.g., Beebe & Cumming, 1996; Sasaki, 1998; Turnbull, 2001; Yuan, 2001). Turnbull's (2001) analysis of native speaker refusal data showed that, compared with DCTs, role-play refusals more closely approximated naturally-occurring refusals regarding the types and distribution of refusal expressions. Sasaki's (1998) study of L2 requests and refusals also found that role plays elicited longer utterances with a greater variety of strategies than DCTs. The moderate correlation between the two methods ($r=0.58$ for the score of appropriateness) in her study implies that they do not measure exactly the same trait.

Although data coming from role plays may reflect naturalistic language use more closely than those from DCTs, the interaction elicited in role plays is still constrained because participants are asked to act out a situation while taking on their imagined roles. In the case of closed role plays, participants are informed about the situation's outcome, but this rarely happens in a real-life interaction. Hence, a lack of established relationships between interlocutors and real-world consequences beyond the task are major limitations of role plays. In addition, compared with DCTs, data obtained through role plays can be more time consuming to analyze because researchers need to transcribe the recorded data.

Points to remember

- Role plays can be open or closed, spontaneous or structured.
- Role plays have an advantage over DCTs because they can simulate real-life communicative encounters.
- Role plays can be done face-to-face, via chat, by phone or video, and even via virtual reality and role-playing software.

- Stimulated recall protocols can be used after role plays in order to gain an understanding of learner's thought processes.
- By means of methods such as CASTs, learners can practice various sides of a role play.
- Role plays are constrained by the fact that they fail to collect naturalistic data due to its hypothetical nature.

3.4 Recording of Authentic Data

Both DCTs and role plays discussed in the previous sections are used for data elicitation. Although these methods help us collect a large number of linguistic samples in one setting, forced-elicitation techniques present a limitation for pragmatics research because pragmatics is about language use in context. Context is critical for pragmatic language use, but the context appearing in an elicitation task is an invented context. To draw generalizations about language use in an invented context, researchers have engaged in discussion about target language use domain (TLU) (Bachman & Palmer, 2010). TLU refers to the degree of correspondence between test tasks and real-life tasks. This means whether test tasks adequately reflect some of the features of real-life language use (e.g., task modality, response format, input characteristics, and settings where test tasks take place). TLU helps address construct validity – whether language use elicited through test tasks can be generalizable beyond the test context to the real-life context.

Task-based language teaching (TBLT), which embraces the value of learning by doing and language in context, makes a similar case for the importance of using authentic materials. Long (2016) notes that one of the advantages of TBLT is that it is not chained to using tasks based on frequency lists or a textbook writer's intuitions as to what a learner needs to know. Instead, TBLT retains authentic models of the use of lexical items, collocations, grammatical structures, pragmatic devices, and so on, which learners need to acquire to successfully resolve tasks and do things with language in the real world.

Researchers have used a variety of methods to strengthen their claims about the construct validity of DCT and role-play scenarios. Bardovi-Harlig's (2009) study on conventional expressions in L2 English collected spontaneous speech samples from local community members. Field notes and recordings were used to identify conventional expressions and the contexts in which they occurred. Scenarios for a spoken DCT were created to elicit the same conventional expressions. Those scenarios were then piloted with native speakers to see if they could indeed elicit the target expressions. Scenarios that did not elicit target expressions were eliminated. In Taguchi, Li, and Xiao's (2013) study on routines in L2 Chinese, the authors added another step: they confirmed commonality of target routines by collecting perceived frequency data from community members via a survey. Garcia (2004) also used TOEFL 2000 Spoken and Written Academic

Language Corpus to construct a pragmatic listening comprehension task that involved tape-recorded dialogues between two native English speakers to assess L2 learners' comprehension of implicature. These efforts are meant to enhance validity of the items used in an elicited task, moving away from intuition-based task construction.

Although these efforts to make tasks valid and reliable are noteworthy, the invented nature of the context does not fully confirm that learners can actually perform pragmatic acts in real-life situations. As Cohen (2004) says, "while any enhancement may make the task more authentic, we must remember it is still a task attempting to simulate reality" (p. 317). Hence, we need to consider alternative methods that can provide access to naturalistic data. Naturalistic data is contextualized. Pragmatic language use arises from participants' interactional goals and needs, and is naturally structured by various contextual parameters. Those parameters reflect both static, contextual elements (e.g., setting) and dynamic elements that change during the course of interaction (e.g., direction of talk). Hence, in naturalistic data, what we can observe in learners' pragmatic behaviors is a direct reflection of the context where those behaviors occur. Corpus pragmatics is a growing field that can offer new possibilities for pragmatics research in terms of authenticity. Corpora such as the British National Corpus (BNC) and the Michigan Corpus of Academic Spoken English (MICASE), for instance, can be used to extract data on discourse markers, routines, and certain speech acts. However, there is a need to have a corpus that is tagged for pragmatic acts. The single large-scale example of a corpus that does this is SPICE-Ireland, briefly discussed in Chapter 2. Such tools would increase the authenticity of pragmatic assessment and data collection tools, and can provide information on frequency and at least some contextual elements (especially co-textual) regarding a particular pragmatic construct that is studied.

In addition to this direct connection between context and language use, authentic data helps us examine a wide range of discourse and interactional features, going beyond isolated pragmatic forms, and can also reveal spontaneous, non-contrived language use. Although authentic data has its own limitations (e.g., practicality, difficulty in collecting sufficient data), given its numerous advantages, researchers should explore creative ways to collect a sizable pool of authentic data in a feasible manner. In the following section, we will present methods for collecting naturally-occurring data in three subcategories: (1) audio/video-recording of naturalistic language use; (2) diaries; and (3) field notes. Conforming to the theme of this chapter, we will limit our discussion to production of pragmatic features.

Naturalistic Language Production

A number of studies have systematically collected authentic tokens of pragmatic features through audio/video-recording of naturalistic or semi-naturalistic interactions. These studies analyzed a variety of pragmatic features: speech acts strategies in office hour conversations (Al-Gahtani & Roever, 2014a, 2014b; Bardovi-Harlig & Hartford, 1993); routines in service encounters (Shively, 2011); acknowledgement and alignment expressions in a classroom (Ohta, 2001); disagreement tokens and arguments in academic discussions (Dippold, 2011; Nikula, 2008; Salsbury & Bardovi-Harlig, 2000); sentence final particles and speech styles among peers and host family members (Cook, 2008; Diao, 2016; Ishida, 2009; Taguchi, 2015a); and humorous utterances (Bell, 2007, 2011; Shively, 2013). In addition to these studies, a growing number of studies have used digital media for collecting authentic data. Particularly notable is the use of computer-mediated communication (CMC), social computing, and multiuser virtual environments as venues to explore pragmatic language use (e.g., Alcón-Soler, 2015; Belz & Kinginger, 2003; Gonzales, 2013; González-Lloret, 2016; Kim & Brown, 2014; Sykes, 2013; Tsai & Kinginger, 2015).

By reviewing the list of existing studies, we can tell that these studies focused on pragmatic features that occur relatively frequently in specific communicative events or settings. As a result, these studies were able to address the challenge of collecting sufficient linguistic tokens for analysis. Bardovi-Harlig and Hartford (1993) and Shively's (2013) studies analyzed institutional discourse that contained highly constrained social interactions. Institutional discourse is replicable because of its recurrent and consequential nature. Because contextual features such as settings, participant roles and relations, expectations, and goals of interaction are relatively fixed in institutional talk, data tokens are comparable across time and place (Bardovi-Harlig & Hartford, 2005). Other studies examined pragmatic features such as sentence final particles, acknowledgement and alignment expressions, and speech styles, which are prime characteristics of colloquial speech, and thus are common in everyday conversations.

Many of these studies analyzed participants' self-recorded conversation data. Researchers gave a recorder to participants and instructed them to record interactions with specific interlocutors (e.g., host family members, roommates, and friends) at certain time intervals. The absence of the researcher during data collection may mitigate the observer's paradox (Labov, 1972), that is, the possibility of the researcher's presence affecting the normal course of interaction. However, even in the researcher's absence, participants are still aware that they are being recorded, and this awareness could influence their linguistic behavior in certain ways. For instance, they may be more conscientious about their speech and monitor their language more closely because of the presence of a recorder. These pros and cons of naturalistic recording should be kept in mind as we present exemplary studies in the following section.

Several studies recorded participants' spontaneous speech across different settings and speech events by having participants wear a microphone clip (Ohta, 2001) or having them carry around a portable digital recorder (Shively, 2011). See Box 3.6 for a description of Shively's study. This study examined changing patterns of service encounter requests among learners of Spanish during their semester of study abroad in Spain. Participants were instructed to record five service encounters in shops, restaurants, post offices, and other local settings at the beginning, middle, and end of the semester (resulting in a total of 15 recorded service encounters per participant). Participants recorded an entire service encounter exchange each time, from beginning to end, with the recorder hidden. They also took notes on the types of shop, purpose of the encounter, and characteristics of the interlocutor (e.g., age, gender).

BOX 3.6 Shively, R. (2011). L2 pragmatic development in study abroad: A longitudinal study of Spanish service encounters. *Journal of Pragmatics, 43*, 1818–1835.

Purpose: To examine L2 Spanish learners' development in their service encounter routines during their semester study abroad and to consider the role of language socialization and explicit instruction in that development.

Participants: Seven undergraduate students from a US university enrolled in a study abroad program in Toledo, Spain.

Data: Naturalistic service encounters between the participants and their service providers recorded in a portable digital recorder (15 encounters per participant recorded over a period of 14 weeks). Student journals, interviews, and a background questionnaire provided additional data.

Data analysis: Service encounters were analyzed for opening sequences and linguistic strategies used to request for products.

Results: Participants' request-making forms changed over time from the dominant use of speaker-oriented strategies (e.g., *¿Puedo comprar eso?* "Can I buy that?") to the increased use of hearer-oriented strategies (e.g., *¿Me puedes poner un café?* "Can you give me a coffee?") and elliptical requests (e.g., *Un café con leche* "A coffee with milk"). The participants' openings were usually brief and contained the canonical greeting sequence *hola-hola* ("hi-hi"), but in a few cases, there were marked, L1-specific sequences (e.g., how-are-you inquires). Some learners acquired the knowledge of appropriate request-making forms in service exchanges by observing other customers' request-making forms and adapted them to their practice, while others learned the request forms through feedback from their host families.

Collection of naturalistic data is the primary strength of Shively's study. Because the service encounter situations had real–life consequences for the participants, data revealed not only the locution and illocution of typical service encounter speech acts, but also the perlocutionary effect of their speech acts, as seen in service providers' reactions to participants' speech or success of a service exchange recorded in the data. Compared with data elicited through DCTs or role plays, participants' service encounter recordings more closely reflected how participants typically engage in real-life service encounters while abroad. In addition, service encounter exchanges were frequent and structurally consistent across time, place, and participants, lending comparability in data collected over time.

However, this comparability is not as stringent as that of elicited data. Because participants made their recordings in a variety of locations, the lack of a common, stable site in data collection reduced the degree of comparability across individuals and over time. In addition, because the researcher was not present at data collection, we do not know what actually went on during recording. Finally, the data obtained at each time point (five encounters per participant) is not particularly large. Hence, a challenge remains as how to collect sufficient quantities of the pragmatic feature under study in naturalistic settings.

Readers may have noted that Shively's (2011) study involved a hidden recorder. This raises ethical issues concerning the use of somebody's speech without their permission. Ethical issues attend any data collection method involving human (or animal) participants. As we discussed earlier in this book in Section 3.1, we are not morally or (often) legally "free" to collect data in naturalistic settings and do what we want with it. Studies need to be designed with ethics in mind at the outset, and approvals sought from relevant institutional ethics committees. As Shively (forthcoming) explains, she made three arguments to her IRB in the US as to why she need not seek informed consent from all parties prior to a recording being made (i.e., why she should be able to use a hidden recorder). The first was that she was recording public service encounter talk. Public talk is not concealed from the various casual overhearers in the particular setting where it is produced. The second was that the identities of the service providers were anonymous. The anonymity of participants is generally a key issue in ethics. The third was that informed consent would have been a barrier to carrying out the research, and the value of the research outweighed the potential risks (as we also discussed when we mentioned the observer's paradox, earlier in the section). Even so, Shively (forthcoming) rightly cautions that ethics committees do not work to some kind of universal guidebook. Different committees could make different judgments about the same data collection method. For a more complete discussion of ethical issues involved in the collection of language and linguistic data, see Mackey and Gass (2015). Some journals, for example, *TESOL Quarterly*, publish comprehensive details on their guidelines for research involving human participants, as do many professional organizations in the field. L2 pragmatics researchers in particular do need to educate themselves about the expectations of their institutions and the venues where they hope to publish their data, as well as of any grant-awarding bodies. This is because L2 pragmatics data can be naturalistic, as well as experimental, and whenever hidden recording or data collection "in the wild" is involved, particular care will need to be taken to satisfy ethics committees that no harm has been, or will be, done to participants.

Diaries

Compared with naturalistic recording, the diary method has been less prominent when it comes to the study of pragmatic production. Second language diaries, also called L2 journals or learner autobiographies, are essentially people's journal entries about, and reflections on, their own impressions and learning experiences. Experiences recorded usually involve the diary writer's attentiveness to specific pragmatic input, interpretation of pragmatic behaviors that he/she observed, and reflection on his/her understanding of pragmatic acts. Because of this self-reported, self-reflective nature, the diary method is probably more suitable for investigating participants' metapragmatic awareness and understanding. We will discuss this use of the diary method in Chapter 5, but here we will review a small body of studies that used a diary as a method for collecting data on pragmatic production.

Cohen's (1997) study reported the author's experience as a student in a Japanese language course in a US university. Data in this study included tape-recorded journals of the author's insights as they occurred (25 journal entries total), written notes, tests, and quizzes taken in class. These data sources were triangulated to reveal the author's self-assessment and monitoring of pragmatics learning in a semester-length beginning level Japanese class. The author reported numerous instances of his own pragmatic language use, both inside and outside of class, combined with his personal reflections about his pragmatic performance.

> When I spoke in class, if I simply mimicked the phrases appearing in the text, I could get by in a paired task but rarely felt that I had full control over choice of the appropriate phrase. For example, if I greeted my drill partner with *ogenki desuka?* (literally, "how is your health?" but meaning "how are you?"), I was not sure whether it was an acceptable utterance. My mind would question whether it was accurate enough in terms of content (i.e., whether it can be used on a daily basis or only if I haven't seen the person for some time) and level of formality (*ogenki* vs. *genki*) to be appropriate for use with a peer in an academic setting, as opposed to using a "safer" greeting relating to time of day, such as *ohayoo* "good morning" or *ohayoo gozaimasu*, if I chose to be more formal.
>
> *(p. 149)*

This excerpt shows that the author was able to produce the appropriate greeting expression to his tutor drawing on the information he gained in class, but he remained ambivalent about this knowledge and choice of expression in a real-life situation in which competing options were available. The diary method was effective at revealing this discrepancy. While the researcher's successful production of the target form shows his pragmalinguistic knowledge, his reflections tell us that his knowledge was not so entrenched. This was because in a real-life situation, multiple sociopragmatic elements, such as formality, familiarity, and timing of interaction, emerge to guide appropriate expression selection. These elements are dynamic and complex, unlike a situation presented in a classroom task.

Hassall (2006) also used the diary method. The author-as-a-participant kept a diary recording of his own production of leave-taking expressions during his sojourn in Indonesia. Indonesian language has two leave-taking forms: *dulu* and *permisi*. The former means "goodbye" and is used among friends. The latter form, *permisi*, literally means asking permission to leave and is directed to someone in authority. Hence, using *permisi* at leave-taking is more than just saying goodbye because *permisi* encodes cultural values of showing respect for those of higher status. The 272-page diary documented that the author exclusively used *dulu* when taking leave, which was too informal for certain occasions. However, after the mid-point, he started using *permisi* because he observed the use of this form among locals and noticed the form in the media. The author's diary excerpt below illustrates such a learning episode.

> As I was trudging home on the final stretch after a long hot walk, I was called over to chat by two women in the yard of a house nearby. We chatted amiably enough, but I suddenly got the impression that I'd over-stayed my welcome – one of them seemed to be casting around rather awkwardly for further questions to ask me. So I rather hastily took my leave, with a *dulu* statement: *Puland dulu ya* "I'm going home for now, okay" (literally, "Go-home for-now, yes"). I said it a bit tensely and unsmilingly and it felt a bit abrupt as I said it. As I then turned to go, one of them said softly, in English, "Excuse me". I turned around in puzzlement. She then repeated it in Indonesian: *Permisi*, and laughed. So her "excuse me" had been a gentle correction; a supplying of what I'd omitted to say. (Diary entry, Padang Week 2, 9/1/02)
>
> *(Hassall, 2006, p. 39)*

The author recorded his production of *dulu* for leave-taking, which was implicitly corrected by a local member through her modeling of *permisi*. After this triggering event, *permisi* entered the author's repertoire. Two weeks later in another occasion of a casual chat with an acquaintance, the author recorded his successful production of *permisi* when he took leave.

The diary method shares similar advantages with naturalistic recording because data reflects participants' real-life language use and provides a contextualized illustration of pragmalinguistic forms produced. Because the diary writer can describe elements of a situation surrounding pragmatic forms under study (e.g., interlocutor relationships, settings, goal of interaction), the data can reveal participants' sociopragmatic understanding alongside their pragmalinguistic knowledge. However, because of the participant-directed nature, data gathered in diaries are bounded by subjectivity. As Kasper and Rose (2002) claim:

> They [diaries] distinguish themselves from any other form of self-report in that they are – in the self-study variety at least – entirely participant-directed, since the diarist decides on the substance, form, and timing of entries without being constrained by a particular task response format, or social interaction.
>
> *(pp.112–113)*

As such, it is possible that diary data do not represent entire instances of language use. In addition, the self-directed characteristic of the diary method makes it difficult to compare data over time or across participants. Although the open-ended format in a diary can generate extensive data with an *emic* perspective (the notion of emic is discussed in Section 6.1), in order to ensure comparability, researchers need to implement specific guidelines that allow systematic data collection by, for example, providing detailed instructions about the type of events to record and manner of recording. Several L2 pragmatics studies have used personal journals to complement interpretation of the topic under study (e.g., Kinginger, 2008; Shively, 2011), and the directions for journal writing used in these studies can serve as useful sources for pragmatics researchers. Technology is also changing the field in relation to diaries – with younger people becoming increasingly confident with video diaries or blogs. Considering these shifts, it is possible that diaries will provide more insight as such means become more available to language learners and researchers.

Field Notes

Field notes are data collected through participant observation. Participant observation is a qualitative method rooted in ethnographic research, which enables the researcher to learn about the perspectives of participants under study by observing and participating in routine activities in a local community (Kawulich, 2005; Schensul, Schensul, & LeCompte, 1999). Different from other methods, participant observation allows the researcher to approach participants in their own environment, rather than having participants come to the researcher. The researcher takes notes on what he/she sees and hears, and records all observations as field notes in a field notebook. Thus, field notes are developed by the researcher to remember behaviors, activities, and events in a community, which help researchers produce meaning and understanding of the phenomenon being investigated (DeWalt & DeWalt, 2002).

Participant observation and field notes help us develop understanding of the context and phenomena under study. However, a recorded observation may not present a full description of the phenomena because, like diaries, field notes are subjective and are affected by the researcher's perceptions about what is relevant and important to record. The researcher's presence in the community may also influence the participants' behavior (the observer's paradox). In addition, being observers and outsiders, researchers may not be accepted fully in the community, which inevitably affects the quality of data obtained through observation (DeWalt & DeWalt, 2002).

A classic pragmatics study that used field notes dates back to the 1980s when Manes and Wolfson (1981) collected over 1,200 instances of naturally occurring compliments in American English. Analysis of compliment tokens in a wide range of situations revealed that complimenting behavior is highly ritualistic: about 80% of compliments fall into three syntactic patterns: [noun phrase] is/looks [adjective] (e.g., Your scarf is beautiful.); I like/love [noun phrase] (e.g., I love your scarf.); and [pronoun] is [adjective] [noun] (e.g., That is a nice scarf).

To our knowledge, this type of systematic, large-scale study that solely used field observation to document occurrence of pragmatic features is rare in L2 pragmatics research. However, a few smaller-scale studies have collected field notes of learners' language use to make inferences about their pragmatic development (e.g., Jones, 2007; Kinginger, 2008; Li, 2000; Schmidt, 1983). These studies implemented data triangulation using the mixed methods approach, with field notes being one part of quantitative and qualitative data.

Jones (2007) documented three English-speaking children's development in L2 Japanese, focusing on grammar and certain pragmatic aspects. The three children were siblings (ages 7, 5, and 2) who moved to Japan with their family. The author collected two sets of data during a 52-week study period: video recording of family dinner conversations and the mother's field notes on the children's language use. The pragmatic aspects analyzed in the study were extensive, including the use of interactional particles, different politeness levels, regional versus standard dialect, gendered language, donatory verbs, and address forms. We will focus on interactional particles to illustrate the author's use of field notes.

Interactional particles (e.g., *ne, yo, na, kana*) occur at sentence-final position to convey the speaker's interactional attitudes and stance. Jones took field notes on these particles as they appeared in the children's utterances. Numerous tokens of interactional particles helped the author illustrate patterns of development over time. She showed that all three children began to produce the common particles *ne* and *yo* relatively early, particularly as part of formulae and chunks. See Week 12 data below for illustration. Interactional particles are in bold.

15) *Eric: ii **yo**.* [week 12]
     That's OK!

16) *Eric: soo **yo**.* [week 12]
     That's right!

After this phase, the children started extending their use of particles to English sentences. See sample tokens:

29) *Miranda*: Kent, wait for me, **ne**? [week 29]
30) *Kent*: Let's see if it works, **ne**? It will, I hope. [week 29]

After the children began reproducing routine expressions with interactional particles, they started using the particles in novel utterances, demonstrating creative language use. At the same time, the children started producing particles different from *ne* and *yo* and expanded their pragmalinguistic repertoire. Weeks 42 to 48's data below show emergence of particles *kana* and **na**.

24) *Miranda*: *oishii kamo shirenai, un, wakaranai* **na**. [week 42]
     It's probably yummy. Hmmm, I don't know . . .
26) *Eric*: *kore moo ikkai yomoo* **kana**. [week 48]
     I wonder if I should read this one again.

As shown above, the children relied on routines in their early production of particles and overused certain particles, but they gradually expanded their linguistic repertoire by incorporating different particles and using them in novel sentences. Their creative use even extended to their L1 English, which indicated that they appropriated pragmatic functions of these particles such as indexing attitudes, affect, and stance. Systematic observations and field notes allowed the researcher to trace these patterns of development over time.

Although tape- or video-recordings of natural conversation may yield more accurate data, field notes are more expedient because no special equipment and setting are necessary. Researchers can take notes of their observations anywhere, anytime. Because notes are taken spontaneously, the observer's paradox is relatively controlled: it is most likely that participants are behaving naturally without being excessively self-conscious. The quality of field notes depends on the researcher's memory, but this is probably not too difficult to manage when the focus of investigation is on relatively simple pragmalinguistic forms, such as sentence final particles in Jones's study. Naturalistic data have ecological validity as their primary advantage.

However, naturalistic data have been far less prevalent than elicited data in the field. Naturalistic data is not as popular as elicited data because pragmatic features under study are not common enough in authentic discourse to form a sizable data set. This is especially true when contextual variables (e.g., power, social distance) become part of the investigation. For example, Garcia (2004) examined speech acts in three corpora of academic discourse: office hours, service encounters, and study group conversations. She found that, while the student-initiated request was the most common speech act in service encounter situations, it occurred only about 30% of the time in the other two corpora. These findings suggest that in naturalistic discourse, not all speech acts are equally represented across registers. Because compiling a sizable database of speech acts across registers is challenging, researchers may turn to naturalistic data when they examine discourse/interactional markers that occur regularly in everyday conversations.

Points to remember

- Forced-elicitation techniques like DCTs and role plays present a limitation for pragmatics research because pragmatics is about language use in context.
- Target language use domain (TLU) helps address the construct validity of elicitation tasks in invented contexts.
- Task-based language teaching (TBLT) highlights the importance of authentic tasks that allow learners to do real things with language.
- Authentic data can reveal spontaneous, non-contrived language use.
- Diaries and field notes are two ways of gathering authentic language data.

3.5 Conclusions

In this chapter, we have presented a survey of how pragmatic production has been elicited and studied. Although speech act strategies have occupied a large portion of production data, other areas of language use – such as routines, speech styles, address forms, and sentence final particles – have shown a steady increase in production data. Existing data largely fall into two categories: elicited data and naturalistic data. DCTs and role plays have been popular methods for eliciting data, while audio/video/digital media-based recording, diaries, and field notes have been used to collect naturalistic data. Both types of data, as well as individual data-gathering methods, have strengths and limitations, as we have discussed in this chapter. Researchers should weigh advantages and disadvantages of different data collection methods and select the most appropriate one(s) for the purposes of their studies and research questions posed.

Discussion Questions

1. Compare the advantages and disadvantages of different types of DCTs discussed in this chapter in terms of collecting production data.
2. What are the similarities and differences between DCTs and role plays?
3. Based on the discussion on the disadvantages of using DCTs for collecting production data, what are some ways to make DCTs more reliable and authentic?

4. Besides the widely used DCTs, what other tools are available for researchers to collect data on language production in pragmatics research?
5. Why is ethics approval needed for surreptitious recordings made of L2 pragmatics data?
6. Which data collection tool(s) would be the most useful for a cross-sectional study investigating L2 learners' production of a certain speech act (e.g., requests, apologies, disagreements)?
7. How does technology affect the methods used to examine learners' production of a communicative act?

Follow-up Activity

A. Consider a situation where you want to elicit requests to borrow money and refusals to lend money between interlocutors of different levels of social standing and familiarity. Based on what you have learned about the elicitation methods in this chapter, think about how you could use each of the following methods to elicit L2 requests and refusals.

A written DCT to be used in a traditional classroom.
An oral DCT to be used in a traditional classroom.
A collaborative dialogue DCT to be used in a traditional classroom.
A traditional role play to be used in a traditional classroom.
A virtual reality role play to be done online by participants in different cities.
A CAST to be done online.

B. Now that you have considered the above elicitation methods, choose one and briefly sketch out the steps you would take to implement it. Consider, for example, the following questions:

Why did you choose this method? What advantages and disadvantages does it have over the other methods listed?
What instructions will you give to the participants?
Will you provide audio/visual support?

C. Now imagine that you wanted to compare the data you elicited to naturally-occurring data. How could you do so? What methods could you use to gather examples of naturally-occurring requests and refusals?
D. Finally, consider the authenticity of the elicitation methods you designed. How do you think they represent real-world situations and how could they be made more authentic?

4

LANGUAGE COMPREHENSION AND AWARENESS: CONCEPTUAL BACKGROUND

Introduction

In the current chapter, we will focus on the hearer and how they go about understanding. Hearers have been neglected in traditional pragmatics research, which has a speaker bias (see Chapter 2). Hearers are particularly important in L2 pragmatics, where listening, as well as speaking, is essential in our understanding of how a second language is learned. We should immediately point out that it is important to be clear that the range of participants in communicative events, the ways in which they can participate and the dynamic nature of those events, are obviously broader than simple categories of speaker and hearer. For example, observers are neither speaker nor hearer, but they can still be parties to conversations.

H.P. Grice's (1975/1989) Conversational Implicature, a theory that purports to account for implied/inferred meanings, is both considered a foundational work in general pragmatics and has been deployed extensively in L2 pragmatics research on learner inferencing. Consequently, this theory will be the first that we attend to in this chapter. However, conversational implicature only accounts for part of the implicational and inferencing activity that participants undertake. For this reason, the following section (Section 4.1) discusses the important area of "associative processes" and the way in which contextual assumptions can be derived from prior knowledge. Here, we will also briefly introduce Relevance Theory (Sperber and Wilson, 1995). Over time, sometimes implied/inferred meanings become associated with specific contexts – they become conventionalized to some degree. We will discuss such processes in Section 4.3, not least because conventionalized pragmatic expressions or formula have become an important topic in L2 pragmatics (see in particular various publications by Kathleen Bardovi-Harlig). Politeness formulae come about in very similar ways, and so we will next discuss this aspect of politeness, and, more generally, judgments of contextual appropriateness. Finally, we consider metapragmatic awareness and metapragmatic expressions in Section 4.5.

4.1 Logical Inferencing: Conversational Implicature

Why study inferencing in L2 pragmatics? As we discussed in Chapter 2, a joke, repeated here for ease of reference, can be used to illustrate why simple decoding is not enough to understand the underlying meaning of many conversations.

[*Context: In a countryside area in the UK, travelling in a car, past a field with cows in it.*]

1. *Jonathan*: They're lying down . . . means it's going to rain.
2. *Emily*: Well, what if it doesn't.
3. *Natalie*: They'd be lying.

Much of the meaning in that joke about cows lying in a field is beyond the words, beyond what was said, beyond semantic meaning. In the discussion of (in) directness in Section 2.4., we also encountered meanings, including politeness meanings, that lie beyond what is in the surface form. Answering simply "yes" to the apparent question "Could you tell me the time?" would be perverse. These areas, though very important, are not the only cases involving meanings that go beyond what is said. An obvious reason for their frequent presence is economy of expression; we can rely on our hearers to fill in the gaps through inferencing. In fact, every utterance is open to some degree of inferencing, in the broadest sense of the word. This is regardless of language or culture, though precisely how that inferencing works may vary across cultures and is a topic of study in intercultural pragmatics.

In the context of general pragmatics, four key terms involving meanings beyond the semantics of what is said are as follows:

Related to the speaker:

Imply: The speaker generates some meaning beyond the semantic meaning of the words.

Implicature: The implied meaning generated intentionally by the speaker.

Related to the hearer:

Infer: The hearer derives meaning from available evidence.

Inference: The inferred meaning derived by the hearer and which may or may not be the same as the speaker's intended implicature.

These four words and their definitions provide a useful categorization of different aspects of pragmatic meaning. However, a key point to note is that native speakers of English do not always follow these definitions. Quite often, for example, people use *infer* to mean *imply*. In this book, and indeed in most general pragmatics, usage follows what we have laid out above.

The title of H. Paul Grice's (1975) key paper is telling: "Logic and conversation." Grice's work focuses on the kind of "logical" inferencing characterized by mechanisms for drawing conclusions or implications from premises, as might be illustrated thus:

[1]   *Premise 1*: Plants die when they are not watered.
      Premise 2: Lilies are plants.
      Conclusion: Lilies will die when they are not watered.

Grice set out to show that there is some kind of logical system operating in natural conversation for working out meanings beyond the semantics. It is not, however, quite the same as the logic in Example [1]. There we see the premises and conclusions that are typical of deductive logic. We are dealing with absolute truths (there is no fuzziness or doubt that "lilies are plants"). In contrast, the logic proposed for conversation is a kind of pseudo-logic based on assumptions that lead to probable conclusions. Conversational logic is often fuzzy and rarely leads to one definite conclusion, though hearers often settle on a single conclusion because of various contextual factors. We will discuss the assumptions that lead to these conclusions in the following section.

Grice's essential mechanism underlying the logic of conversation is the Cooperative Principle (CP), which is as follows:

> Make your contribution such as is required, at the stage at which it occurs, by the accepted purpose or direction of the talk exchange in which you are engaged.
>
> *(1989, p. 26)*

The title of the principle and the wording of it are unfortunate. It sounds like a prescription to talk in such a way that we cooperate with each other, and, to the uninitiated, "cooperate" is likely to have a sense of social cooperation, that is, doing what the other person wants. In fact, it is much better to view Gricean cooperation as informational cooperation, namely, giving enough information for the needs of the conversational exchange. The first part of the exchanges in [2] was said by a person in London, whilst waving an empty tin can at a passer-by in an attempt to gain some money (see Figure 4.1).

[2]   (a)   *A*: Any spare change please.
            B: Sure.
      (b)   *A*: Any spare change please.
            B: No.
      (c)   *A*: Any spare change please.
            B: Go away.

FIGURE 4.1 "Any spare change please"

We will concentrate on the B responses here: [2a] contains a response, *Sure*, that is cooperative in informational terms (it provides enough information to count as a full response to the request), and also in social terms (it complies with the requestive goal of gaining money); [2b] contains an answer, *No*, that is cooperative in informational terms (it provides enough information to count as a full response to the request), but is not cooperative in social terms (it does not comply with the requestive goal of gaining money); [2c] contains an answer, *Go away*, that is not cooperative in informational terms (it does not, on the surface, provide enough information to count as a full response to the request) or in social terms (it does not comply with the goal of gaining money). The key point about [2c] is the fact that its lack of informational cooperation on the surface is a signal to the hearer to work out informational cooperation at a deeper level. It is a short step to infer that if somebody is saying *Go away* as a response to your request, then that response is likely to be negative (they do not have any spare change for you).

Grice's Cooperative Principle is comprised of four maxims. They are as follows (the phrasings are quotations from Grice, 1989, pp. 26–27):

1. *Maxim of Quantity*: (1) Make your contribution as informative as is required (for the current purpose of the exchange); (2) Do not make your contribution more informative than is required.
2. *Maxim of Quality*: (1) Do not say what you believe to be false; (2) Do not say that for which you lack evidence.
3. *Maxim of Relation*: Be relevant.
4. *Maxim of Manner*: (1) Avoid obscurity of expression; (2) Avoid ambiguity; (3) Be brief; (4) Be orderly.

Again, the prescriptive flavor of the wording is unfortunate. It is better to consider these maxims as assumptions that people make about how conversation works. Consider Example [2c], *Go away* is not the most relevant response one could make to a request; it flouts the Maxim of Relation (be relevant). But we are assuming that this person is abiding by the Cooperative Principle, so there must be informational cooperation (relevance) at a deeper level (i.e., relevance is assumed to be there but needs to be inferred). We are also making assumptions about the context, and, at a higher level, an assumption that all these assumptions are available to both participants. Given all this, we can work out a likely inference that the answer is "no." What we have constructed, in simplified form, is the speaker's implicature. A feature of all implicatures is that they can be cancelled, at least in principle. Thus, in [2c], the speaker of *Go away* could add: "I'm trying to concentrate, I'll be back later with some money," thereby cancelling the inference of a simple "no."

> **Points to remember**
>
> - Much of the meaning in what we say is beyond words (beyond semantic meaning). The speaker often **implies** something beyond that surface meaning, leaving the hearer to **infer** what is being meant. In the field of pragmatics, the outputs of these processes are called **implicature** and **inference**, respectively.
> - Utterances that **flout** (blatantly break with) Grice's Cooperative Principle encourage inferencing. Namely, if a hearer receives a response to an utterance that is not cooperative (it does not provide enough information to count as a full response to the request), this is a signal to the hearer to work out cooperation at a deeper level. Namely, the hearer must **infer** what the speaker was trying to get across (i.e. the **implicature**).

The other maxims can be used to describe other kinds of linguistic triggers for the hearer to work out an implicature. Quantity implicatures are triggered by a lack of or too much detail ("what did I do . . . well, one thing"); quality implicatures are triggered by such things as metaphors, sarcasm and hyperbole ("what did I do . . . well, everything in the world"); manner implicatures are triggered by lack of clarity of expression ("what did I do . . . well, more than I assumed but less than I thought"). It is useful to note that the Maxims can overlap, and that is especially true of the Maxim of Relation. If any of the other three maxims are broken, that necessarily makes the utterance less relevant, and therefore the Maxim Relation is also broken. It is not surprising, therefore, that later work focused on the notion of relevance, and the influential Relevance Theory (Sperber & Wilson, 1986, 1995) emerged. Relevance Theory argues that a hearer will search for meaning in any communicative situation, and once they have settled on a meaning that fits their expectation of relevance, they will stop searching and settle on an interpretation. All this is perhaps why in L2 pragmatics, the Maxim of Relation seems to have special focus (see Chapter 5).

As we have shown, people can *flout* the maxims to trigger an implicature (Box 4.1). Note that: one utterance can trigger multiple implicatures; implicatures can vary in strength; and implicatures can consist of various types of meaning, including, for example, social or emotional meanings. Breaking multiple weak maxims is typical of poetry, with all its subtle and multiple ambiguities of meaning. Breaking maxims in exaggerated ways and/or conveying implicatures that the audience works out, but the characters do not, can be an effective source of comedy. In the famous "Roger schoolboy sketch" (the clip is available in various places on the internet), the comedians Peter Cook and Dudley Moore play a schoolboy son and father in a gentile, old-fashioned setting. The comic target is the traditional British taboo on discussing sex, as epitomized by the conventionally oblique reference (flouting the Maxim of Relation) to discussion of the birds and the bees. Over a cup of tea (cf. Figure 4.2), the father is trying to explain to the son, who is nearing 18 years of age, how he was created (i.e., through sexual intercourse), but cannot bring himself to do it explicitly. Instead, he does it through implicatures, largely triggered through repeatedly flouting the Maxim of Manner with obscure utterances such as "the method whereby you came to be brought about." The comic target is the traditional British taboo on discussing sex.

FIGURE 4.2 The birds and the bees: Flouting manner

BOX 4.1 Flouting Maxims

Maxim of Quantity

Lara: Where does Professor Yarow live?
Margaret: Somewhere past where the train reaches.

To avoid breaking the maxim of quality – providing information she knows to be untrue – Margaret flouts the maxim of quantity – obviously providing less information than was asked for. Possible implicatures might be that Margaret doesn't know exactly where the professor lives, or that she wants to discourage Lara from going there because it is very far.

Maxim of Quality

Karen: Tehran's in Turkey, isn't it?
Aysenur: Uh-huh, and Boston's in Tokyo.

By providing the obvious falsehood that Boston is in Tokyo, Aysenur triggers the possible implicature that Tehran is, in fact, not in Turkey.

Maxim of Relation

Bill: I don't understand why everyone is complaining about Jim being sexist.
Pete: Well, look at this great weather we're having today.

Pete gives a seemingly irrelevant response, but it can trigger the implicature that he does not want to engage in a conversation about Jim's sexism.

Maxim of Manner

Jeff: How was the movie last night?
Meg: Starting with the musical score, I thought the composer borrowed too
generously from Santollalla, though the vocals were top-notch. Moving on to the cinematography, I thought Hollander's wide angles made the landscapes come alive, but the apartment scenes felt constricted and dull. There must have been some tension between him and the director, who typically works in a very different style.

Meg's response is unnecessarily detailed and long, which flouts the expectation of brevity. The content of implicatures always depends on the specifics of the context, but here might be a criticism of Jeff for assuming that she did not have the ability to offer a critical opinion.

Flouting happens when a speaker violates a conversational maxim "not with any intention of deceiving or misleading, but because the speaker wishes to prompt the hearer to look for a meaning which is different from, or in addition to, the expressed meaning" (Thomas, 1995, p. 65). Box 4.1 gives many examples. On the other hand, a *violation* of a maxim refers to cases where there is no intention to generate an implicature, but there is an intention to surreptitiously mislead the hearer. The most obvious example is a lie, an utterance that violates the Maxim of Quality.

One further important way of breaking the maxims explicitly refers to L2 learners. If a speaker *infringes* a maxim they fail to observe a maxim because of:

> an imperfect command of the language (a young child or a foreign learner), because the speaker's performance is impaired in some way (nervousness, drunkenness, excitement), because of some cognitive impairment, or simply because the speaker is constitutionally incapable of speaking clearly, to the point, etc.
>
> *(Thomas, 1995, p. 74)*

It is not difficult to imagine how infringements of the maxims might lead a learner to generate unintended implicatures or fail to generate intended implicatures (see Greenall [2009] for some interesting remarks in this area).

There is also a particular distinction between two different types of implicature that underpins some important issues in L2 pragmatics, as we will explain in Section 4.3. Grice (1975/1989) proposed a distinction between "particularized" and "generalized" implicatures. Particularized implicatures, which have characterized our discussion so far in this section, require special knowledge of the features of the context in order to work out the implicature it has in that context. Consider Example [3]:

[3] *Sam*: Am I late?
     Elena: Graeme's just left.

Clearly, Elena's answer flouts the Maxim of Relation. But what is the answer: is Sam late or not? We only know this if we know the particulars of the context, notably, the relationship in time between Graeme's leaving and being late (if Graeme usually leaves long before Sam does, and so Sam is not late; or if it is the case that Graeme usually leaves after Sam, and so Sam is late).

Generalized implicatures, on the other hand, require no special contextual knowledge to work out. See, for example, the exchange in [4]:

[4] *Xue*: Who ate all the nuts?
     Nic: Well, I had some.

The issue here is the word *some*. It carries an implicature that Nic did not have *all* the nuts. That implicature has the potential to arise in whatever context we find the word *some*. Thus, it is a generalized implicature. This particular example involves a subgroup of generalized implicatures called "scalar implicatures." As the name suggests, they derived from items that are positioned on scales such as the following:

- Quantity – some, most, all
- Frequency – sometimes, often, always
- Coldness – hot, warm, tepid, cool, cold, freezing
- Likelihood – possibly, probably, certainly, etc.

Using an item on a scale potentially generates the implicature "not the other items on the scale." Hence, *some* implicates "not all," "not most," and so on.

4.2 Associative Processes, Inferencing, and Relevance Theory

Much implicit meaning is constructed on the basis of associative processes. Such processes enrich our understandings of what people say, make what they say cohere and even enable predictions about what they are going to say. The pseudo-logical inferencing of conversational implicature discussed previously does not take place in a vacuum. Running alongside such inferencing are associative processes enriching, constraining, or supporting the kind of inferences being made. Pragmatics scholars such as Recanati (2004) and Mazzone (2011) argue for a key role for associative processes. The relevance of this to L2 pragmatics is that learners may lack the relevant knowledge to feed associative processes in their target language in the same way that the L1 speaker can. Example [5] and the associated Figure 4.3 illustrates this:

[5] Contextual assumption 1: It often rains in Lancaster.
Contextual assumption 2: My umbrella often keeps me dry.
Conclusion: My umbrella will probably keep me dry in Lancaster.

FIGURE 4.3 It often rains in Lancaster

Contextual assumptions 1 and 2 are based on things that regularly go together in a person's experience (rain + Lancaster; umbrellas + dryness) and become associated in their head. Complex bundles of experience-driven knowledge have been described in terms of schema theory (Rumelhart, 1984; Schank & Abelson, 1977), a theory of knowledge that accounts for bundles of (usually generic) knowledge and how they affect processes of comprehension. Contextual assumptions are the default values of a particular schema (a schema of life in Lancaster may well incorporate rain experiences, which become a default value of a Lancaster schema). These assumptions are not premises, absolute truths feeding a logical process, as we saw in [1]; they are probabilities based on our experience. We can derive conclusions from such assumptions, as [5] illustrates. Such conclusions might be thought of as implications. Some implications are implicatures – remember that implicatures are intentional meanings conveyed by a speaker to somebody else, not simply cognitive processes in a person's head.

We will now return to Example [2c], repeated below as [6] for convenience:

[6]   *A*: Any spare change please.
      B: Go away.

Depending on one's particular experiences, the first utterance allows various assumptions to be made. Someone asking to borrow money might be assumed to be: in a needy state; less powerful than the person they are talking to; embarrassed by having to ask for money; sensitive to refusal. Moreover, and we will return to this particular issue in the following section, the specific phrasing of this utterance has the potential to generate the assumption that it is a request from a homeless person in a city begging or pan handling for money. The second utterance also allows various assumptions to be made. Someone saying *Go away* at that point might be assumed to be: posing a response to the request (responses regularly follow requests); offensive (dismissals like this are regularly used to be impolite; there is no reciprocal politeness); insensitive to the other's needs. On the basis of just some of these assumptions, we can draw a conclusion: the request is denied (e.g., compliant request responses are not usually offensive). There is no claim here, of course, that these are the exact assumptions that everyone will make, but they illustrate how pseudo-logical inferencing of the Gricean type is interlaced with interpretative support from associative processes.

> **Points to remember**
>
> • Associative processes play a key role in understanding implicit meaning. Certain things that regularly co-occur in a person's experience become associated with one another and coalesce into a mental schema. People then make inferences about their interlocutor's intended meaning based on these schemas.

In the previous section, we briefly mentioned Relevance Theory (Sperber & Wilson, 1986, 1995), a theory that has had some impact on L2 pragmatics (see Section 5.1), though perhaps not as much as one might expect, given its importance in pragmatics generally. Relevance Theory is not simply a principle regarding the communication of meaning. The striking thing about Relevance Theory is that it incorporates aspects of cognition, including contextual assumptions, which is why we discuss it here.

Relevance Theory consists of two principles. The first is the Cognitive Principle of Relevance: "Human cognition tends to be geared to the maximisation of relevance" (Wilson & Sperber, 2012, p. 6; see also the expanded version Sperber & Wilson, 1995, pp. 260–266). What this is saying is that our minds are predisposed to attending to what is most relevant in what we see hear, see, or perceive. But what exactly counts as relevant? Sperber and Wilson have a specific understanding of relevance. Essentially, it concerns extracting the most information for the least effort. So, poetry is typically difficult to understand (it needs effort), but there can be rich meanings (cognitive rewards). The resulting communication would count as relevant. Conversely, an L2 speaker might produce something that is difficult to understand (it needs effort), but there may be relatively trivial meanings (cognitive rewards) to be gained. In which case, the L2 speaker's speech is not counted as relevant (in this technical sense). Cognitive rewards are what Sperber and Wilson refer to as "cognitive effects." They are considered adjustments you make to your assumptions about the world, and are of three kinds: (1) strengthening an existing assumption (you thought it was going to rain in Lancaster, and it duly did when you arrived); (2) weakening or eliminating an existing assumption (you thought it was going to rain in Lancaster, but there was sunshine the whole time you were there); and (3) deriving a contextual implication to create new information (you discovered umbrellas are useless in Lancaster because the wind blows them inside out).

The second is the Communicative Principle of Relevance: "Every act of overt communication conveys a presumption of its own optimal relevance" (Sperber & Wilson 2012, p. 6; see also the expanded version Sperber & Wilson 1995, pp. 266–272). "Act of overt communication" simply means acts by which somebody intends to communicate something (if somebody has blood-shot eyes, we might infer that they were up all night working on a paper, but that would not be something they intended to communicate). The key claim is that every such act carries a guarantee that it will be worth it, while working out what they intend to communicate; that is, the mental effort taken to work it out will be matched by sufficient cognitive effects. Return to Example [6]. "Go away" directed toward the beggar is likely to be taken as an act of overt communication, and so it has guaranteed relevance. For reasons mentioned in the previous section and earlier in this section, it is relatively easy to work out that this person is refusing the request for money. The mental cost is rewarded by the new information derived from the contextual implication (saying "Go away" is not compatible with giving money, therefore no money will be given).

4.3 Conventionalized Forms and Generalized Implicatures

In the next chapter, we will discuss the methods deployed in Bouton's (1992, 1994) work testing L2 English speakers' comprehension of various types of implicature. One type of implicature he addressed is the so-called "Pope implicature," which involves using the utterance "Is the Pope Catholic?" (see Figure 4.4) to mean that something is obviously the case. Another example of this kind of implicature is "Does a bear defecate in the woods?" where defecate is usually replaced by a less formal term. How does this work? On the surface, the interrogative form seems to be acting as a yes/no question performing a rogative – a speech act that elicits missing information (cf. Leech, 1983). However, the information that is being asked for cannot reasonably be missing. The Pope is the head of the Catholic Church – it is inconceivable that he would be anything other than Catholic; and bears do not have any alternative for the location of their bodily functions!

These questions flout the Maxim of Quality ("Do not say that for which you lack evidence"); in other words, the speaker is ostentatiously pretending not to know something that she or he in fact does. Assuming the Cooperative Principle to be followed, we search for cooperation at a deeper level. It is a short step to infer the implicature that the speaker views something in the context as obviously the case. This interpretation is crucially supported by associative processes.

FIGURE 4.4 "Is the Pope Catholic?"

For example, note that in the above description we included knowledge of the information that the Pope is the head of the Catholic Church. From this knowledge, we can generate the contextual assumption that the head of the Catholic Church is Catholic. Most people do not know the legal framework by which popes are appointed; it is an assumption that the person inhabiting that role is Catholic, an assumption based on previous associations, notably that previous popes have been Catholic. Without the knowledge that enables us to generate this assumption, it would be difficult to infer the speaker's implicature. Importantly, however, there is another route to the speaker's implicature.

For at least the majority of native speakers of English, inferring the Pope implicature is a more straightforward process than was suggested above. Over time, the question "Is the Pope Catholic?" becomes increasingly associated with the meaning "that is obviously the case." So, rather than working through the inferential steps to derive the implicature, people can go straight to the implicature's meaning because the utterance has become conventionally associated with it. The idea that particular forms can become associated with particular implicatures, or indeed meanings generally, is a widespread phenomenon, a normal part of language change.

We have already encountered a specific context where implicatures often become conventionalized for particular forms, and that is indirect speech acts. In Section 2.4, we noted how in Searle's account, the notion of conventional indirectness does not refer to regular ways of doing particular speech acts, but to a systematic relationship with the direct speech act's felicity conditions. Thus, *Can you pass me the salt* orientates to the preparatory condition of the speaker having the ability to perform the act referred to in the request. Hearers, as Searle proposed, work through inferential steps in a Gricean fashion to derive the underlying requestive meaning. An alternative approach is simply to note regularities of co-occurrence, or associations between utterances and their meanings. For example, based on the analysis of London-Lund Corpus of Spoken English, the most frequent way of asking for something in British English is to use the "could you" structure (e.g., *Could you pass me the salt*) (Aijmer, 1996). The high frequency with which this structure is used for requests by British native speakers means that it is very likely that they do not need to go through any kind of full-blown Gricean logical inferencing to retrieve the implicature. Instead, they can short-circuit the inferencing processes and go straight to the implied meaning, a request via associative processes (cf. Morgan, 1978).

What type of knowledge is relevant to associative processes surrounding conventionalized forms? A good starting point is to consider Aijmer (1996), who undertook comprehensive analyses of particular speech acts in British English using corpus data. She described the "pragmatic frames" of speech acts, schema-like clusters that are constructed out of the situational features that regularly accompany particular speech acts. In fact, in contrast with what the somewhat decontextualized account of speech act theory offered by Searle may suggest (see Section 2.3), people's knowledge of speech acts is indeed bound up with knowledge of the contexts in which they occur. Ervin-Tripp, Strage, Lampert, and Bell (1987) and Gibbs (1981) both emphasize the general importance of social context in speech act interpretation. Moreover, Holtgraves (1994) empirically demonstrated its importance. He showed that knowing that a speaker was of high status was enough to prime an interpretation that the speaker's utterance would be directive (in speech act terms) in advance of any remark having been actually made. If we consider the idea of pragmatic frames in relation to Example [6], and specifically the utterance, *Any spare change please*, a rich array of assumptions can be generated, some of which we have already noted in the previous section. The core of this utterance, *Any spare change (please)*, is conventionalized for a very specific context: it is regularly heard in large cities in the UK Merely hearing this utterance allows people with knowledge of the relevant pragmatic frame to assume that it is a request, a request for money, produced by a homeless person, addressed to passers-by (often office workers), and so on.

We might ask whether in cases such as these an implicature is still involved. Is it not now part of the conventional meaning of the expression? Not quite. Implicatures in these cases become conventionalized, but not necessarily fully conventional (i.e., part of the semantic meaning). Importantly, the implicature can still be cancelled. Utterances such as *Could you pass me the salt* can still be meant and/or understood in specific contexts as a genuine question about ability to pass the salt. Nevertheless, the implicature here could be described as being of a particular kind. Recall from the end of Section 4.3 that generalized implicatures require no special contextual knowledge to work them out. Particularized implicatures are worked out from scratch on the basis of the particular context the utterance appears in; generalized implicatures have a more stable association with particular linguistic forms (cf. Grice, 1989, p. 37). So, what we are dealing with here might be described as a kind of generalized implicature. This does not mean that they are context free. Terkourafi (2003), in particular, makes a case for connecting generalized implicatures with minimal contextual structures, not unlike the pragmatic frames discussed above. In fact, Terkourafi is the one scholar who has taken the view of conventionalization outlined here, added the notion of generalized implicatures, made a link to frames, and accounted for politeness.

Points to remember

- Over time, some implicatures become directly associated with their implied meaning, so rather than working through the inferential steps to derive an implicature, people can go straight to its meaning. Once this occurs, people need minimal context to interpret its meaning, and it may be referred to as a generalized implicature.

4.4 Appropriateness and Politeness

What does it mean to be appropriate? In this section, we will outline two principal ways of approaching appropriateness. Simultaneously, we will consider how the notion of politeness overlaps with appropriateness.

One way of viewing appropriateness is in terms of social norms concerning what should happen. Consider this exchange that took place in a swimming pool changing room in the UK between a boy, around 5 years old, and a male adult (presumably his father):

[7]   *Boy*: I want my Kinder chocolate right now.
      Adult: You're not getting anything if you're being rude.

The boy's use of a relatively forceful request ("I want X") coupled with the aggravator "right now" transgressed social norms. In the context of family social norms, certain members are accorded certain forms of language with certain values, and transgressions count as rude, impolite, and so on. "Social norms" is in fact a somewhat ambiguous term. What we are really talking about here are social "oughts": the prescriptive side of social norms (see Culpeper, 2011). Social oughts are norms that relate to authoritative standards of behavior, and entail positive or negative evaluations of behavior as being consistent or otherwise with those standards. They are underpinned by culturally dominant ideologies/belief systems that can sustain and normalize the social conventions that serve power hierarchies. Ideologies are evaluative and prescriptive assumptions about: "what is 'correct', 'normal', 'appropriate', 'well-formed', 'worth saying', 'permissible', and so on, but also about what indexical expression x has as its default meaning (Silverstein, 1998)" (Coupland & Jaworski, 2004, pp. 36–37). The notion of indexical expressions being linked to some aspect of the context overlaps with the points we were making in the previous two sections concerning particular pragmatic expressions being associatively linked with meanings and aspects of context (and we will return to the notion of indexicals in the following section). Those links can be links to evaluative assumptions. Thus, the word *please* is linked to a polite evaluation. This does not mean, of course, that every particular occasion of use results in a polite evaluation overall (e.g., the word *please* can be used sarcastically, just like the US English term "Have a nice day"). In Example [7], the 5-year-old is using forms that do not have associations with the particular context of usage; he is challenging and transgressing a particular dominant parenting ideology. It is important, of course, to notice that such ideologies and oughts can be culturally specific. In a US daycare setting, one of the British authors visited her 4-year-old child's classroom at lunch time, and was horrified to see children raising their hands and saying, "I need help" when they could not open their juice boxes or sandwiches and receiving help from the teachers without comment. For a British person, teaching a 4-year-old to say "please" is an important parenting ideology (see Figure 4.5),

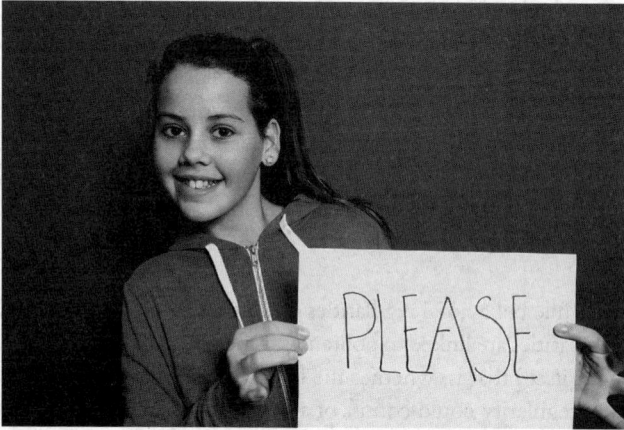

FIGURE 4.5 Manners can be fun

thus, the expectations are that children will say "I need help please" in the UK and if they do not, a parent or caregiver will correct them.

This view of social norms ties in with the social-norm view of politeness, as discussed in Section 2.5. Politeness, in this sense, subsumes notions such as "good manners," "social etiquette," "social graces," and "minding your Ps and Qs." As we can see in the examples above, British parents typically prescribe the use of *please* in requests their children make, and proscribe requests that are not accompanied by that word.

Another way of viewing appropriateness is in terms of social norms concerning what normally happens. We are talking about social habits here rather than social oughts. Opp (1982) argues that regular behaviors develop into expectations. Those expectations give people a sense of certainty, and it is this certainty that has value. People generally like to know what will happen next – a point made forcefully in social cognition in relation to schema theory (see Fiske & Taylor, 1984, 1991). However, such claims are claims about *general* expectations. What about expectations in specific situations? In fact, the best account of appropriateness in specific situations was designed to account for politeness. Terkourafi (2001) places statistical behavioral regularities or habits at the heart of her frame-based politeness approach. She suggests that it is through that regularity of co-occurrence that we acquire "a knowledge of which expressions to use in which situations," that is, "experientially acquired structures of anticipated 'default' behaviour" (Terkourafi, 2002, p. 197). This echoes our discussion in the previous two sections of prior knowledge and associative processes, the conventionalization of particular forms, and the role of generalized implicatures. How these phenomena are connected with politeness is neatly summarized here:

Politeness is achieved on the basis of a generalized implicature when an expression *x* is uttered in a context with which – based on the addressee's previous experience of similar contexts – expression *x* regularly co-occurs. In this case, rather than engaging in full-blown inferencing about the speaker's intention, the addressee draws on that previous experience (represented holistically as a frame) to derive the proposition that "in offering an expression *x* the speaker is being polite" as a generalized implicature of the speaker's utterance. On the basis of this generalized implicature, the addressee may then come to hold the further belief that the speaker *is* polite.

(Terkourafi, 2005a, p. 251, original emphasis)

However, while behavioral regularities do play a major role in politeness, not all behavioral regularities are linked to politeness. One important factor is the "valence" of the behavior itself, that is, whether the behavior is judged to be socially positive or negative. A regularity could consist of a string of behaviors perceived as socially negative; this is hardly likely to be judged as polite. For instance, continuously insulting fellow guests at a dinner table can become regularized, but will never be considered positive. Terkourafi's (2005a) solution is to argue that "[i]t is the regular co-occurrence of particular types of context and particular linguistic expressions *as the unchallenged realizations of particular acts* that creates the perception of politeness" (p. 248, our emphasis; see also Terkourafi, 2005b).

We conclude this section by emphasizing two points. One is that the two approaches to appropriateness described here are not unconnected. Whatever is a social ought constrains people to act accordingly, and then it is likely to become a social habit. Thus, we may say the word *please* because we should in many English-speaking cultures and also because it is habit. Conversely, doing what is habitual offers comforting security – a habit can easily develop into a social ought. Appropriateness typically involves simultaneous orientations to both social oughts and habits. The other point is that appropriateness does not straightforwardly lead to politeness. Whilst some scholars, most notably Meier (1995), have argued that politeness should be framed in terms of appropriateness, there are some clear differences. We have already hinted at one: a string of negative behaviors could be appropriate in some contexts, such as interrogations, army recruit training, or certain reality TV shows (cf. Culpeper, 2011). Furthermore, sometimes being polite goes beyond what might be considered appropriate for a particular context. Cases in point might include effusive thanks or a compliment out of the blue (cf. "surplus" approaches to politeness, such as Watts, 2003). In addition, it seems plausible that some linguistic actions might be neither polite nor impolite and simply appropriate. An example might be an information leaflet containing linguistic actions that are appropriate and non-(im)polite.

4.5 Metapragmatics

The prefix *meta-* is used in somewhat different ways in English. In the context of linguistics broadly conceived, it denotes that the item to which it is affixed is *about* the item to which it is affixed. For instance, "metalanguage," probably the most commonly used meta-label in linguistics, is language about language; "meta-discourse" is discourse about discourse; "metacommunication" is communication about communication; while "metapragmatics" is, presumably, pragmatics about pragmatics. However, what "about" actually means and how the items it connects are related could be rather variable and even problematic, especially for metapragmatics. Let us first dispatch two minor uses, and caution against another possible use. Then we will outline two major uses, both of which have potential for L2 pragmatics.

The first minor use involves an early use of the *meta-* prefix in linguistics. Jakobson (1960, p. 356) deployed the prefix for his "metalinguistic" function. What this meant was the use of language to "gloss" language. A dictionary, for example, uses language to gloss and define words. Linguists, including those working in pragmatics, need to do this too when they clarify or define terms (just as we have begun to do in this section). However, discussion of meta-related notions in linguistics and pragmatics clearly goes well beyond this limited function. The second minor use is restricted to metatheory. For metapragmatics, this con-sists of scholars reflecting on the theoretical apparatus accounting for pragmatic phenomena. All academic fields of enquiry have their theories and engage in debate about those theories (i.e., metatheory). Pragmatics is no different. If, for example, we object to the distinction between pragmalinguistics and sociopragmatics, we are engaging in metapragmatics in this sense. Perhaps because this is such a general academic phenomenon, it has not been singled out in pragmatics for specific attention under the heading of metapragmatics. Finally, a cautionary note. As Hübler (2011) points out, we should avoid using the term metapragmatics when the term pragmatics will suffice. If pragmatics is about communicative behavior, then any accounts of communicative behavior informed by pragmatic theory will necessarily be metapragmatic. In this sense, then, all of pragmatic scholarship is metapragmatic already, so there is not much point in using the term for this. More detail about metapragmatics can be found in Caffi (1998, 2006), Hübler and Bublitz (2007), Hübler (2011), and Culpeper and Haugh (2014, chapter 8).

Most studies of metapragmatics focus on aspects of pragmatic reflexive aware-ness, that is, awareness of the pragmatic features that participants and their inter-actants use and the potential meanings they have in context (including the context of interaction). In this section, following a division made in Hübler (2011), we will divide those studies into two according to how explicit the metapragmatic expressions are. Explicit metapragmatics involves expressions that are about some pragmatic aspect of the communication in hand. Examples include orientations to: speech acts (e.g., "Is that an apology?"), Grice's maxims (e.g., "Cut to the chase"), politeness (e.g., "That's so rude"), text structure (e.g., "To conclude . . ."), and turn-taking (e.g., "Don't interrupt"). Many studies, but especially Hübler and Bublitz (2007), have investigated the way such expressions are used in communication.

> Points to remember
>
> - Pragmatic reflexive awareness refers to an awareness of the pragmatic features that participants and their inter-actants use, and the potential meanings they have in context. Most studies of metapragmatics focus on this very issue.

Metapragmatic expressions seem to have largely escaped the attention of L2 pragmatics scholars with a few exceptions (see Chapter 6). However, they are interesting and important, and should not be overlooked. First, many methods in L2 pragmatics use explicit metapragmatic expressions in order to elicit particular responses. For example, the choice of labels on a rating scale used to assess perceptions of a pragmatic behavior is usually a choice of metapragmatic expressions (e.g., more appropriate, less appropriate, most polite, least polite). Thus, for a politeness rating scale, one may choose to place the label *polite* at one end and *impolite* at the other end. But how do we know that these are the most relevant labels for the informants? Maybe they mean something different to the informants compared with researchers? In fact, while *impolite* appears to be the obvious anto-nym to polite, *rude* is far more frequently used in British English, for instance.

Second, studying the usage of metapragmatic expressions by L2 learners and native speakers could offer a window into communicative issues. Metapragmatic expressions do not simply reflect what is going on in communication but help structure it. This point is neatly made by Jaworski, Coupland, and Galasinski (2004):

> How people represent language and communication processes is, at one level, important data for understanding how social groups value and orient to language and communication (varieties, processes, effects). This approach includes the study of folk beliefs about language, language attitudes and language awareness, and these overlapping perspectives have established histories within sociolinguistics. Metalinguistic representations may enter public consciousness and come to constitute structured understandings, perhaps even 'common sense' understandings – of how language works, what it is usually like, what certain ways of speaking connote and imply, what they <u>ought</u> to be like.
>
> *(p. 3)*

Implicit metapragmatics does not involve easily identifiable expressions, or even a clear separation between communicative levels, that is, one bit of com-munication being about another bit of communication. Instead, the key advo-cates in this group (e.g., Lucy, 1993; Silverstein, 1993; Verschueren, 2000) focus on indicators that interlocutors are metapragmatically aware, that they are articu-lating beliefs and understandings about language use in language. In particular, scholars such as Silverstein (2003) argued for metapragmatics as awareness of the relationships between linguistic forms and situated contexts, something that requires continual updating in the ebb and flow of language and contexts. Not surprisingly, indexicals are mentioned as a key area, in other words, items that "index" some aspect of the context. For example, *you* and *I* point to specific interlocutors in specific contexts. Another area that is often mentioned as key is that of contextualization cues (Gumperz, 1982). These refer to subtle features of speech, such as intonation, which help interlocutors infer contextually adequate meanings in conversation. The important point to note here is that Gumperz's notion of contextualization cues very much overlaps with the conventionalized pragmatic phenomena we described in Section 4.3. Gumperz (1982) elaborates:

> The identification of specific conversational exchanges as representative of socio-culturally familiar activities is the process I have called "contextualization" [. . .]. It is the process by which we evaluate message meaning and sequencing patterns in relation to aspects of the surface structure of the message, called "contextualisation cues." The linguistic basis for this matching procedure resides in "cooccurrence expectations," which are learned in the course of previous interactive experience and form part of our habitual and instinctive linguistic knowledge. Cooccurrence expectations enable us to associate styles in speaking with contextual presuppositions. We regularly rely upon these matching processes in everyday conversation. Although they are rarely talked about and tend to be noticed only when things go wrong, without them we would be unable to relate what we hear to previous experience.
>
> *(p. 162)*

Points to remember

- Explicit metapragmatics involves expressions that are about some pragmatic aspect of the communication in hand. Studying the explicit usage of metapragmatic expressions by L2 learners and native speakers could offer a window into how these groups orient to language and communication.
- Implicit metapragmatics focuses on indicators that interlocutors are metapragmatically aware, namely that they are articulating beliefs and understandings about language use in language. Key areas of study include indexicals and contextualization cues.

Researchers in L2 pragmatics have not studied implicit metapragmatics in quite the same way as its protagonists have, as described in the previous paragraph. They have not normally focused on pragmatic awareness *in situ*, in the on-going dynamics of interaction because they typically use a task or instrument to elicit such awareness. However, they have focused a great deal on one component that feeds into pragmatic awareness, that is to say, metapragmatic knowledge, knowledge about pragmatic aspects of communication. The methods by which they have done this will be fully explained in the following chapter.

4.6 Conclusions

This chapter has focused on the hearer and what they do in constructing meanings. We outlined the kind of (pseudo) logical influencing described by Grice, covering the Cooperative Principle and its constituent maxims, as well as the various ways of breaking them. It is well known that flouting maxims can be a means of triggering the hearer's search for cooperation at a deeper level and the retrieval of an implicature. Less well known, even in L2 pragmatics, is the notion of infringing the maxims, in other words, unintentionally breaking them, despite the fact that this is pertinent to language learners generating unintended implicatures or failing to generate intended implicatures. We elaborated on associative processes, processes based on schema-like prior knowledge that are used to generate contextual assumptions. We demonstrated how such associative processes enrich, constrain, and echo the kind of logical inferences described by Grice. We illustrated this with the Pope question. The point to note, of course, is that L2 learners may lack the relevant prior socio-cultural knowledge to generate contextual assumptions via associative processes that help them understand such implicatures. We then discussed pragmatic conventionalization: forms that become associated with their pragmatic contexts. We suggested that those pragmatic contexts could be described in terms of pragmatic frames, and that the kind of link between forms and contexts that constitutes pragmatic conventionalization could be described as a generalized implicature. We then turned to the notion of appropriateness, and suggested that there were two main, though linked, approaches to this notion, one being social oughts and the other social habits. We also explained how differing views of politeness could be linked to these approaches to appropriateness. Finally, we discussed the topic of metapragmatics. We explained how there are two main camps in metapragmatics, largely depending on whether they involve explicit or implicit indicators of pragmatic reflexive awareness. We claim that L2 pragmatics has not yet exploited the potential for the field offered by studying explicit metapragmatics. As for implicit metapragmatics, a large amount of work in L2 pragmatics has investigated mostly metapragmatic knowledge, rather than *in situ* metapragmatic awareness.

Discussion Questions

1. Select a comedy show that is popular in your region and identify some examples of characters flouting the Maxims of Quality, Quantity, Relation, and Manner. What effect does this flouting achieve? Discuss the implicatures

that are generated through the flouting of these maxims. Are there any examples of L2 speakers infringing a maxim? How is maxim flouting by native speakers and infringement by L2 speakers portrayed differently on TV? Furthermore, does this have any resonance with your own conversational experience?

2. Consider this conventionalized utterance: "Do you have a minute for [gay rights/the environment/healthcare]?" What are the contextual assumptions that go along with this phrase? Describe how you imagine someone might develop a schema associated with this form and illustrate the resulting pragmatic frame.

3. According to your understanding, how does politeness relate to appropriateness? In what contexts do these refer to the same thing, and in what contexts can they be disambiguated? Can you name a situation in which impolite actions may be considered appropriate and vice-versa?

4. What can studying the use of metapragmatic expressions teach us about L2 learners? How would you design a study exploring a research question you have about L2 learners' use of metapragmatic expressions?

Research questions	Participants	Data collection tools	Data analysis
Explore a research question about an L2 learner's use of metapragmatic expressions			

5

DATA ELICITATION METHODS IN L2 PRAGMATIC COMPREHENSION AND AWARENESS

Introduction

In this chapter, we describe methods that have been used to investigate pragmatic comprehension in L2 research. It is important to realize that for L2 learners, as for L1 speakers, pragmatic competence not only involves production but also understanding, because successful communication requires both. The advantages and disadvantages of different comprehension elicitation techniques should be kept in mind at the design stage of a study and we outline them here, following our description of each technique.

5.1 Multiple-choice Tests

When trying to understand meaning, people typically select the most relevant interpretation based on contextual information. Communication involves decoding linguistic and contextual cues, and using them as evidence to understand the speaker's intention. There are a range of different ways to research this, such as multiple-choice tests and recognition tasks that ask learners about the right meaning or appropriate pragmatic form in a given situation. On the other hand, open response methods, such as interviews and diaries, allow the examination of metapragmatic awareness. We will begin here with multiple-choice tests, which have been the most widely used tasks in L2 pragmatics comprehension research to date. Multiple-choice tests were first used to measure L2 learners' comprehension of implicature. Comprehension of implicature is a challenging task for language learners because they have to recognize the gap between the literal utterance and the intended meaning and re-process literal cues to infer implied meaning. For example, in English someone may say, "Are you gonna eat that?" which can imply that the speaker would like to eat whatever is being referred to.

Non-native speakers inexperienced with the pragmatics of this statement may understand its literal meaning, but many may not also understand that the speaker is requesting to eat the hearer's food.

Written Multiple-choice Tests of Implicature Comprehension

Early research on implicature comprehension goes back to the 1970s when Carrell (1979) examined comprehension of indirect responses among ESL learners. She used a multiple-choice test in which items had a situational description followed by alternative statements for the target indirect utterance. Learners were asked to choose the statement that best represents the meaning of the indirect reply to Bob's question. In the sample item below, Ann provides an indirect response to Bob's question.

> Bob says: "Did you go to the movies last night?" Ann says: "I had to study last night."
>
> a. Ann went to the movies last night.
> b. Ann did not go to the movies last night. (correct option)
> c. I have no idea at all whether (a) or (b).

Bouton (1992, 1994) also used multiple-choice questions to assess L2 comprehension of implicature. L2 English speakers in a US university completed a multiple-choice test consisting of short written dialogues involving different types of implicature: relevance implicature, Pope implicature (saying "Is the Pope Catholic?" to mean something obvious), irony, indirect criticisms, and sequence implicature (Box 5.1).

Participants were asked to read each dialogue and select the correct meaning of the target utterance. Sample items adapted from Bouton (1992, 1994) appear below. In the first item, Mark's response flouts the relevance maxim (Grice's Maxim of Relation) and does not provide the straightforward comment to David's problem. However, Mark's comment is relevant at an underlying level because this is an indirect suggestion. In the second item, Speaker B's reply generates sarcasm because he refrains from commenting on the content of the paper and instead comments on the writer's typing skills.

> Relevance implicature
>
> *David*: Mandy just broke our date for the play. Now I've got two tickets for Saturday and no one to go with.
> *Mark*: Have you met my sister? She's coming to see me this weekend.
>
> (a) Mark can't remember if David has met his sister.
> (b) There is nothing Mark can do to help David.
> (c) Mark suggests that David take Mark's sister to the play. (correct option)

BOX 5.1

Relevance implicature

Relevance implicature is when the implied meaning surfaces due to the relevance of the statement to the context or previous statement (this orients to Grice's Maxim of Relation, rather than Sperber and Wilson's (1995) Relevance Theory). In the following example, Speaker B's statement is only relevant if we understand that the implied meaning is that B does not have enough clothing for cold weather.

> A: I thought the weather would be warmer this month.
> B: I need to buy some new clothes.

Pope implicature

As noted in the previous chapter, Pope questions are used to indicate that a question has been asked to which the answer is very obvious, usually in a joking manner, as in Speaker A's response in the following exchange.

> A: I have been waiting my whole life for this concert.
> B: Oh yeah? Are you excited?
> A: Can a duck swim?

Irony

Irony is traditionally defined as when the literal meaning of a speaker's words is used to express an opposite or alternative meaning. In the following exchange, Speaker B agrees with Speaker A's comment, but then makes a statement that contradicts that position. However, the implied meaning is the opposite of the literal meaning: Speaker B agrees with Speaker A and does not feel good about the exam.

> A: This exam is going to be awful.
> B: Yeah I feel great about it.

Indirect criticism

Indirect criticism is when a speaker veils a negative comment directly by using implicature to avoid making such a comment (this is roughly equivalent to Brown and Levinson's (1987) off-record politeness strategy; see Section 2.5). In the following exchange, Speaker A asks Speaker B for an opinion, but Speaker B avoids a direct response to Speaker A's question.

A: What do you think of this dress?
B: Well it's certainly . . . colorful.

Sequence implicature

Sequence implicature occurs when a certain order of events can be assumed from the statement.

For example, an implicature of the statement "José graduated and got a job" is that José graduated before getting a job, but the sentence would still be strictly true if José got a job before he graduated.

Indirect criticism

A: What did you think about Mark's paper?
B: I thought it was well typed.

(a) He liked the paper; he thought it was good.
(b) He thought it was certainly well typed.
(c) He thought it was a good paper; he did like the form, though not the content.
(d) He didn't like it. (correct option)

Following Bouton's format, Roever (2005) developed a web-based test that assessed ESL and EFL learners' comprehension of implicature, recognition of routine formulae, and production of speech acts in English. More recently, Roever's instrument was used by Roever, Wang, and Brophy (2014), who investigated the effects of English proficiency, length of residence in an English-speaking country, gender, and language background on the same targets (Box 5.2).

Online Listening Tests and Response Time Data

The studies cited above used written multiple-choice tasks to test L2 implicature comprehension. More recent work by Taguchi (2008, 2011b) has used audio input to assess listening comprehension of implicature in L2 English. Instead of a written test, an aural pragmatic listening test was used to reflect the target language use domain (conversational implicature is often heard, not read). Similar online listening tests have also been developed in other L2s: Japanese (Taguchi, 2008), Chinese (Taguchi, Li, & Liu, 2013), and Spanish (Taguchi, Gomez-Laich, & Arrufat-Marqués, 2016).

This audio format has allowed Taguchi and colleagues to test claims made in Sperber and Wilson's (1995) Relevance Theory. This theory holds that implicature is more difficult when more processing is required for comprehension.

> ## BOX 5.2   Roever, C., Wang, S., & Brophy, S. (2014). Learner background factors and learning of second language pragmatics. *International Review of Applied Linguistics, 52, 377–401.*
>
> **Research question:** What are the effects of proficiency, length of residence in an English-speaking country, gender, and language background on comprehension of implicature, recognition of routine formulae, and production of speech acts in English?
>
> **Participants:** Two hundred and twenty-nine ESL and EFL students living in Germany and the US
>
> **Instrument:** A web-based pragmatics questionnaire that was also used in Roever (2005). Three sections of 12 items each on implicature, routines, and speech acts.
>
> **Data analysis:** Responses were scored as correct or incorrect. Then the researchers entered the proficiency, length of residence, gender, and language background variables into separate Poisson regressions for each section of the test.
>
> **Results:** Of these factors, only proficiency (determined by course level) was significantly associated with implicature comprehension. The effect was quite strong: EFL learners with four years of experience were two times more accurate on implicature items than third-year learners, and EFL learners with six to nine years of experience were up to four times more accurate.

Comprehension is easier and faster when the proposition is immediately accessible, but when the proposition is not salient, listeners need to decode a greater number of contextual clues to make sense of the heard utterance and its implied meaning. As a result, comprehension becomes more difficult and takes a longer time. Conventionality encoded in the utterance (via conventionalized linguistic forms or discourse patterns) is a feature that can facilitate comprehension. Because conventions trigger routinized associations in long-term memory, conventional utterances do not require extensive processing and thus are accessed quickly.

Taguchi (2008) explored this theoretical claim by using online measures of comprehension response times along with accuracy scores as shown in Box 5.3. A computer-delivered listening test assessed L2 English learners' comprehension of conventional implicatures (in this case, indirect refusals) and non-conventional implicatures (in this case, indirect opinions). Note that we use the term

BOX 5.3   Taguchi, N. (2008). The role of learning environment in the development of pragmatic comprehension: A comparison of gains between ESL and EFL learners. *Studies in Second Language Acquisition*, 30, 423–452.

Research question: Are there differences in the comprehension of implied speaker intentions between learners in ESL and EFL environments?

Participants: Fifty-seven ESL students at a US university and 60 EFL students at a Japanese university.

Instrument: A 60-item computerized listening test assessing comprehension of indirect refusals and indirect opinions was given to the students at the beginning and end of their program.

Data analysis: Accuracy of comprehension (scores) and speed of comprehension (response times) were compared between the EFL and ESL groups over time.

Results: Both groups significantly gained on accuracy and response times over time. For the ESL group, the effect size of the response time gain was larger than that of the score gain, but the pattern was reversed for the EFL group. The EFL group showed significantly greater improvement than the ESL group in the accurate comprehension of indirect refusals. There was no group difference on response times of either item category.

"convention" here, in order to be consistent with what was used in Taguchi (2008). Strictly speaking, we are talking about semi "conventionalized" implicatures, as explained in Section 4.3, rather than fully conventional non-cancellable implicatures, which would be difficult to distinguish from semantic meaning. Indirect refusals are conventional because they follow a common, predictable discourse pattern: giving an excuse for a refusal. In contrast, indirect opinions are non-conventional because meaning is not embedded in predictable discourse patterns, and linguistic options for expressing an opinion are wide open. The sample items below illustrate this difference. In the first item, Barbara indirectly refuses Ben's suggestion in the last utterance by giving a reason for refusal. In the second item, Barbara indirectly conveys her negative option about the movie in the last utterance by saying that she was glad when the movie was over. The results of Taguchi (2008) confirmed the facilitative effect of conventionality in comprehension: indirect refusals were easier and faster to comprehend than indirect opinions.

Indirect refusal (conventional implicature)

Ben: Hey, what are we doing for dinner tonight?
Barbara: I don't know.
Ben: How about if we go out to eat tonight. How about Chinese food?
Barbara: Don't you think we should finish the leftovers?
Question: Does Barbara want Chinese food?

Indirect opinion (non-conventional implicature)

Ben: I can't believe I fell asleep in the middle of the movie last night. Did
   you watch it till the end?
Barbara: Yeah, I did.
Ben: Did you like it?
Barbara: I was glad when it was over.
Question: Did Barbara like the movie?

Response times have been used widely in psycholinguistics research. Response time data have been argued to provide an indirect reflection of the ease or difficulty of processing the stimuli, as well as the relative amount of linguistic, cognitive, and affective resources required for processing. Taguchi's (2008) study shows how response time data can be used in L2 pragmatics research to reveal the relation between the degree of indirectness and the amount of effort required for comprehension. Conventionality, once activated, is considered to reduce processing effort (Sperber & Wilson, 1995). In Taguchi (2008), shorter response times were obtained with conventional implicature. In contrast, non-conventional implicature required more extensive processing of linguistic and contextual cues to derive meaning. Taguchi (2008) argued that non-conventional implicature requires both bottom-up processing of linguistic information and top-down processing of contextual cues, leading to longer response times.

In summary, existing studies have used written or spoken multiple-choice tests to assess L2 comprehension of implicature and indirect speech act utterances. Recent technology has made it possible to measure response times as an additional dimension of comprehension beyond accuracy. Language learners' speedy selection of the correct implied meaning has served as an alternative indication of implicature comprehension.

Multiple-choice tests have several advantages for studying implicature comprehension. Like DCTs, they serve as quick and convenient ways to collect a large amount of data in one setting. In addition, researchers can compare learners' comprehension across different implicature types by designing each item type to reflect different indirectness levels, such as conventional versus non-conventional implicature as in Taguchi (2008). In addition, the controlled nature of multiple-choice tasks allows for comparisons among learner groups over time points, allowing for cross-sectional and longitudinal investigations. The multiple-choice format also allows researchers to conduct a *post hoc* error analysis to investigate why learners make a wrong choice. Taguchi (2005) developed distractor options for each question based on three principles: (1) The option containing a meaning opposite to the implied meaning; (2) the option containing the words taken from the last part of the dialogue; and (3) the option related to the overall conversation but not to the target. She found that when learners made a wrong choice, they most often selected option (2), indicating that learners' comprehension was bound to short-term memory.

While multiple-choice tests have some advantages, there are also limitations. One limitation relates to their narrow construct operationalization. Following Gricean maxims, existing studies have operationalized implicature as utterance-level deviation from the maxims. However, in real-life conversations, implicitness often manifests at discourse level through various sequential and cumulative features of spoken discourse, such as ellipsis, incomplete utterances, deixis, and pronoun references. Implicitness is also conveyed in an extended discourse over multiple turns, not restricted to a brief exchange of a few turns. To date, research has not attended to these discourse-level features (we will have more to say about them in the following chapters). As a result, data is limited to the comprehension of utterance-level implicitness.

In addition, multiple-choice tests can only assess L2 learners' comprehension as observers of a conversation; it does not assess their ability as participants in a conversation. While taking the test, learners are eavesdropping on someone else's conversation and making inferences about someone else's intention. Hence, the test neglects the fact that intention often emerges in discourse, as the speaker and listener co-construct and negotiate what is communicated. This emergent view of intention has been articulated by several scholars. For example, Kecskes's (2014) socio-cognitive approach combines the cognitive-philosophical perspective, which incorporates the Gricean view of intention as a priori mental state of the speaker, and the sociocultural-interactional perspective, which views intention as a *post factum* phenomenon jointly constructed by the speaker and listener during interaction. Because existing methods do not address this co-constructed nature of intention, the future agenda of L2 pragmatic research involves developing new methods that can reveal how L2 learners disambiguate indirect meaning in collaboration with their interlocutors.

In addition to the limitations with test format (i.e., multiple-choice test), there is a limitation with input source used in the existing instruments. Most studies used highly controlled, artificially created dialogues to assess implicature comprehension. As a result, it is questionable whether the test items represent a sample of real-life language use. Only a few studies used authentic dialogues to assess implicature comprehension. Yamanaka (2003) used video segments taken from TV sitcoms to develop a test on implicature comprehension in English. Walters (2009) applied a conversation analytic approach to reveal how indirect meaning is communicated turn–by–turn and used that analysis to assess L2 English learners' comprehension of implicature. Several other studies have used corpora of spoken English. For example, Garcia (2004) used the TOEFL 2000 Spoken and Written Academic Language Corpus (Biber, Conrad, Reppen, Byrd, & Helt, 2002) to locate samples of implicature in naturalistic conversations, while Taguchi (2011b) used the Santa Barbara Corpus of Spoken American English (DuBois, Chafe, Meyer, & Thompson, 2000). Authentic measures have the potential to elicit rich samples of L2 comprehension data, but those measures have thus far seen limited practice.

Another weakness of the current instruments is the lack of multi-modal cues encoded in test items. Multiple-choice tests use highly controlled items to reduce the effect of extraneous variables that may affect comprehension (e.g., vocal features, visual cues). But this is a threat to construct validity because real-world inter-actions usually involve multi-modal processing of linguistic, visual, and auditory cues. Without including these features, existing tests fail to assess how learners attend to gestures, head nods, or gaze directions and use them as cues to draw inferences. One exception is the study of Taguchi et al. (2016), which used audio-visual input via videos to assess L2 Spanish learners' comprehension of implicature and irony. Retrospective verbal interviews revealed that participants did attend to visual and vocal cues (e.g., facial expressions, intonation) to derive indirect meaning conveyed by the speaker. More studies can incorporate visual and auditory features into an instrument to assess implicature comprehension. Researchers can, for example, construct test items that assess learners' ability to understand the speaker's emotion, feelings, and attitudes based on paralinguistic cues displayed in input. Such an advancement in methods will help us examine how learners process meaning at discourse-level, regulated by all forms of semiotic activity, including texts, images, gestures, and spaces.

Multiple-choice Tests Assessing Recognition of Pragmalinguistic Forms in Context

Multiple-choice tests can be used to test L2 learners' knowledge of pragmalinguistic forms in context, similar to the DCTs discussed in Chapter 3. While a DCT tests a learner's productive ability to use appropriate forms, a multiple-choice test assesses a learner's receptive ability to recognize appropriate forms. As in DCTs, multiple-choice items present a scenario with a prompt for a response. But unlike DCTs, the items do not provide an opening for the participant to fill in with their own utterances. Instead, the items provide a list of alternative forms from which participants select. Hence, these items are intended to assess knowledge of appropriate pragmalinguistic forms and the sociopragmatic factors associated with the forms. In order to judge whether a form is appropriate, one needs to know the form, its function, and its associated contextual values, and then work out whether the use of the form is appropriate in a given context. Below is a sample from Liu's (2007) study, which examined English learners' recognition of appropriate apology expressions.

Situation:

You are a student. You are now rushing to the classroom as you are going to be late for the class. When you turn a corner, you accidentally bump into a student whom you do not know and the books he is carrying fall onto the ground. You stop, pick the books up, and apologize.

(A)   Oops, sorry, my fault. I'm in such a hurry. Here let me help pick these up for you. (correct option)

(B)   I'm sorry, I will be late if I'm not in a hurry. I'll pay attention to this when I turn the corner next time.

(C)   Oh, I'm very sorry. I'm going to be late for my class, and if I'm late, I won't be allowed to enter the classroom. But I like this course very much. So, sorry again!

(p. 415)

The test development process for Liu's study involved several stages. Each stage was necessary in constructing the multiple-choice test in a reliable and valid manner. First, Chinese EFL students were asked to report common apology situations from their daily lives. Second, the students and native English speakers assessed social variables in apology scenarios (e.g., severity of the situation, power relationship, and social distance between interlocutors). This was followed by a pilot study in which EFL students and native speakers responded to a DCT involving 15 apology-eliciting scenarios. Two native speakers rated their responses. Data from the pilot study were used to develop the multiple-choice options. Responses from native English speakers were coded as the "key" (correct option), whereas those from the students rated as inappropriate were coded as "distractor." The "key" and "distractor" options in each item were confirmed in another pilot.

The final version of the test ($k=12$) was administered to 105 university students studying English in China. The results showed satisfactory reliability (Cronbach's alpha=0.83), meaning that the test was internally consistent with each item measuring the same construct. A Rasch analysis detected no poorly fitting items, although there was variation in item difficulty. Verbal protocols showed that the participants drew on construct-relevant knowledge, that is, apology expressions and sociopragmatic variables, when selecting the appropriate option. However, distractor options were sometimes difficult for the participants to rule out because of L1 transfer of cultural norms.

While Liu's (2007) study created multiple-test items assessing learners' recognition of appropriate speech act strategies, some studies used the same test format assessing learners' recognition of formulaic expressions and routines (e.g., Bardovi-Harlig & Bastos, 2011; Davies, 2007; Roever, 2005; Taguchi, 2011b).

In Roever (2005), participants read a situational scenario and selected the appropriate routine in the situation, as in the sample item below (p. 317).

Situation:

The person ahead of Kate in line at the cafeteria drops his pen. Kate picks it up and gives it back to him. He says, "Thank you."
What would Kate probably say?

1. Thank you.
2. Please.
3. You're welcome. (correct option)
4. Don't bother.

Bardovi-Harlig and Bastos (2011) extended research on L2 learners' knowledge of routines but used a different format of a multiple-choice test. Instead of providing a list of alternatives, they used an audio recognition task that presented listeners with target conventional expressions. Participants were asked to indicate their degree of familiarity with the expressions by selecting a response from three choices, as in the sample item below (Bardovi-Harlig & Bastos, 2011, p. 360).

"Good morning."
I often hear this/I sometimes hear this/I never hear this

As a variation on the multiple-choice test, other studies have used a judgment task in which participants were asked to read a target pragmalinguistic expression and judge the appropriateness of the expression by responding to a yes/no question. See the sample item from Bardovi-Harlig and Dörnyei's (1998, p. 361) study below. Participants watched a series of video clips, each involving a short dialogue with the target speech act utterance appearing at the end. Participants were first asked to indicate whether the target utterance was pragmatically appropriate by selecting the box for "yes" or "no." If they selected the box for "no," they were asked to rate the severity of the problem on a six-point scale ranging from "not bad at all" to "very bad."

It's Anna's day to give her talk in class, but she's not ready.

Teacher: Thank you, Peter, that was very interesting. Anna, it's your turn to give your talk.

Anna: I can't do it today, but I will do it next week.

Was the last part appropriate/correct?   Yes   No

If there was a problem, how bad do you think it was?

Not bad at all   Very bad
___:___:___:___:___:___:

Eight of the dialogues included the pragmatically inappropriate but grammatically correct utterance, another eight included the grammatically incorrect but pragmatically appropriate utterance, and the remaining four included the appropriate and grammatically correct utterance. This test was used to reveal whether participants were able to detect pragmatic errors. Results showed that ESL learners detected more pragmatic errors than EFL learners in Hungary.

Multiple-choice items in a pragmatic recognition task assess learners' understanding of situational characteristics (e.g., interlocutors' power difference and social distance) and their knowledge of preferred linguistic forms in the situation. In multiple-choice items, the construct under study is well-defined. Researchers can incorporate the exact situational variables in the stimulus scenarios and pre-select the pragmatic forms to evaluate learners' knowledge of the forms, which allows a direct examination of L2 knowledge of specific form-context mappings.

The multiple-choice format is appealing when assessing recognition of pragmatic forms. Some reasons are similar to those for the assessment of implicature comprehension. One obvious reason is its practicality. Researchers can administer a test in a short amount of time, collect data from a large number of participants in one setting, and quickly and easily score the responses. The uniform format of a test also allows for replication studies. In addition, unlike production-based items (e.g., DCTs, role plays), multiple-choice items can directly evaluate learners' knowledge of appropriate pragmatic forms, suppressing other extraneous factors affecting the demonstration of that knowledge (e.g., knowledge of grammar and vocabulary, performance constraints). Complete linguistic processing may not be necessary when selecting appropriate pragmatic forms because the learners' job is to compare linguistic alternatives and to select the pragmatically appropriate option over the other. Hence, if researchers are purely interested in the pragmatic knowledge that learners possess – rather than whether they can or cannot implement the knowledge – the receptive-skill based multiple-choice test is an attractive option.

Challenges

Despite their advantages, the multiple-choice test has several disadvantages. First, the receptive-skill format of the test, described as an advantage above, is also a disadvantage because the test does not reveal what learners can actually do with the knowledge. Learners' test performance may not be a direct indication of their performance in actual communicative settings. Another limitation is that the development of answer options is time-consuming and involves several steps, as we saw in the description of Liu's (2007) study. This is because the options are not about right or wrong but rather reflect degrees of appropriateness. Because people's judgment of appropriateness is often subjective, reflecting their personality, style, and experience, a great amount of variation naturally occurs in these judgments. Using native speakers' judgments as the norm is problematic because the norm itself is elusive and variable. Hence, investigation into appropriateness in the key and distractor options require substantial time and effort. The low reliability of multiple-choice tests sometimes reported in studies assessing recognition of appropriate pragmatic forms (e.g., Hudson, Detmer, & Brown, 1995; Yamashita, 1996) is probably a result of this difficulty in designing good response options. Alternative expressions might be too ambiguous to distinguish from each other. This was noted by Hudson et al. who said, "for many items, the distractors had to be modified due to their not being clearly incorrect from a pragmatic perspective" (1995, p. 54). Another challenge that comes with multiple-choice format is the chance factor. The participants can choose an answer through guessing. Multiple-choice tests also restrict the number of possibilities that can happen in speech. It is typical to see three to five options provided in multiple-choice tests, and it might be the case that test takers were unsure about the options in the test but knew another alternative that would be appropriate to say or comprehend in real life. Finally, it should be noted that multiple-choice tests are still indirect measurement tools. For instance, in a multiple-choice conversational implicature test, we ask language learners to pretend to be listening to, or participating in, a conversation and imagine what they would think, feel, understand, or say in a particular situation. Therefore, researchers should bear in mind these strengths and limitations of multiple-choice tests when choosing data collection instruments for the recognition of pragmatic forms.

5.2 Measures for Metapragmatic Awareness

The previous section described how multiple-choice tests have been used to investigate L2 pragmatic receptive skills in two areas, both of which were discussed in Chapter 4: implicature comprehension and recognition of appropriate pragmalinguistic forms in context. Continuing with the theme of pragmatic knowledge in receptive skills, this section will review the tasks and methods available for assessing metapragmatic knowledge, that is, what learners know about pragmatic acts (see Section 4.5). Existing methods have revealed L2 learners' understanding of the pragmatic implications of a communicative act. For example, which sociocultural elements make up a certain situation? Which speech act strategies are appropriate in a given context? Which social meanings are projected by certain pragmalinguistic forms? What kind of information do learners consider when they make a linguistic choice in a given situation? We will analyze three types of available methods: (1) scaled-response questionnaires for metapragmatic assessment; (2) metapragmatic discussions, interviews, and verbal protocols; and (3) diaries, journals, and blogs.

Scaled-response Questionnaires for Metapragmatic Assessment

In scaled-response questionnaires, participants evaluate the degree of appropriateness of target pragmalinguistic expressions on a Likert scale. For example, participants may be presented with a five-point scale in which a rating of 5 represents "very appropriate" and a choice of 1 represents "not at all appropriate." Scaled-response questionnaires help researchers gain insights about how learners evaluate the contextual parameters in a communicative act (e.g., interlocutor relationship, degree of imposition) and how they assess linguistic realizations of the act in terms of appropriateness, politeness, and formality.

Several studies have used scaled-response questionnaires to investigate L2 perception of speech acts. An early study by Maeshiba, Yoshinaga, Kasper, and Ross (1996) used scaled-response items to complement data obtained from a DCT. The authors examined the degree of correspondence between L2 English learners' production of apology strategies and their assessment of contextual factors affecting their strategy choice. They collected learners' assessments of seven contextual variables: severity of offense, offender's face loss, offended person's face loss, offender's obligation to apologize, social distance, and dominance. When learners' assessments converged between L1 and L2, positive transfer of strategies was assumed to have occurred from L1 to L2.

Maeshiba et al. (1996) is one of few studies that have used scaled-response items to examine learners' sociopragmatic awareness in terms of their assessment of contextual factors. Other studies of this sort include Barron (2003), which examined sociopragmatic assessments of social distance and dominance in the speech act of refusals by L2 learners of German. Ishihara (2010) used a similar assessment tool targeting sociopragmatics. In the sample item below (Ishihara, 2010, p. 222), learners read a situational scenario and accompanying apology expressions. Then, they evaluated the situation for contextual variables on a scale. This was followed by two questions tapping into learners' metapragmatic assessment of the apology expressions in terms of their perceived impact on the interlocutor and appropriateness of the expressions.

Scenario:

Michelle completely forgets a crucial meeting at the office with the boss at her new job. An hour later, she shows up at his office to apologize. The problem is that this is the second time she's forgotten such a meeting in the short time she has been working at this job. Her boss is clearly annoyed when he asks, "What happened to you this time?"

Michelle: So sorry, Mr. Peterson. I have sleeping problems and then I missed the bus. I can make it up to you.

1.   Indicate your analysis of the situation by placing Xs on the lines.
     Social status (boss's status) lower ←——X——→ higher
     Distance   close ←—X——→ distant
     Intensity of apology less intense ←——X——→ intense
2.   How would the boss interpret Michelle's utterance?
3.   Imagine that Michelle is your friend. What suggestions would you give her about the way she spoke?

While the studies cited above focused on the sociopragmatic factors (e.g., social status, distance), other studies used scaled-response times to elicit learners' assessments of pragmalinguistic forms (Ishida, 2007; Martínez-Flor, 2006; Takimoto, 2009; Tan & Farashaiyan, 2012). These studies asked learners to rate the degree of appropriateness of pragmatic forms. The scaled appropriateness rating task is different from the multiple-choice and appropriateness judgment tasks for the recognition of pragmatic forms described in the previous section. Multiple-choice tasks ask participants to select the appropriate form from a list of alternatives and appropriateness judgment tasks ask them to make a forced judgment between "appropriate" and "not appropriate." Scaled rating tasks, on the other hand, ask participants to rate the degree of appropriateness of a specific expression in a situation. Hence, the scaled rating task can tap into a learner's *degree* of certainty or confidence when evaluating the pragmatic appropriateness of linguistic forms. Because the multiple-choice test and the appropriateness judgment task are constructed to have just one correct response, the learners' scores serves as indication of their pragmatic knowledge. In contrast, the scaled rating task does not have one correct response. Therefore, interpretation of learners' responses often draws on native speakers' base-line data. The closer the learners' responses are to the baseline ratings, the better their knowledge approximates the target norms.

Takimoto's (2009) instructional studies on requests used appropriateness rating scales both as instructional materials and assessment measures of instructional outcomes. See Box 5.4 for the study summary. A sample item from a listening test is presented below. Learners listened to a dialogue and rated the appropriateness of Taro's request form on a five-point scale.

Listening test, sample item:

Taro is working in a restaurant. The owner has asked Taro to get each customer to complete a very long questionnaire about the quality of the food and the service in the restaurant. Taro has given the questionnaire to a customer. Taro notices that the customer has not filled it in but is about to leave in a hurry. Taro needs to have the questionnaire filled in by the customer.

Taro: Excuse me. I can see you are in a hurry. But please fill in this questionnaire.
Brown: Oh, look. I'm sorry I really haven't got the time.

not appropriate at all 1—2—3—4—5 completely appropriate

(Takimoto, 2009, p. 1044)

Martínez-Flor (2006) also used an appropriateness rating scale, but inspired by an approach used in an earlier study by Takahashi (2001), this was combined with confidence ratings for each judgment. Learners rated their confidence level when judging the appropriateness of suggestion expressions on a five-point scale (1=confident; 5=not confident).

BOX 5.4   Takimoto, M. (2009). Exploring the effects of input-based treatment and test on the development of learners' pragmatic proficiency. *Journal of Pragmatics, 41,* 1029–1046.

Research questions: (1) What are the relative effects of comprehension-based instruction, consciousness-raising instruction, and structured input instruction on the development of Japanese learners' pragmatic proficiency? (2) To what extent do the effects of the different input instruction vary according to the method of testing?

Participants: Sixty EFL learners were divided into three treatment groups and one control group. The treatment groups included a comprehension-based instruction group, a consciousness-raising instruction group, and a structured input instruction group.

Instructional targets: Request downgraders (e.g., syntactic downgraders such as "I am wondering if" as well as lexical downgraders such as "possibly").

Instructional treatments: The comprehension-based instruction group received explicit information on request downgraders followed by structured input tasks, which involved selecting appropriate request forms or rating appropriateness of the forms. The structured input group completed the structured input tasks without explicit information. The consciousness-raising group compared request forms across different dialogues and evaluated the forms.

Measures of learning outcomes: Four tasks were used: (1) a DCT; (2) a role play; (3) an aural appropriateness rating task; and (4) a written appropriateness rating task.

Results: All treatment groups outperformed the control group, but the comprehension-based instruction group did not maintain the gains at the delayed post-test.

While the studies by Maeshiba et al. (1996), Ishihara (2010), Takimoto (2009), and Martínez-Flor (2006) targeted speech acts, other studies examined learners' perceptions of speech styles. Ishida (2007), for example, examined how L2 Japanese learners developed understanding of two primary speech forms, the polite form and the plain form, in relation to various contextual features. He administered a questionnaire of eight situational scenarios (provided in English) with a target utterance in Japanese at the end of each scenario. The utterance took either the polite or plain form. Learners were asked to rate the appropriateness of the form on a 5-point scale. They were also asked to provide reasons for their ratings. Several scenarios required learners to attend to both static and dynamic contextual features when rating appropriateness. For instance, when talking to a teacher whom one feels close to, one needs to decide whether it is acceptable to show a less formal stance using the plain form, or whether it is still expected to display a formal stance with the polite form by attending to the static contextual feature of the teacher-student hierarchy.

Learners' appropriateness ratings were then evaluated by native Japanese speakers based on a four-point Likert scale, in which 4 represented an "agreeable rating with valid reason for the rating"; 3 represented an "agreeable rating but with no clear or valid reason for the rating"; 2 represented a "disagreeable rating but not without valid reason for the rating"; and 1 represented a "disagreeable rating with no valid reason for the rating." These rating descriptions closely reflect the construct of metapragmatic awareness because they tap learners' knowledge and understanding of an appropriate pragmatic act.

Scaled-response questionnaires share many of the advantages of multiple-choice tests described in the previous section. In addition to the practicality advantage, scaled-response items can represent well-defined constructs under study, controlling for construct-irrelevant variables. In addition, the scales can be constructed to address metapragmatic assessment on both pragmalinguistic and sociopragmatic dimensions. Moreover, scaled-responses can be used in concert with other instruments or as part of the process of creating and validating other instruments. When developing DCTs, role plays, or multiple-choice items that involve a situational scenario, it is critical to understand how participants assess contextual variables involved in the scenarios because their assessments essentially influence their linguistic choices. Scaled-response items offer additional information about participants' assessments, which can help a researcher to ensure that items are empirically grounded. It should also be noted that the scenarios or situations used in pragmatic assessment tools, such as scaled-response questionnaires, should be based on a careful test development process. One way to ensure this is checking corpora that include construct-relevant authentic examples of daily exchanges and then pilot the scenarios with competent speakers who live in the target language environment. Otherwise, the test may include scenarios that are not relevant for the learners' profile and this decreases the validity of the assessment tools.

Verbal Data for Metapragmatic Awareness

This section will discuss methods that can reveal learners' metapragmatic awareness through their verbalizations of their thought processes. These include metapragmatic discussions (talk around pragmatic acts), interviews (researcher-directed questions that aim at revealing learners' understanding of pragmatic acts), and verbal protocols (a type of interview that takes place during or immediately after completion of a task). All of these methods record learners' shared verbal narratives, so they usually require audio/video-recording and transcription of the data prior to analysis.

Metapragmatic Discussions

Metapragmatic discussions occur when participants are engaged in a dialogue about pragmalinguistic forms, sociopragmatic factors, and the connection between them, and eventually develop a joint understanding of the principles underlying the connection. Metapragmatic discussions prompt a deeper level of cognitive processing by requiring learners to think through pragmatic rules and explicitly verbalize their thoughts about the rules. Moody (2014) is an example study that used a peer-to-peer discussion as a means of generating metapragmatic awareness. The author developed an instructional model to teach the plain and polite forms in Japanese. These two forms appear at the end of an utterance and project social meanings related to politeness. However, rather than describing these forms as a single binary choice motivated by politeness, the author developed a task that assumed that these forms were influenced by four social dimensions: formality, familiarity, social position, and affective stance. For instance, on the dimension of formality, there are two situational possibilities: formal (e.g., giving a public speech) and informal (e.g., chatting with a close friend). In these situations, either the polite or plain form is expected. Similarly, on the dimension of affective stance, two situational possibilities (psychologically close or distant) influence the choice of the speech form.

After explicit metapragmatic explanations of these situational dimensions and the associated speech forms, participants (beginning-level learners of Japanese) received a series of situational scenarios, each presenting several dimensions in conflict. In the sample scenario below (adapted from Moody, 2014), the dimensions of formality, familiarity, and social position indicated the choice of the plain form (speaking to a host father). However, the dimension of affect does not conform to this choice because of the situation where the Japanese host father is annoyed.

Situation:

You are studying abroad in Tokyo and staying with a host family who are very nice but who explained at the beginning that they all stick to strict rules about curfews because they worry. You have returned home 30 minutes past curfew because the train was delayed. Before you have a chance to explain, your host father begins to lecture you for being out late. Tell him the train was late.

After reading a scenario like this, learners are asked to discuss which speech style they would use and explicitly justify their choice by considering all of the four social dimensions. Learners' discussions of problems like this often include metapragmatic concerns, such as politeness, authority, social positioning, and so on. Learners draw on their L1-based sociopragmatic knowledge and knowledge of L2 norms in determining the appropriate speech style, which eventually develops into a sophisticated understanding of linguistic choices in context. Critically, learners develop more nuanced understanding of speech styles by attending to a complex matrix of multiple social dimensions. Metapragmatic discussion is advantageous when researchers want to examine how learners respond when they are presented with new metapragmatic information – specifically what resources they draw on to deepen their understanding of the new information and how they modify pre-existing knowledge.

Metapragmatic Interviews

Another example of verbalization is found in a series of metapragmatic interviews conducted by Kinginger and Blattner (2008) and van Compernolle and Henery (2014). Kinginger and Brattner's study used a Language Awareness Interview (LAI). L2 French learners in a semester-long study abroad program were presented with a series of texts involving French sociolinguistic variations and were asked to comment on the language use in each text. For instance, in the section of colloquial expressions, learners were presented with a list of ten colloquial phrases (e.g., *canard* for "newspaper"). The learners were asked to provide a meaning for these phrases, along with information about who would use them in which context. Three points were given for each colloquial expression, with one point awarded for the partial comprehension of the phrase, another point for the referential understanding of the phrase, and the last point for identifying the appropriate context in which the phrase occurs.

Kinginger and Blattner (2008) contended that the choice of variable sociolinguistic features such as colloquial versus formal forms is indexical. That is, the choice of one particular form over another can index a speaker's identity – how he or she wants to be perceived in the particular interaction. For example, the speaker may want to appear friendly or establish distance with others. The authors contend that the use of a particular form reflects not only a speaker's pragmatic knowledge about what forms are appropriate in certain situations, but also the speaker's desire to project his or her identity in certain ways. Speakers may make a conscious decision to use certain forms even when they are not appropriate in the majority norm. For this reason, the authors claim that a recognition task with interviews like the LAI is more effective than a production-based task for gathering data about learners' metapragmatic awareness.

Van Compernolle and Henery's (2014) study also used interviews to examine metapragmatic awareness in L2 French. Following Vygotsky's sociocultural theory, this study deployed concept-based instruction, which aims at developing learners' control over concepts through a sequence of tasks (Gal'perin, 1989).

Learners were introduced to sociopragmatic concepts of power, distance, and self-presentation via diagrams illustrating two peoples' relationship and stance to each other. These sociopragmatic concepts were mapped onto the pragmalinguistic forms of *tu* and *vous*, two French address forms representing the concepts. Learners' metapragmatic awareness from pre- to post-instruction was assessed using three measures: (1) language awareness questionnaires; (2) appropriateness judgment tasks; and (3) strategic interaction tasks (a type of role play in which learners act out a scenario after strategizing their acts). These tasks asked learners to select *tu* or *vous* in a situation.

What is common among these measures was that the analytical focus was placed on the quality of the learners' explanations when making a choice, rather than their choices themselves. For instance, the first task asked participants to explain the difference between *tu* and *vous*. Scoring procedures involved assessing concepts that guided learners' choices based on three categories. The first category, "awareness of concepts," was used to assess the extent to which the concepts of self-presentation, social distance, and power were integrated into learners' responses. The second category included "types of awareness," that is, whether awareness was meaning-, function-, or context-based. The last category, "agency," assessed the learners' awareness of the effects of the pronoun choice on the listener.

An analysis of learners' interviews showed that their metapragmatic awareness of French pronouns improved between the pre- and post-test, as seen in their longer and more articulate explanations at the post-test. The excerpts below illustrate this. Responding to a situation about talking to a friend in a café, this learner (Katie) selected *tu* at both the pre- and post-instruction phase. However, the post-instruction data revealed that the learner integrated the concepts of power and social distance into her explanation, indicating that her understanding of informality and solidarity related to the pronoun *tu* improved.

Pre-instruction data

Jean is my friend, and the setting of our conversation is casual.

Post-instruction data

We are both on the same level of power because we are young kids who are friends, we have a close relationship, and we are in a casual setting at a café. It makes the most sense to be casual in this scenario.

(van Compernolle & Henery, 2014, p. 564)

The studies by Kinginger and Blattner (2008) and van Compernolle and Henery (2014) provide exemplary approaches to eliciting and analyzing metapragmatic awareness by using interviews combined with an elicitation task (e.g., a recognition task, questionnaire, or judgment task). In these studies, participants' verbalizations about their understanding of linguistic forms in context or reasoning behind their linguistic choices, which were guided strategically by researchers, served as indications of their metapragmatic awareness. The studies generated developmental insights by comparing the extent of awareness at the beginning and end of a study abroad period or instructional phase. Scoring specific aspects of learners' verbalizations and explanations during interviews has proven a useful method for assessing learners' metapragmatic awareness.

However, as many methodology books note, quantification of interview data requires caution, particularly when data is used to compare learners across time points. The unit of analysis used in these studies was the presence or absence of learners' verbalization of target items. Kinginger and Blattner (2008) gave a score when learners were able to *mention* the context in which a target colloquial phrase occurs. When there was no such mention, their score for this category was zero. Similarly, van Compernolle and Henery's (2014) study rated learners' responses as "yes," "no," and "somewhat" depending on whether or not they were able to explicitly verbalize the pragmatic concepts taught. However, interviews involving learners' voluntary accounts indicate that whether learners can actually verbalize certain phenomena or not may depend on factors other than their metapragmatic awareness. For instance, learners' personalities (for example, in terms of how expressive or reserved they usually are), task familiarity (whether they are used to or comfortable with verbalizing their thoughts), and practice (repeated instances of verbalization) may affect the resulting data. These limitations must be taken into consideration when using interviews to investigate learners' metapragmatic awareness.

Verbal Protocols for Metapragmatic Awareness

So far, we have presented metapragmatic discussion and interviews as two methods for exploring L2 metapragmatic awareness. Another method that has been widely used is verbal protocols or verbal reports, which are based on stimulated recall interviews (Gass & Mackey, 2016). Verbal protocols, as they explain, are a form of introspection consisting of participants' verbalized thought processes after completion of a task, with some sort of stimulus used to refresh their memories. They are used to gain insights into the reasoning and cognitive processes behind learners' written or spoken linguistic behaviors at the time of those behaviors. Participants are asked to verbalize whatever they are thinking. These sorts of interviews can be carried out in whatever language their thoughts are occurring, or seems easiest for them to use (assuming the researcher shares both languages). Think–aloud (concurrent) verbal protocols tap into learners' thought processes during a task, as in, for example, the line of research popularized by Rosa and Leow (2004), where learners carry out a language-related but not oral production requiring task, like a crossword puzzle, and think aloud about the process as they do so. Some studies have used these two methods together (e.g., Robinson, 1992).

In L2 pragmatics, a number of studies have used verbal protocols (e.g., Cheng, 2011; Cohen & Olshtain, 1993; Félix-Brasdefer, 2004, 2008; Hassall, 2008; Ren,

2014; Robinson, 1992; Taguchi, 2002, 2012; Taguchi et al., 2016; Woodfield, 2010, 2012; see Félix-Brasdefer, 2010, for a review). The intent has been to gain insights into the reasoning behind learners' written or spoken pragmatic perform-ance (e.g., perceptions of the situation and influence of the perceptions on their linguistic choice), as well as planning processes of their responses. Because learners' internal processes while performing a pragmatic task are not directly observable, verbal protocols are useful in determining underlying cognitive processes. The researcher has access to learners' mental processes that are unavailable by other means (Gass & Mackey, 2016).

Despite these advantages, the use of verbal protocols requires caution because several factors can undermine the reliability and validity of the data. One limita-tion is the accuracy of verbal reports as a reflection of cognitive processes (Ericsson & Simon, 1993; Nisbett & Wilson, 1977). Participants' reports may be biased by the researcher's assumptions or task instructions. Reactivity, which occurs when the act of completing the verbal report has an effect on the performance data being collected, is also a potential problem, because interrupting participants to ask them to report their thoughts may change the nature of their thought pro-cesses (Russo, Johnson & Stephens, 1989). Memory is another possible threat to the accuracy of reporting. Bloom (1954) showed that reporting accuracy declined and memory loss occurred in the time between the event and the recall. Also, participants may provide limited information due to unfamiliarity with the task of verbal reporting. Talking about a task while thinking about the task is a complex activity, so training is necessary. Van Someren, Barnard, and Sandberg (1994) also point out that the language for reporting (L1 versus L2) and task complexity can affect the amount of reporting obtained. In L2 pragmatics research, some research-ers have used previously completed DCT items and playback of audio or video recorded role plays and interviews as cues during stimulated recalls.

Now that we have overviewed the factors to keep in mind when adopting ver-bal protocols in a research project, we will highlight one recent study that carefully considered the advantages and disadvantages of the retrospective verbal protocols for investigating metapragmatic awareness. Ren's (2014) study involved a novel use of introspective data in a longitudinal design with the aim of studying L2 learners' changing cognitive processes while engaged in a multimedia DCT (see Chapter 3). Box 5.5 displays a summary of this study. The DCT was designed to elicit the speech act of refusal in a variety of situations. The task was administered three times to L2 English participants during the course of a one-year study abroad in England. Immediately after each DCT, audio recordings of participants' responses were replayed in the retrospective verbal interview phase. The researcher asked the par-ticipants what they were focusing on when they responded to each refusal scenario and why they replied in the manner they did. Data were coded for any socioprag-matic variables that participants noticed and that guided their refusal production.

The percentage of verbal protocols showing participants' attention to socio-pragmatic variables increased over time, from under 37% at Time 1 to 45% at

BOX 5.5   Ren, W. (2014). A longitudinal investigation into L2 learners' cognitive processes during study abroad. *Applied Linguistics, 35,* **575–594.**

Research questions: (1) To what extent does one year of study abroad influence L2 learners' noticing of the sociopragmatic features of a situation? (2) To what extent does one year of study abroad influence learners' perceptions of the factors that affect their refusal production?

Participants: Twenty Chinese learners of English in a graduate program in England.

Instruments: Two instruments were administered three times over one academic year: a computer-delivered multimedia DCT and retrospective verbal protocols. The DCT involved eight refusal-eliciting situations of varying situational characteristics (i.e., equal vs. unequal power relationship between interlocutors). Immediately following the DCT, participants were asked to report their thought processes based on the instructions below (p. 8):

> Now I would like to ask you some questions. I am interested in what you were thinking when you were responding to the speakers. I can hear what you were saying by listening to the recordings, but I don't know what you were thinking. So what I'd like you to do is tell me what you were thinking, what was in your mind while you were responding.

Data analysis: The verbal protocols were coded according to three themes: (1) sociopragmatic factors noticed; (2) difficulties that participants experienced when completing the DCT; and (3) source of pragmatic knowledge they used when responding to the DCT items (e.g., formal classroom instruction, outside class information).

Results: Participants reported paying more attention to sociopragmatic factors in situational scenarios when completing the DCT. Participants also reported decreased pragmatic difficulties, indicating that study abroad had an effect on their pragmatic development.

Time 3, which suggests that participants' metapragmatic awareness increased during their stay in the target country. In addition, more learners reported attending to sociopragmatic variables in unequal-status situations than in equal-status situations. The verbal protocol data below illustrates learners' inaccurate sociopragmatic understanding at Time 1. This is a response to a status-unequal scenario involving refusing a tutor's suggestion for taking an optional course. We can see that both accounts reflect learners' choice of direct refusal strategies (explicit "no") based on the learner-side reason, without consideration for the tutor's rationale for the suggestion.

> (1) I thought that she might try to persuade me if I were indirect, so I replied to her directly. It was good to do it this way because I might need to find reasons if I were indirect. (S4, Phase 1, [Course])

> (3) It should be fine to be direct in this situation because I couldn't go since I had something to do. She might think I didn't want to go if I were indirect. (S6, Phase 1, [Course])

> *(Ren, 2014, p. 11)*

Ren's (2014) study reveals various advantages and disadvantages of retrospective verbal interviews for investigating L2 metapragmatic aware-ness (Box 5.5). To enhance the validity and reliability of the data obtained, he adapted the following suggestions from the literature (e.g., Cohen, 1997, 2014; Ericsson & Simon, 1993; Félix-Brasdefer, 2008; Gass & Mackey, 2016; Woodfield, 2012): (1) the verbal protocols were collected immediately after the DCT task; (2) participants' DCT performance was replayed to assist their memory and recall; (3) participants were given explicit instructions for their recall processes; and (4) participants were offered choices of L1 (Chinese) or L2 (English) as the language used for the recall to reduce the influence of L2 proficiency levels. Together, the data collection tools were able to provide valuable information about learners' internal processes and L2 metapragmatic awareness.

Written Measures for Metapragmatic Awareness: Diaries, Journals, and Blogs

In Chapter 3, we talked about diaries and journals as methods for collecting data on pragmatic production. Here, we will discuss these methods as tools for recording and documenting learners' metapragmatic awareness and under-standing. Because diaries are individuals' written entries about past experiences and reflections on their experiences, they are useful tools for collecting introspective data. By using diaries, individuals can keep a record of their obser-vations and analyses of specific pragmatic acts, as well as their insights gained from those observations. Narrative accounts of observations and interpretations of pragmatic acts are a reflection of learners' metapragmatic awareness. Drawing on this advantage, a number of studies have used diaries, journals, and blogs to reveal learners' metapragmatic awareness over a period of time (e.g., Cohen,

1997; Hassall, 2006, 2015a, 2015b; Jin, 2012; Kinginger, 2008; Shively, 2011; Takamiya & Ishihara, 2013).

Hassall's (2015b) study collected learners' diary entries to examine fellow learners' influence on pragmatics learning in a study-abroad context. This study described experiences of a cohort of 12 Australian learners of Indonesian during a five- to seven-week sojourn. A triangulated dataset of a written pre- and post-test, diary entries, and interviews revealed how learners' shared time together affected their noticing and understanding of pragmatic acts in naturalistic settings. This was notable because eight of the participants had shared homestay arrangements and spent a good deal of time at home with their homestay partners. The shared time inevitably contributed to their pragmatics learning through observation of each other.

While in Indonesia, the learners were asked to keep a diary to describe and reflect on pragmatics learning episodes related to Indonesian address terms, leave-taking expressions, and the speech act of complaining. A total of 40 reports illustrated learners' observations of target pragmatic features in communication between fellow learners and their Indonesian interlocutors, as well as between fellow learners. When they noticed pragmatic features in other learners' output, they often assessed the output critically rather than taking it for granted, which contributed to their development of metapragmatic awareness. In the diary entry below, the learner is skeptical about his homestay partner's leave-taking expression, *sampai jumpa* "until-meet" ("good-bye"). The learner compares alternative leave-taking forms, associating them with the speaker and setting (who uses which forms when), and draws his own conclusion about social meanings (i.e., formality) behind different forms.

> (8) I have noticed that when Jacinta leaves she will say, most commonly, "*sampai jumpa*" and Ibu ['mother'] will respond with "*sampai nanti*" ['until-later', i.e., 'See you later'] or even "*sampai besok*" ['until-tomorrow', i.e., 'See you tomorrow']. However, I have not noticed Ibu respond with "*sampai jumpa*". I think this may be because it is too informal [. . .].
> [David: diary, Day 16/48]
>
> *(Hassall, 2015b, p. 429)*

Diary data also revealed instances in which the learners engaged in a metapragmatic discussion with their peers by talking about pragmatic problems they had experienced in their daily lives, or by jointly planning a pragmatic action to perform. For example, two participants in a shared homestay setting decided to refuse certain foods at the dinner table that they strongly disliked. They decided to use a hinting strategy to their host mother. According to the author, a range of sociopragmatic and pragmalinguistic dimensions emerged in their discussions. They shared their perceptions about the acceptability of the face-threatening act in the given situation (sociopragmatics). They also discussed the force of pragmalinguistic forms to be used in the situation. These discussions helped shape learners' metapragmatic knowledge of refusals in context for an incipient communicative purpose. The diary data in Hassall's study successfully captured moments of metapragmatic awareness as learners observed and critically assessed each other's pragmatic acts, reflected on the relevant target norms, and often modified their pragmatic knowledge as a result.

Another study by Jin (2012) used the diary method to reveal L2 Chinese learners' metapragmatic awareness during a semester abroad in Shanghai. This study charted four learners' change in their knowledge of Chinese compliment response patterns in relation to participant agency and affordances in a study abroad context. Along with interviews and the researcher's observation journals, participants' weekly blog entries formed the main source of data. Participants were asked to reflect on their linguistic and cultural learning during study abroad by writing blogs on the class website. The participants' entries about compliment responses were extracted for analysis.

The results of Jin's study revealed how various influences from context helped participants develop *emic* understanding of compliment responses, that is, an understanding that takes the participant's perspective rather than that of the researcher (see Section 6.1, for a discussion of the terms emic and the contrasting etic). Although their textbooks taught that rejecting a compliment by saying 哪里哪里 ("no no") is the norm in Chinese, learners' repertoire of response strategies expanded over time to include other expressions (e.g., 谢谢, "thank you") and strategies (e.g., shifting credit to others). These learners developed metapragmatic understanding of form-function-context mappings through observation and participation. Below is one such instance obtained from a reflective blog of one participant, Anli.

> In week 1, Anli noticed that besides 哪里哪里 ("no no"), Chinese people also used 谢谢 ("thank you") as a CR [compliment response], just like in English. In week 2, she learned from an American friend who was a veteran learner of Chinese and lived in China for years that deflecting a compliment by saying "you are better than I anyway" can "avoid any awkward transitions that may follow a compliment, such as attempting to think of an irrelevant return compliment, or ending with a quick 'thank you'" (Anli's 2nd reflective blog).

> *(Jin, 2012, p. 222)*

Takamiya and Ishihara (2013) also used blogs to explore learners' development of metapragmatic awareness. Unlike the other two studies, this study was conducted as part of a regular class project called the blog-mediated cross-cultural telecollaboration project. Advanced-level learners of Japanese studied speech acts in Japanese such as refusing and thanking. They were then instructed to write blog entries on the speech acts four times a semester, reflecting on their understanding of the speech acts. Blogging also served as space for the learners to exchange ideas with Japanese college students in Japan. The learners wrote their blogs in Japanese, which were responded to in Japanese, whereas Japanese students' blogs were written and responded to in English.

One learner posted her observations of a white lie as a refusal strategy, which she found to be dishonest and unappealing. Her blog entry below, translated into English, illustrates her sophisticated sociopragmatic analysis of Japanese refusals. She identified three refusal strategies in Japanese and concluded that lying is not acceptable in American culture, even as a face-saving strategy.

> English translation of a learner's blog entry
>
> According to blog X [link], refusals in Japanese can be classified into three types: (1) conveying an honest reason if the person wishes to maintain a trusting relationship in the future; (2) conveying [a reason] indirectly in the event that speaking honestly may result in friction; and (3) if it's a person you'll only meet once, being blunt with the refusal. According to blog X, the first type of refusal is the most important. Even so, the author writes that in the occasional event that supplying an honest reason is inappropriate, it's okay to use a formulaic expression.
>
> *(Takamiya & Ishihara, 2013, p. 199)*

Subsequent blog entries showed this learner's developing metapragmatic awareness about white lies. Japanese students explained the cultural reasons behind the use of white lies, which helped the learner gain *emic* insights about this refusal strategy. After this instance, this learner became more tolerant of white lies.

The studies by Hassall (2015b), Jin (2012), and Takamiya and Ishihara (2013) exemplify how diaries, journals, and blogs can serve as tools for revealing metapragmatic awareness. Rich qualitative data can illustrate how metapragmatic awareness has occurred in a specific moment and setting by presenting a situated illustration of metapragmatic understanding. Because learners' metapragmatic awareness and understanding are deeply embedded in their everyday thoughts and experiences, diaries, journals, and blogs are effective methods in revealing learners' introspections and reflections about their own and others' pragmatic behaviors.

The commonality across these three studies is that the authors employed data triangulation by using multiple data collection methods (e.g., interviews, field notes and observations, recording of class sessions). Although data triangulation naturally enhances the validity of the conclusion drawn from the analysis, when considering data collection methods individually, the contribution of the diary method alone to metapragmatic awareness is uncertain. A review of these studies shows that the actual data cited in these papers are mostly from interviews rather than diary entries. Hassall's study listed a total of 80 reports of pragmatic-related incidents by participants from a combination of diary entries, interviews, and spoken remarks during the post-test. Out of 20 data extracts presented in the paper, only four were from diaries; the remaining were from interviews (ten excerpts) and post-test remarks (six excerpts). Jin's study showed similar tendencies. Out of 26 references to data points, 21 came from interviews, four from the researcher's field notes, and only one from participants' blogs (above excerpt). Although we were not able to determine the actual proportion of diary data in the database, these tendencies indicate that the diary method alone may not yield a sufficient amount of data for metapragmatic awareness.

As we discussed in Chapter 3, the self-report, participant-directed nature of diaries can mean that the resulting data are heavily subjective. Because diary writers decide on the content, form, and timing of entries, diary data may not reveal sufficient instances of the target forms of language use under study (Kasper, 2008). To obtain a sizable pool of metapragmatic instances, researchers can be more strategic in their directions. Hassall asked his participants to record specific pragmatic acts (address forms, leave-takings, and complaints). This type of approach might help enrich diary data. However, raising participants' consciousness toward specific pragmatic features can be a threat to the validity of the findings because it may function as an instructional intervention rather than purely naturalistic occurrences of the phenomena under study. By making the target pragmatic features explicit, learners might pay more attention to those features. As a result, they might become more conscientious about those features and monitor their behaviors more closely when those features occur in their interactions. Like other methods, these pros and cons of diaries, journals, and blogs need to be considered carefully, along with the purpose of the study, when researchers make a decision about which research methods to employ.

5.3 Conclusions

In this chapter, we have examined methodological approaches to investigating language learners' receptive pragmatic competence and knowledge, focusing on pragmatic comprehension, perception, and awareness. We have discussed an array of data collection methods and tasks, starting with multiple-choice tests used to assess L2 comprehension of implicature. We examined how multiple-choice items are designed strategically to assess the comprehension of different types of implicature and how response time data can be included to assess speed of comprehension. We also reviewed methods used to assess learners' pragmatic recognition and metapragmatic awareness. These included questionnaire-based methods such as fixed-response items for the recognition of pragmatic expressions and scaled-response items for appropriateness ratings. Finally, we discussed methods for eliciting metapragmatic awareness both in spoken mode (metapragmatic discussion, interviews, and verbal protocols) and written mode (diaries, journals, and blogs).

- **Points to remember**

- Multiple-choice tests have several advantages over other methods. Like DCTs, they serve as a quick, convenient, and controlled way to collect a large amount of data in one setting. The uniform approach makes replication and comparison of data easier while making it easier to score them. If researchers are purely interested in the pragmatic knowledge that learners possess, a multiple-choice task is a viable option.
- Multiple-choice tests also have several disadvantages, including potential inauthenticity, a time-consuming development process, and sometimes low reliability due to the subjective nature of responses and chance factor that comes with the test format.
- Response time data can be collected along with multiple-choice tasks to provide an indirect reflection of the ease or difficulty of processing the stimuli, as well as the relative amount of linguistic, cognitive, and affective resources required for processing pragmatic input.
- Scaled-response questionnaires help researchers gain insights about how learners evaluate the contextual parameters in a communicative act (e.g., interlocutor relationship, social distance, degree of imposition) and how they assess linguistic realizations of the act in terms of appropriateness, politeness, and formality.
- Verbal responses such as metapragmatic discussions, interviews, and verbal protocols can tap into learners' L2 pragmatic awareness.
- To enhance the validity and reliability of verbal data obtained, it is a good idea to: (1) collect verbal protocols immediately after the performance task; (2) replay participants' performance to them to assist their memory and recall; (3) give participants explicit instructions for the reporting or recall process; and (4) offer participants the option of speaking in whichever language they prefer.
- When using verbal reports, the researcher should keep in mind the potential for reactivity and memory loss to occur.
- Diaries, journals, and blogs can serve as tools for revealing metapragmatic awareness and result in rich qualitative data that can illustrate how metapragmatic awareness has occurred in a specific moment and developed over time.
- The participant-directed nature of diaries can mean that the resulting data are heavily subjective. It can also be difficult to catch instances in diaries that are relevant to metapragmatic awareness as exemplified in Hassal's study. Finally, diaries can take time to transcribe if they are handwritten.
- The advantages and disadvantages of each method should be carefully considered during the design stage of a study. Data triangulation can be one way to enhance the effectiveness of data collection methods.

Discussion Questions

1. What is the difference between a multiple-choice task and a scaled response task used in speech act studies?

2. Compare the advantages and disadvantages of each of the following types of instruments for use in L2 pragmatics research:

   - Written input and audio input when examining comprehension of implicature
   - Multiple-choice task versus scaled response task when examining recognition of speech act utterances
   - Interview versus retrospective verbal report when examining metapragmatic awareness
   - Interview versus diary when examining metapragmatic awareness

3. Of the methods discussed in this chapter, which would be best for a longitudinal study in a study abroad context investigating learners' development of, and metapragmatic awareness about, requests in an L2? Why do you think so?

6

INTERACTION: CONCEPTUAL BACKGROUND

Introduction

In this chapter, we focus on the speaker and the hearer together in the interactive process that comprises the production and comprehension of meaning. Some scholars describe what we discuss here as interactional pragmatics.

While there is no single theoretical framework that seeks to establish or define a field of interactional pragmatics, some researchers such as Thomas (1995), Linell (1998), and Clark (1996) share a common vision of interactional pragmatics as an alternative way of looking at pragmatics, one that emphasizes the indeterminacy of meaning as well as its dynamic construction. We focus here on three core areas in interactional pragmatics. The first concerns *contexts*, where we note that the relationship between language and contexts is dynamic and reflexive. The second concerns *co-acts*, and here we look at how meaning emerges in the flow of inter-action, and how placement within a sequence lends meaning. The third concerns *activities*, and here we think about how constellations of communicative contri-butions combine to form activity types, how they play a role in shaping and being shaped by context, and how they influence meaning. But first we consider inter-actional pragmatics in the context of broader shifts in the social sciences.

6.1 From Etic to Emic, and the Case of Politeness Phenomena

Over the last two or three decades, criticism of the epistemological and methodo-logical foundations of much of social science, for example, in the work of Harré (1995) (see also Harré & Gillett, 1994), a social psychologist, has led to greater acceptance of a range of different types of research, which can be represented for simplicity as shown in Table 6.1, but is more accurately seen as a continuum.

TABLE 6.1 Evolving approaches to research in social science

	Etic	Emic
Research ethos	Scientific	Non-scientific
Research perspective	Observer	Participant
Research scope	Macro	Micro
Research metalanguage	Use of "academic" terms	Use of "lay" terms
Research methods	Quantitative	Qualitative/mixed
Conceptualization of meanings	Abstract	Situated
	Inherent	Emergent
	Essentialist	Contested
	Static	Dynamic
	Pre-planned	Spontaneous
	Cognitivist	Anti-cognitivist

There are no perfect labels for the second and third columns of Table 6.1. They could be labeled "more traditional" and "more recent," respectively, thereby flagging up the chronological shift. However, the characteristics in each column are not unrelated to each other – they represent fairly cohesive research approaches. Consequently, we have labeled these approaches etic and emic, using the terminology coined by Pike (1967). Definitions of these terms have varied in emphasis, but, fundamentally, an etic approach involves positioning the researcher as a cultural "outsider," whereas an emic approach involves positioning the researcher as a cultural "insider." Thus, a researcher pursuing an etic approach would apply pre-existing theories and notions to socio-cultural phenomena. They would take an observer's perspective. In contrast, a researcher pursuing an emic approach would seek to find out the notions and theories used by the members of the cultural group for the socio-cultural phenomena in hand. In doing this, they would be taking a participant's perspective.

For example, in cross-cultural pragmatics, an etic researcher might present members of different cultural groups with speech act utterances assumed to be apologies and ask them to rate them in particular ways, such as the degree of politeness. They might measure reaction times to uncover information about cognitive processes involved in rating politeness. They might use eye-tracking devices to see what participants are looking at, and for how long, when they are asked to rate degrees of politeness. They might be asked to specify how confident they are about their responses. In contrast, an emically oriented researcher might investigate whether the members of those different cultural groups conceive of apologies and politeness in the same way through one-to-one, participant led, unstructured interviews, focus groups, or observations of naturally-occurring data.

Etic and emic approaches, like the individual characteristics in Table 6.1, cannot be straightforwardly separated. For example, members of a particular culture also use etic approaches of their own to approach socio-cultural phenomena.

But they are useful terms for capturing general types of research approach. Pragmatics, especially of the narrow Anglo-American kind, was traditionally rooted in an etic approach, but has more recently seen a shift toward emic approaches, including the varieties of pragmatics termed "interactional pragmatics" and "discursive pragmatics." This shift is in tune with shifts in approach to methodology and the collection and analysis of data in the social sciences generally. In the rest of this section, we will describe the effect of the more recent emic approach to research on one sub-field of pragmatics, namely that of politeness. Our choice of politeness is due to the fact that here the shift in research approach has been dramatic.

We talked about classic politeness frameworks in Chapter 2. Brown and Levinson (1987) is considered the archetype of the etic approach to politeness. An outsider derived set of notions are applied by researchers to the politeness productions and perceptions of various cultures. With respect to the characteristics of traditional social science research in Table 6.1, it is generally considered at least semi-scientific, because of its empirical basis and its amenability to quantitative research. The researcher acts as an observer/analyst of politeness phenomena. The scope is certainly macro (witness the title of their book: "Politeness: Some universals in language usage"). Some key terms are academic, including "negative face" and "positive face," which have no parallels in everyday talk.

Meanings are discussed in relatively abstract terms and contexts rarely accompany their examples. Although Brown and Levinson (1987) do not explicitly claim the politeness values of particular structures to be inherent, much gives the impression that they are considered to be so, and certainly there is no discussion that such meanings are contested. Similarly, such structures are discussed as static and preplanned entities. In fact, preplanning is very much the business of calculating face threat, before one selects and delivers a particular strategy. That preplanning clearly takes place in the mind. Moreover, the cognitive grounding of this politeness framework is present in its reliance on speech act theory, a theory to which the cognitive notion of intentions is central. However, whilst all this seems to paint quite an extreme traditional picture, it is not quite so. For example, some terms and notions, such as *face* and *off-record*, do have a degree of lay person currency, at least in most English speaking cultural settings, and a host of terms are widely used (e.g., *polite*, *hint*, *direct*), albeit with definitions that may depart somewhat from lay understandings.

Points to remember

- Both etic and emic approaches play roles in politeness research.
- The more traditional approach has been etic, with researchers acting as outside observers.

In recent years, there have been different approaches to politeness (e.g., Eelen, 2001; Locher, 2006; Locher & Watts, 2005; Mills, 2003; van der Bom & Mills, 2015; Watts, 2003; Watts, Ide, & Ehlich, 2005). We have already briefly seen some criticisms of the classic pragmatics-based politeness theories in Chapter 2. The scholars Elen, Watts, Locher, and Mills, for example, argue that the classic politeness theories articulated pseudo-scientific theories of particular social behaviors. In contrast, they claim that their more recent politeness work emphasizes that the very definitions of politeness itself are contested. In emic fashion, these researchers argue that a lay person's conception of politeness can be revealed through their use of such terms as *polite* and *politeness* to refer to particular social behaviors. Politeness in this approach is situated or contextualized, meaning that it exists – indeed emerges – in interaction. One study, for example, that pursues this specific line is Haugh (2007a). His study undertakes an emic analysis of "(im)politeness" and "face" in Japanese culture and highlights the importance to these concepts of the interactional achievement of "place" (*basho*): "one's contextually contingent and discursively enacted social role and position" (Haugh, 2007a, p. 660). In other words, speakers' "place" is not some abstract notion that is predetermined, but rather is shaped and decided by interaction. This kind of understanding reflects interactional pragmatics.

As an antidote to the classic politeness theories, the more recent politeness work has been a valuable corrective. In particular, it has drawn attention to the fact that (im)politeness is not inherent in particular forms of language in the sense that a judgment of politeness is solely determined by the usage of particular linguistic forms. Instead, emic (or so-called discursive) politeness argues that it is a matter of the participants' evaluations of particular forms as (im)polite in context. It has also been influential: indeed, many recent studies have at least some of the characteristics of newer, more emic approaches.

Conversation Analysis (CA) (e.g. Heritage, 1984; Sacks, Schegloff, & Jefferson, 1974), which emphasizes the understandings displayed by participants themselves, would be the obvious approach for more emic, more interactional politeness studies. CA reveals how participants co-construct an action sequentially turn-by-turn, and designs their turns to jointly accomplish the action at hand (Hutchby & Wooffitt, 2008; Pomerantz, 1984; Schegloff, 1984, 1996). CA can reveal how a communicative act emerges in a conversation through sequences of talk, a sequence being a linguistic action co-constructed by participants over multiple turns (Schegloff, 1996). CA has been applied to the study of interactional linguistics and discoursal-functional linguistics, which examine social activities and sequential contexts in which linguistic forms occur (e.g., Mori, 2006). Studies in these areas reveal how a particular linguistic form emerges from the "moment-by-moment unfolding of talk-in-interaction and in conjunction with other types of multimodal semiotic resources available for interactional participants" (Mori, 2009, p. 344).

However, few politeness studies have adopted this approach (but see the notable example of Piirainen-Marsh, 2005). Chief amongst the reasons for this is because politeness scholars still need to interpret a participant's understanding of politeness as relevant to politeness. In other words, conversation analysts are interested in the emergence of meanings of any kind from the conversational interaction, but politeness scholars are only interested in those relevant to politeness. Thus, they need a notion, a theory about what politeness is. Instead of the wholesale adoption of CA, some politeness scholars have used hybrid models, which draw on elements of CA. These models are in the spirit of interactional pragmatics. A case in point is the Conjoint Co-Constituting Model of Communication (Arundale, 1999, 2006), which Haugh (2007b) has argued has much to offer as a framework for the study of politeness. This approach encompasses a wider context than the local structures of conversation analysts, including aspects of identity and the history of particular identities. Also, in this approach, evidence for politeness evaluations involves the analyst not just in looking at explicit metalinguistic comments made by participants (e.g., "that's so rude," "he wasn't polite"), as some emic or discursive politeness theorists have argued for, but also at "the reciprocation of concern evident in the adjacent placement of expressions of concern relevant to the norms invoked in that particular interaction" (p. 312). In other words, the evidence is in what people do in interaction after, for example, a norm has been violated (e.g., that an insult has been perceived may be evidenced by a following counter-insult). The general idea here of looking for pragmatic meanings in the context of interaction is what interactional pragmatics is all about. The following four sections elaborate on this area.

Before leaving this section, an important corrective is necessary. So far, we have given the impression any approach in pragmatics is either of the etic kind or of the emic kind, each being characterized by the relevant features listed in Table 6.1. However, it need not be so. Culpeper and Haugh (2014) proposed "integrative pragmatics," a kind of pragmatics that specifically rejects the old dichotomies of etic and emic, Anglo-American and European pragmatics, and so on. It views pragmatic phenomena as multi-layered. It is not just about pragmalinguistics, just about sociopragmatics or just about interaction – these are simply some of the layers that constitute pragmatic phenomena. It is strongly empirical in orientation, favoring mixed methods approaches, but always embedded in at least some aspects of pragmatic theory.

Points to remember

- The shift from etic approaches to more inclusive emic approaches in social science has heavily influenced research in general pragmatics, as well as L2 pragmatics as will become clear in Chapter 7.
- Interactional approaches to pragmatics are partly informed by CA.
- Integrative pragmatics is one example of a more inclusive theoretical and methodological approach in pragmatics research.

Term to Remember

• *Etic approaches* position the researcher as an objective outsider while *emic approaches* position the researcher as a subjective insider.

6.2 Meaning Making in Interaction: Contexts

Back in 1972, Erving Goffman was clearly dissatisfied with contemporary treatments of context:

> At present the idea of the social situation is handled in the most happy-go-lucky way. For example, if one is dealing with the language of respect, then social situations become occasions when persons of relevant status relationships are present before each other, and a typology of social situations is drawn directly and simply from chi-squaredom: high-low, low-high and equals. [. . .] An implication is that social situations do not have properties and a structure of their own, but merely mark, as it were, the geometric intersection of actors making talk and actors bearing particular social attributes.
>
> *(Goffman, 1972, p. 63)*

Goffman was clearly not a fan of essentialist approaches to context (revolving around the idea that context is "out there" waiting to be coded), or reductive approaches to context (revolving around the idea that context can be reduced to a limited set of variables amenable to quantification). Goffman died in 1982. By then, the situation, from his point of view, would have been looking worse, and would deteriorate further. This state of affairs was largely driven by the methodological flavor of the overwhelmingly dominant sociolinguistics paradigm, that of Labov (1972), with its emphasis on quantification. Social context is reduced to social variables such as power, social distance, and rank of imposition (as Goffman wryly observes: "high-low, low-high and equals"). As we noted in Section 2.5, these social variables are a key feature of the politeness frameworks being developed in the late 1970s and early 1980s (e.g., Brown & Levinson, 1987), and politeness, of course, was enthusiastically being researched in both cross-cultural pragmatics and L2 pragmatics, often through questionnaires or tasks involving situational scenarios (e.g., DCT) or Likert-type rating scales for those social variables (see, for example, the papers in Blum-Kulka, House, & Kasper, 1989a, and Spencer-Oatey, 1996, for many references).

What was the alternative? Goffman (1972) defined a "social situation" as:

> an environment of mutual monitoring possibilities, anywhere within which an individual will find himself accessible to the naked senses of all others who are 'present', and similarly find them accessible to him.
>
> *(p. 63)*

Although an explicit connection has not been made, this definition is somewhat similar to the notion of context in a leading pragmatics theory, namely, Relevance Theory:

> Any shared cognitive environment in which it is manifest which people share it is what we will call a *mutual cognitive environment*.
>
> *(Sperber & Wilson, 1995, p. 41)*

These definitions share the idea that *context is mutually constructed*. That is, participants not only construct the context themselves but are simultaneously available for construction as part of the context reiteratively. Thus, part of the context we construct of others is their likely constructions of us (including what we think they think we are thinking), which could include our likely constructions of them (including what we think they think we think we are thinking), and so on.

Although Brown and Levinson's (1987) politeness framework seems to be an exemplar of the essentialist and reductive approach to context, their views are more complex and in line with this vision of a mutually constructed context:

> We are interested in D[istance], P[ower], and R[anking of imposition] only to the extent that the actors think it is mutual knowledge between them that these variables have some particular values. Thus, these are not intended as *sociologists'* ratings of *actual* power, distance, etc., but only as *actors'* assumptions of such ratings, assumed to be mutually assumed, at least within certain limits.
>
> *(Brown & Levinson 1987, pp. 74–76, original emphasis)*

Thus, as Myers (1991) notes, the values for all variables are not given, but are constructed in interaction. For each variable "there is not one value, but a tension between at least two interpretations of the situation" (p. 44). Intersubjectivity is key. Brown and Levinson (1987), however, offer no method for achieving this vision. Subsequent researchers chose to ignore it and adopted their own approach, an approach that was inevitably more essentialist and reductive.

However, both Goffman's and Sperber and Wilson's definitions of context are flawed in one crucial respect. They both give the impression that context is a one-way process – a matter of speakers "monitoring" the context or simply being aware that a "cognitive environment" is potentially "shared." In fact, context influences understandings of language, and language influences understandings of context. The former is the more traditional approach involving a relatively passive view of context; the latter is the newer approach involving a relatively dynamic view of context. Although this newer approach had been noted by sociolinguists for some time (Gumperz, 1982; Hymes, 1974), it was not until the early 1990s that it took off, propelled, for example, by the paper published in

Duranti and Goodwin (1992). In their work, Duranti and Goodwin (1992) pointed out that the notion of "context" is not static as it is shaped by the interactional nature of language.

Let us briefly consider Gumperz (1982) as an example of the language influencing understandings of context approach, and in particular his important notion of "contextualization cues." Gumperz (1992) defines these cues as "those verbal signs that are indexically associated with specific classes of communicative activity types and thus signal the frame of context for the interpretation of constituent messages" (p. 307). Readers will be quite right to note that this sounds reminiscent of the conventionalized formulae and pragmatic frames (schema-like clusters of situational features that accompany such formulae) that we discussed in Section 4.3. For example, in most cultures within the UK, conventionalized formulae such as "ladies and gentlemen," "on your marks, get set, go," and "let us pray" are utterances that seem to carry their typical contexts with them (respectively, initiating an announcement at a formal occasion; signaling the beginning of a race; directing a church congregation to begin prayer during a church service). Users can deploy such language to shape the context they are in. For example, in an English-speaking culture, a user might deploy a first name term of address to another in order to accelerate familiarity. The basis of this tactic is that first name terms of address are typically associated with contexts involving closer relationships. Similarly, a Turkish speaking person can use the formal form of address to maintain the distance between themselves and the addressee. A simple example can be observed in a commonly used question *nasılsınız* (how are you) in Turkish. For instance, a speaker can use the formal form "nasılsınız" instead of the informal form of addressing "nasılsın" in a greeting. This could signal the other interlocutor to use the formal form of addressing in exchange.

Of course, in reality, meanings are generated through a two-way interaction between context and language, that is, involving both context influencing understandings of language and simultaneously language influencing understandings of context. So, first names can backfire. For example, a new employee in a business might call his boss by her first name, then notice coworkers addressing her by a more formal title. This important reflexive relation between language and contexts is deemed to be a superordinate principle of dialogue (Linell, 1998).

> **Points to remember**
> - Context is essential in investigating meaning making in interaction as it directly influences understandings of utterances.
> - Context is mutually constructed by the participants of social interactions, and it directly shapes language use.

6.3 Meaning Making in Interaction: Co-acts

In Chapter 2 we talked about speech acts as individual acts, constituted as isolated items and flowing from single speakers. Here, though, we illustrate how speech acts, and other pragmalinguistic material, do not have fixed meanings in context, but instead their meanings are contingent on surrounding discourse and context. We will also pay attention to the co-construction of acts, and the role of sequentiality. Our springboard will mainly be two examples drawn from Walker, Drew, and Local (2011). This paper is more than a mere source of these examples. It pioneers an alternative approach to indirect speech acts, one that is based on the analysis of sequential environments in everyday conversation.

Consider this utterance: "He'll be back again tomorrow." What kind of speech act is it? Perhaps somebody is asserting that this is the case in order to put someone in the picture; or perhaps somebody is warning that this is the case in order to encourage someone into doing something. The point is that we do not really know the speech act value of this utterance until we see it in its co-text and context. This is where meaning emerges. So the first case of "he'll be back again tomorrow" could be said by a mother to a child who is waiting for the postal worker to deliver a parcel, which has not arrived. In the second scenario, a janitor could be warning another janitor that although the boss has gone, and he is skipping cleaning the whole floor, the boss will be back the next day and so perhaps it is not such a good idea not to clean thoroughly.

The indeterminacy of utterances out of context was only occasionally acknowledged by the early pragmatics theorists. Leech (1983), discussing a very similar example, not only acknowledged pragmatic indeterminacy, but pointed out an important motivation. He writes that:

> The indeterminacy of conversational utterances [. . .] shows itself in the NEGOTIABILITY of pragmatic factors; that is, by leaving the force unclear, S may leave H the opportunity to choose between one force and another, and thus leaves part of the responsibility of the meaning to H.
>
> *(pp. 23–24)*

Note well the final words: part of the responsibility for meaning lies with the hearer. The idea that meanings are jointly constructed by both speaker and hearer is an important idea that was articulated by people such as Clark (1996) and Arundale (1999). As Arundale (1999) elaborates, this runs counter to Grice's (1957, 1989) key vision for pragmatic meaning, namely, that it is a matter of reconstructing what the speaker intends to mean in saying something. For instance, the intended speaker's meaning in saying, "The weather forecast says it'll rain all day" in a particular context might be "We won't be going on a picnic." Indeterminacy and the idea that the hearer is involved in co-constructing meaning run counter to Grice's vision because the speaker's preconceived intended meaning becomes less central.

Now consider Example [6.1] (in the examples, the lines of the transcription are numbered and the key parts of interest are in bold text):

[6.1]

1. MrsH: O: keh-eh Oh he i:s coming back t'[morrow i[s he?
2. Edg: ['t!   **[He'll be back**
3.   **again tomorrow** I would think about mid da:y so if you: you
4.   could pho:ne throu:gh,

(Walker et al., 2011, p. 2437)

Quite obviously, this example is not easy to understand because we do not know about the context, and thus are unable to retrieve referents for the pronouns (e.g., "he," "I," "you") or anchorage points for the deictic expressions (e.g., "coming back," "tomorrow," "be back"). What we are interested in, however, is the utterance "he will be back again tomorrow." We can now see a particular co-text: it follows a yes-no tag question. Thus, its sequential placement suggests that it is an answer or response question. A question-answer adjacency pair, like all adjacency pairs, is a co-constructed entity. In CA, it forms a basic unit of sequence (Sacks et al., 1974). Walker et al. (2011) suggest, the most direct way of responding to the literal question is to say simply "yes" or "no." So, from that point of view this utterance is indirect. However, Walker et al. (2011) propose another perspective. They argue that there is a sense in which it is a "'direct,' clear and obvious, response" (Walker et al., 2011, p. 2437). It clearly gives the confirmation that is sought, and is clearly connected to the question, as indicated by the fact that it repeats material from it. Walker et al. (2011) suggest that it "requires no inferencing" (p. 2437). That is a moot point. One might argue that it flouts the Maxim of Manner being unnecessarily wordy, and thereby triggers an implicature to the effect that the answer to the confirmation request is affirmative. Nevertheless, there certainly is a sense in which it is "clear and obvious."

Let us contrast Example [6.1] with an indirect case, at least from the point of view of Walker et al. (2011). Example [6.2] takes place between Dana and Gordon.

[6.2]

1. Dana: Becuz (0.3) I'm g'nna go see nice Mister Chemist 'n ask
2.   im what 'ee c'n do about my eye. Becuz it itches a lot.
3.   ...7 lines omitted
4. Gordon: =hmhhhh Could it be pollen.

5.   (0.8)
6.   Dana: Par↑d<u>o</u>n?
7.   Gordon: P<u>o</u>llen:.
8.   (0.3)
9.   Gordon: . k As in: uh h<u>a</u>y f<u>e</u>ver.
10.   (0.2)
11. **Dana: It's in one e<u>ye</u>:.**

(p. 2435)

Gordon's question in line 4, "Could it be pollen," is obviously a polar yes/no question. The following pause (0.8 second) is significant: we do not get the preferred answer, but instead a further question/answer adjacency pair is inserted. Gordon's answer to Dana's "pardon" recycles material from his original question. But Dana still does not respond, as indicated by the pause, and so in line 9, Gordon clarifies, "as in uh hay fever." Then eventually we get Dana's response to Gordon's question in line 11, "it's in one eye." As in the previous example, this does not contain a yes or no, as would be expected after such a question. However, unlike Example [6.1], there is no repetition, ellipsis, or pronominalization tying it back to Gordon's question. Nevertheless, Walker et al. (2011) argue that such turns are as follows:

> [I]nterpretable as responses to the preceding inquiry, not only because of their sequential location, but also because of the way in which the talk contained in the turns instructs the co-participants to draw inferences based either on prior talk, their shared knowledge, or both.
>
> *(p. 2440)*

In fact, Dana's response in line 11 links back by repetition of what she has already said in line 2, "my eye . . . it itches." She reinforces the point that she has already provided information about one eye. But more than this, she invites the inference that the diagnosis of hay fever is wrong, appealing to "knowledge" that hay fever would affect both eyes. This is not actually true, but that is not an issue here: she presents it as if it were true and that Gordon got it wrong.

Adjacency pairs were not something Searle had tried to account for in his theory. Questions are only briefly treated, and answers/responses are neglected. This is not entirely surprising because their status as speech acts is highly controversial. In contrast, for conversation analysts they are central. Similarly, the whole issue of indirectness in speech act theory is mainly discussed in relation to requests; it was not worked out for answers/responses. In fact, responses generally contain assertions of some kind, and assessing how assertions relate to context in terms of conversational implicature can be useful, as we briefly illustrated previously. Nevertheless, Walker et al. (2011) are quite right to focus our attention on the fact that literal meaning may not deserve the ascendancy as it is given in speech act theory. Recollect from Section 2.4 that in speech act theory, indirectness is essentially a matter of whether the illocutionary force matches the syntactic structure (if it does, it is literal). But there may be other ways of defining directness, ways that involve the positioning of acts within a sequence of acts and the collaborative work of more than one speaker to create the sequence. Speech act theory does not address this.

> **Points to remember**
>
> - Meaning making is continuously co-constructed by the speakers and the hearers during interactions.
> - Analyzing sequentiality and co-acts in conversations affords a more in-depth understanding of the conversation participants' language usage.

6.4 Meaning Making in Interaction: Activities

As Linell (1998) points out, "[a]cts, utterances and sequences in discourse are always essentially situated within an embedding activity (dialogue, encounter) which the interactions jointly produce" (p. 87). Similarly, in *Philosophical Investigations* (1958, section 23), Wittgenstein positions sentences and speech acts as part of language games:

> [B]ut how many kinds of sentence are there? Say assertion, question, and command?—There are countless kinds: countless different kinds of use of what we call "symbols," "words," "sentences." And this multiplicity is not something fixed, given once for all; but new types of language, new language-games, as we may say, come into existence, and others become obsolete and get forgotten.

Activities are really a specific kind of context, one principally constituted by acts. In fact, we are not a stranger to such a notion, as it is similar to that of the pragmatic frame, introduced in Chapter 4. More widely in the literature, there are other overlapping notions, of which perhaps the best-known is Hymes's (e.g., 1972a) "speech event." However, in this section we will focus on "activity types" (Levinson, 1979, 1992). A feature of all of these notions is that they are "meso" level, that is to say, they are not a broad macro notion context, such as "culture," or a narrow micro notion of context, such as the conversational exchange (e.g., question-answer), but somewhere in the middle. They are also situated in context (as we discussed in Chapter 5). Indeed, Goffman's (1961) notion of "situated activity system" (p. 96) is similar to the notion of activity type. Also, activity types, and many of the other notions, involve reflexive two-way interaction between context and language, that is, context influencing understandings of language and simultaneously language influencing understandings of context.

In a nutshell, an activity type is a bundle of communicative contributions that regularly co-occur and form a semi-conventionalized whole. Levinson's (1979, 1992) definition is as follows:

> [The notion of activity type] refers to any culturally recognized activity, whether or not that activity is coextensive with a period of speech or indeed whether any talk takes place in it at all [. . .] In particular, I take the notion of an activity type to refer to a fuzzy category whose focal members are goal-defined, socially constituted, bounded events with *constraints* on participants, setting, and so on, but above all on the kinds of allowable contributions. Paradigm examples would be teaching, a job interview, a jural interrogation, a football game, a task in a workshop, a dinner party, and so on.
>
> *(p. 69)*

Subsequent researchers have worked on what constitutes these activity types. Thomas's (1995) book, *Meaning in Interaction*, did much to spell out the pragmatic constituents. Her list includes participant goals, allowable contributions, contextual weighting of Gricean maxims, weighting of interpersonal maxims (including politeness), turn-taking and topic control, and the manipulation of pragmatic parameters (e.g., power, social distance) (1995, pp. 190–192). For example, in an interrogation activity type, Grice's maxims of quality and quantity are suspended, because, as is well known, people are prepared to say whatever is necessary to avoid continued pain. Conversely, whilst in a (Catholic) confessional activity type, those maxims, especially quality, are salient, partly because it is considered morally wrong to lie or mislead and partly because the priest is expected not to broadcast further anything he hears.

Activity types are social and interactional: they are dynamic, situated, and co-constructed. But they are also cognitive and interpretative: they account for the participants' use of knowledge about interactions. Their cognitive side is clearly stated in Levinson (1992):

> [T]o each and every clearly demarcated activity there is a corresponding set of *inferential schemata*.
>
> *(p. 72, original emphasis)*

> [Activity types] help to determine how what one says will be "taken" – that is, what kinds of inferences will be made from what is said.
>
> *(p. 97)*

For example, the utterance "how are you?" said to a colleague in the workplace might be taken as a polite enquiry requiring a phatic response (e.g., "fine thanks") even if you are not feeling great, whilst the same utterance said to a doctor in a medical clinic might be taken as a "real" question, and lead to a listing of symptoms.

One thing activity types lack, however, is a means of characterizing the forms of talk that occur within them. Sarangi (2000) compensates for this deficit with the notion of "discourse types":

> [S]pecific manifestations of language form in their interactional contexts (e.g., ranging from utterance types such as "how are you?", "what are we doing here?" to the sequential organization of questions and answers as in a cross-examination, to stylistic features as in promotional talk). While activity type is a means of characterizing settings (e.g., a medical consultation, a service encounter, a university seminar), discourse type is a way of characterizing forms of talk (e.g., medical history taking, promotional talk, interrogation, troubles telling, etc.).
>
> *(pp. 1–2)*

We would argue that discourse types also have counterpart "inferential schemata." In fact, discourse types seem to amount to Gumperz's (1982) "contextualization cues," as discussed in Section 6.2. Recollect that they are: "those verbal signs that are indexically associated with specific classes of communicative activity types and thus signal the frame of context for the interpretation of constituent messages" (Gumperz, 1992, p. 307). Furthermore, in Section 6.2, we reminded readers that contextualization cues are reminiscent of the conventionalized formulae and pragmatic frames we discussed in Section 4.3. There we glossed pragmatic frames as schema-like clusters of situational features that accompany such formulae. Those "schema-like clusters" are these "inferential schemata."

Let us deepen and illustrate the discussion thus far. Our data are drawn from *The Pragmatics and Intercultural Communication Project* (for details, see: www.lancaster.ac.uk/fass/projects/pic/). The aim of this project was to analyze the cultural and linguistic issues affecting communication between language teaching assistants and the permanent staff in French and English schools, especially those who act as mentors. A key activity type is the initial orientation meeting between the language assistants and their school mentors. This usually occurs in a school office. It is the first non-casual extended meeting, and typically takes place within the first week of the language assistant's arrival at any point during the working-day. The following is a list of the typical features of this activity type, and it follows the headings for activity types devised and utilized in Culpeper and McIntyre (2010):

- *Participants and their social roles*: One older adult, who is mentor, manager, and colleague. One younger adult, who is mentee, managed member of staff and colleague.
- *Goals*: For the mentor, to swiftly complete the meeting (i.e., enact institutional goals); for the language assistant, to learn survival skills (gain guidance).
- *Social parameters*: Asymmetric power relations (mentor is more powerful with respect to institutional power and age, but the language assistant has the power of the expert, the native speaker); strangers.

- *Norms of information exchange*: For both the mentor and language assistant, information is relevant to the assistant's role in the school (e.g., the timetable, teaching techniques).
- *Politeness norms*: The mentor uses Tact (give a low value to Self's wants) (Leech, 1983, p. 91) or Negative politeness (Brown & Levinson, 1987) to soften the asymmetric power implications of managerial talk. The language assistant is deferential (uses Negative politeness). Both mentor and assistant may use Positive politeness to accelerate social closeness.
- *Discourse types*: The mentor is informing/advising/directing, as well as solidarity enhancing. Language assistant is seeking advice/responding.
- *Conversational structure*: The mentor initiates and closes the interaction, and takes the longest turns.
- *Norms of interpretation*: When the mentor informs the language assistant, it is often taken to be more than a point of information, usually a direction of some kind. When the assistant asks the mentor about something, it is usually a reflection of a worry and plea for help.

Of course, remember that these are typical features that form the basis of expectations. Not every encounter of this type will be comprised in this way.

Example [6.3] is a fragment from a first meeting between a French language assistant and an English mentor:

[6.3]

Assistant: And do I have to prepare something in advance or . . . er when I come, just tell me what I have to do
Mentor: Probably a bit of both
Assistant: Mmm
Mentor: In . . . first of all in the first few weeks I think it'll be um, having . . . you'll be sort of in lessons seeing how the students work [yeah] and so on and you can go round and help them [yeah] and after a couple of weeks maybe start taking some groups out. [yeah] We can tell you what we want you to do in advance if you want us to, or it maybe just something when you arrive. [Mm-hmm] We can always use e-mail if you need to know in advance.

A rather large quantity of hedging is evident in the mentor's talk – "probably," "a bit," "I think," "sort of," and "maybe." Some of this may simply reflect the fact that the mentor does not know the answer, but the mentor also seems to be politely keeping options open for the language assistant (see Leech, 1983, on optionality). The latter motivation is supported by the conditional "if you want us to." In doing this, he avoids the asymmetric power implications of managerial talk. All this, we should remember is in the context of the mentor having been invited to be directive by the assistant: "just tell me what I have to do."

So, from the language assistant's perspective, was this the perfect first encounter with her mentor? She later commented in a diary entry:

> J'aurais bien aimé savoir . . . Qu'est-ce que je peux faire, est-ce que je peux en mettre un à la porte, donner des avertissements . . . Je suis restée un petit peu sur ma faim parce que je veux savoir qu'est-ce que je peux faire, mon intervention personnelle.

> (I would really have liked to know . . . what I'm able to do, whether I can send one of them out of the class, give them warnings . . . I'm still a little bit frustrated because I want to know what I can do personally, my personal intervention.)

In this context, the language assistant's need for practical survival skills outweighs the value of being given optionality or receiving general "face" support.

Example [6.3] involves an activity type that is not stable and documented. The physical environment, the buildings, are not designed with the assistants in mind; there is no manual outlining how to conduct activities; and knowledge of professional responsibilities tends to be hazy. Consequently, participants draw from their knowledge of neighboring activity types in the conduct of this one. Given that the participants' knowledge arises from different experiences, it is not surprising that communication can be less than successful. One needs to learn the characteristics of the activity types that populate a particular culture. What seems to lie behind the interactional problems of Example [6.3] is a mismatch in role conception: mentors view themselves as "mentor-colleague," whereas language assistants view them as "mentee-managed member of staff." Thus, mentors value optionality and solidarity-enhancement more than directive and powerful talk, whereas assistants prefer practical and explicit direction. Regarding French-English cross-cultural differences, generally, there are, of course, many more similarities than differences. However, Culpeper, Crawshaw, and Harrison (2008) observe a slight tendency for the in-France activity type to have less informing discourse and slightly more advising discourse. The in-France activity type thus perhaps has a more "directive" style. This would be in tune with the French language assistant's expectation in Example [6.3] of more direction from their English mentors.

Points to remember

- Activity types are culture-specific activities that play an important role in decoding and constructing meaning during interaction.
- Activity types are dynamic, situated, and co-constructed, and they frame and guide the speakers' and the hearers' respective interactional contributions.

6.5 Multimodality

The transcriptions of Examples [6.1] and [6.2] were designed to capture more than the words and grammatical structures of the talk. We see, for example, elongated vowels, stress, and rising intonation contours marked. Yet, in transcriptions that appear in earlier pragmatics works, this kind of marking was entirely absent. Searle (1969, 1985) does briefly mention intonation as an illocutionary force indicating device; Brown and Levinson (1987) do make a few remarks about prosody – but this is precisely the point: they are only occasional and brief comments. Regarding non-verbal visual phenomena, there was no evidence of that in Examples [6.1] and [6.2]. Grice does have some non-verbal examples, but most early pragmatic works steer clear of such phenomena. Full pragmatic agreements of *multi*modal data are strikingly scarce in interactional pragmatics work. Wharton (2009) does provide a thoroughly pragmatic treatment of both prosody and gesture, though he is mostly preoccupied with theoretical considerations. A comprehensive treatment is Arndt and Janney (1987), who argue that "utterances become 'meaningful' – by which we mean interpretable – only through the interaction of verbal, prosodic, and kinesic actions in context" (p. 248). Indeed, given that interactional pragmatics takes a more holistic approach to data in general, it is not surprising to see richer transcriptions. Interactional pragmatics, as we already observed, partly draws from Conversation Analysis, where transcription is a window on participant categories and meanings, and thus has to be rich. However, as noted above with respect to Examples [6.1] and [6.2], even here the concentration is on prosody, not visual phenomena.

Let us examine two examples. Example [6.4] is a brief interaction that takes place between two pre-teenage sisters:

[6.4]   *A*:   Do you know anything about yo-yos?
        B: That's mean.

On the face of it, Speaker A's utterance is an innocent enquiry about Speaker B's state of knowledge. However, the prosody triggered a different interpretation. Speaker A heavily stressed the beginning of "anything," and produced the remainder of the utterance with sharply falling intonation. This prosody is marked against the norm for yes–no questions, which usually have rising intonation (e.g., Quirk, Greenbaum, Leech, & Svartvik, 1985). It signals to B that A's question is not straightforward or innocent. It triggers the recovery of implicatures that Speaker A is not asking a question but expressing both a belief that Speaker B knows nothing about yo-yos and an attitude toward that belief, namely, incredulity that this is the case – something which itself implies that Speaker B is deficient in some way. Without the prosody, there is no clear evidence of the interpersonal orientation of Speaker A, whether positive, negative, or somewhere in between. This example illustrates the fact that prosodic features play an important role in disambiguating messages, as research in communication has repeatedly demonstrated (e.g., Archer & Ackert, 1977).

Consider Example [6.5], which occurred in the changing room of a gym in the UK. A and B are strangers, and at the time of this interaction, they were the only people in the changing room. B stands in front of his locker and has his locker door open. Immediately below the lockers, level with the bottom of the doors, is a long bench. To B's left is A's locker, in front of which is placed a single towel on the bench. A arrives in the changing room and walks over to his locker. He looks at the towel, which is partly blocking his locker door.

[6.5] A: Is that your towel?
B: [*Slowly shakes head. No eye-contact is made.*]

A's interrogative involves rather more than a question. By orientating to the ownership of the towel, A is establishing responsibility for the towel, and indirectly requesting that it be moved. B uses a conventional gesture in UK culture, a head shake, to answer "no" that it is not his towel. Simultaneously, the implied meaning is one of refusal of the request to move it. The minimal nature of the response, the lack of eye contact, the absence of an attempt to commiserate – all these things lead A, one of the authors of this book, to feel that the response was not appropriate and not polite.

Perhaps the dearth of pragmatics studies going beyond words and grammatical structures is a result of perceived difficulties in analyzing prosody and/or visual aspects such as gesture. Recently, however, more help is being provided from a technical point of view. As far as prosody is concerned, the leading program for its analysis, *Praat* (www.praat.org), is freely available. Programs such as this provide visualizations of the acoustic profiles of utterances. Although "reading" those profiles does require some training, they are an invaluable descriptive tool (the alternative is an inevitably highly subjective description of what you think you heard). Figure 6.1 shows the Mandarin utterance /han hao/ (a name). Acoustic analysis can reveal not only segmental articulation, but also voice quality, which is often used for pragmatic effect. Here, the spectrogram and waveform reveal the breathiness (noise) of the /h/'s, the periodic modal voicing in the regular striations of /a/ and /n/, and the irregular glottalized voicing of the final diphthong.

Images can be invaluable for the simple representation of non-verbal aspects. Such programs as ELAN (https://tla.mpi.nl/tools/tla-tools/elan/) allow the alignment of audio-video elements and a transcription. There is also more academic attention and guidance regarding how to proceed with a pragmatic analysis of non-verbal aspects and what it all means. A good example is the handbook chapter by Brown and Prieto (2017).

With L2 pragmatics in mind, sounding and looking pragmatically appropriate are important considerations. They are not simply "extras" in communication, but can lie at the heart of it. Furthermore, particular prosodies or gestures can

h　　　a　　n　　h　　　　　　ao

0　　　　　　　　　　　　　　　　　　　　　　　0.7

Time (s)

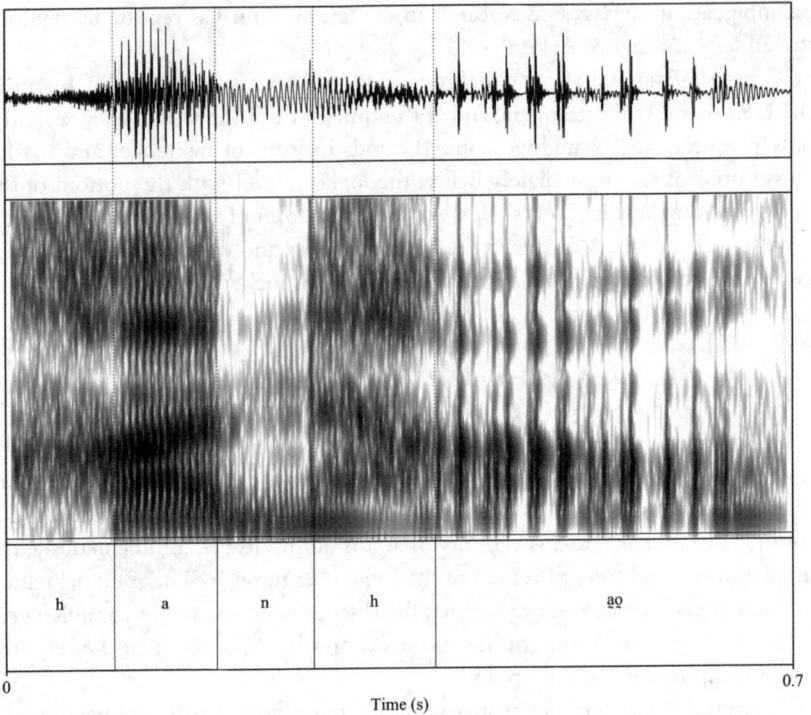

FIGURE 6.1 A spectrogram of the Mandarin utterance /han hao/

carry conventionalized associations in particular situations in particular cultures, just as can happen with words and grammatical structures (see Section 4.3). In his work on "pressed voice," which is characterized by, amongst other things, a rasping vocal quality due to tensed vocal folds, Sadanobu (2004) shows that "utterances of kyoshuku (in the cases of request and rejection) with pressed voice are much more polite than those with verbal expression of kyoshuku" (p. 42). In contrast, Shochi, Auberge, and Rilliard (2007) show that the same voice quality is viewed negatively by Americans and the French. This contrast reinforces the point that pragmalinguistic phenomena are conventionalized for particular situations in particular cultures.

> **Points to remember**
> - Most pragmatics research lacks multimodal data analyses of language exchanges during interaction.
> - L2 pragmatic competence involves not only using the correct vocabulary and grammar, but also *sounding* and *looking* appropriate.

- Examining prosody and non-verbal visuals in conversation provides a more holistic picture in understanding implied meaning.

6.6 Conclusions

We have outlined three key areas of interactional pragmatics. First, we examined contexts, and the importance of conceiving their relationship with language as two-way and reflexive (language shaping context and context shaping language). Second, we looked at co-acts, and the emergence of meanings in the flow of interaction as a result of the fact that they are contingent upon their discoursal and contextual placement. We also emphasized the co-constructed nature of acts and meanings. Third, we discussed activities, and in particular, activity types. We described both the interactional side and the cognitive side of activity types. Finally, we briefly considered multimodality, and the importance of taking channels of communication into consideration.

Questions About Interactional Pragmatics

1. What is interactional pragmatics? What is the relationship between interaction and pragmatics?
2. What are the characteristics of *contexts*, *co-acts*, and *activities* in interactional pragmatics?
3. How do context, co-acts, and activity types affect meaning making during conversational interaction? What is the significance of investigating these constructs in pragmatics studies?
4. Do speakers have pre-determined intentions (a priori) or do they construct intentions during interaction (post-facto)?
5. Why is investigating prosodical and non-verbal visual phenomena important in interactional pragmatics? What does previous research have to say about their role in pragmatic competence?

Questions About Research Methods in Interactional Pragmatics

1. What are *etic* and *emic* approaches? How can these approaches be implemented in pragmatics studies? Can you give an example study in L2 pragmatics for each approach?
2. What are the defining characteristics of an integrative/multi-method pragmatics approach?
3. What is a multimodal data analysis and how can it be utilized in L2 pragmatics studies? Given the cost-benefit analysis, is it worth conducting in interactional pragmatics studies?

162 Interaction: Conceptual Background

4. How can prosodical and non-verbal visual phenomena be investigated and assessed in pragmatics research?
5. To what extent does current research in L2 pragmatics use an integrative approach with a multimodal data analysis?
6. Is there an ideal approach and a method when it comes to interactional pragmatics research? How can researchers determine their methodology?

7

DATA ELICITATION METHODS IN L2 PRAGMATIC INTERACTION

Introduction

In this chapter, we survey interactive data collection methods beginning with open role plays, eliciting an extended interaction around a pragmatic act. These are different from the role plays and studies we described in Chapter 3 because here we focus on research that has analyzed interaction and communication. We discuss the use of authentic and semi-authentic data (i.e., elicited and naturalistic conversation), again focusing on interactional features in the data and illustrate and explain how these types of data can illuminate the co-construction of pragmatic meanings.

> **Points to remember**
>
> • The construction of pragmatic meanings refers to how a pragmatic act unfolds across turns and participants.

While providing information about a range of methods used to examine L2 pragmatics interaction is the primary goal of this chapter, an additional goal involves introducing readers to research in interactional pragmatics, which has been under-represented in the field so far. The key concepts of interactional pragmatics, namely, co-acts and activity types, which we outlined in the previous chapter, have been underrepresented in the L2 pragmatics literature as frameworks for collecting and analyzing data (see Taguchi & Roever, 2017, for the review of L2 studies under interactional pragmatics). The concept of contexts, albeit common, is often understood from an essentialist perspective in the L2 pragmatics area. Researchers sometimes reduce contexts to a limited set of a-priori social variables without considering how those variables are constructed in inter-action. The reflexive relationship between language and contexts, where context influences understandings of language and language influences understanding of context, has rarely been addressed in the analysis of L2 pragmatics behavior. However, we believe this line of research holds great promise for the field and thus we spend time here on the methods, as well as building on some of the theoretical issues discussed in Chapter 6.

7.1 Structured Data for Pragmatic Interaction

In Chapter 3, we discussed role plays as a method to investigate pragmatic pro-duction. Role plays involve an interaction played out by two or more people based on a situational scenario. Although "interaction" is the primary feature that distinguishes role play from other language elicitation tasks, the studies reviewed in Chapter 3 mainly provided utterance-level analyses of role-play data that focused on the types of pragmalinguistic forms produced, and did not attend to interactive features that contribute to the overall success (or not) of communica-tion. These studies often analyzed how learners' forms approximated or deviated from native speakers' forms (base-line data) on the levels of directness and formal-ity. The categorical systems used in these studies may impose pre-determined structures, "thereby obscuring or distorting the features of interactional phenomena" (Psathas, 1995, p. 8).

In this chapter, we will turn to the studies that have analyzed role-play data beyond the utterance-level by attending to the kind of interactional features out-lined in the previous chapter, such as those often considered in Conversational Analysis (CA), like context, turn-taking, sequential organization, and the co-construction of meaning. We will also look at the (few) studies that have exam-ined L2 pragmatics in the context of the interaction approach to L2 learning, including features such as negotiation for meaning, corrective feedback, and recasts. Some of these studies have used open role plays (as opposed to closed role plays) for data collection.

Points to remember

- Role-play data can be analyzed beyond the utterance level by attending to interactional features, like turn-taking, sequential organization, and the co-construction of meaning.

The difference between closed and open role plays is that the former specifies the outcome of interaction, while the latter does not (Kasper & Dahl, 1991). Because the outcomes of communication are not predetermined in a situational scenario, open role plays are thought to simulate a real-life interaction more closely and elicit a number of turns over a longer stretch of discourse. This is because in open role plays "sequential organization is contingent on the interlocutor's uptake" (Kasper & Rose, 2002, p. 87), as the speaker and listener coordinate their contributions through turn-taking. In addition, open role plays enable researchers to investigate how contextual features may affect interaction. By specifying roles and settings that can characterize a communicative event in a situational scenario, researchers can examine how contextual variables, such as interlocutor relationship, social distance, and degree of formality, influence participants' realizations of a communicative act. Researchers can also analyze how those variables shift corresponding to the changing course of interaction.

> **Points to remember**
>
> - The difference between closed and open role play is that the former specifies the outcome of interaction, while the latter does not.
> - Open role plays are thought to simulate real-life interactions more closely because the outcomes of communication are not predetermined.

Using open role plays, previous studies have generated a rich qualitative analysis of L2 interaction when performing a pragmatic act. An important early study by Gass and Houck (1999) examined refusal scenarios role played by three L2 English learners and their native speaker interlocutors (Box 7.1). Role plays were video-taped and transcribed. The authors' analysis went beyond the linguistic categorizations of refusal strategies, extending to the analysis of vocal and non-verbal features, turn-taking, and the use of communication strategies. The learners negotiated their way through the completion of a refusal by using various means to establish solidarity with their interlocutors. For instance, they used communication strategies such as backchannel cues (e.g., nodding, affirmative response) as an emphatic response. The learners used non-verbal cues of affect (e.g., laughter) to mitigate refusals. They also called the interlocutor's attention to their non-nativeness (e.g., limited linguistic and sociocultural knowledge) as a sympathy-soliciting strategy. These features of interaction generated a number of turns in the obtained data, illustrating that a speech act emerges from a negotiation among participants toward a common communicative goal. These findings point to the importance of analyzing a speech act as a discourse unit rather than a

BOX 7.1 Learning to Refuse

Gass, S. M., & Houck, N. (1999). *Interlanguage refusals*. Berlin: de Gruyter.

Purpose: To analyze the dynamic discourse involved in complete refusal sequences between L2 learners of English and native speaker interlocutors.

Participants: Three Japanese learners of L2 English (low to intermediate proficiency), and three native English speaker interlocutors.

Study design: The researchers investigated refusals to four types of situations: (1) suggestions; (2) offers; (3) invitations; and (4) requests. Two situations requiring refusals were created for each of the four situation types. Each role play consisted of an interaction involving a native speaker of English, who was the person making an unfavorable suggestion, offer, invitation, or request, and a Japanese non-native speaker of English, who was expected to refuse the proposition. All sessions were videotaped.

Results: The researchers categorized the L2 learners' refusal strategies and analyzed the interactants' use of vocal and non-verbal features, turn-taking, and communication strategies. They found that the L2 learners used various strategies to establish solidarity with their interlocutors, such as backchannel cues (e.g., nodding, affirmative response), laughter, and calling attention to their non-nativeness. They emphasized the importance of analyzing a speech act as a discourse unit rather than a fragmented exchange, since this illuminates how interlocutors work together strategically toward a common communicative goal.

fragmented exchange. Role-play data can be analyzed for a wider range of communicative resources than speech act strategies, such as discourse tactics and turn-takings to capture interactional features of a communicative act.

7.2 Interaction Approaches to Role-play Data

The Interaction Approach, Role Plays, and L2 Pragmatics

While role plays can provide rich qualitative data of L2 pragmatic interactions, they have also been usefully employed to examine how interactional processes influence SLA. A small body of previous literature has utilized open role plays to examine the effects of interaction on L2 pragmatic development. The interaction approach to SLA identifies key features of interaction that support second language development: access to comprehensible input, output, opportunities to negotiate for meaning, and the provision of corrective feedback (Gass & Mackey, 2006; Long, 1996; Mackey, 2012). Corrective feedback, or the negative evidence that learners receive on their output from their interlocutors, in particular, has been widely investigated with researchers seeking to understand how different types and targets of corrective feedback affect L2 development (Brown, 2016; Li, 2010; Lyster & Saito, 2010; Mackey & Goo, 2007). While the majority of the studies have examined the effects of corrective feedback on morphosyntactic or lexical development and less so in terms of pragmatic development (Mackey, Gass, & McDonough, 2000), some patterns have emerged (Fukuya & Hill, 2006; Guo, 2013; Koike & Pearson, 2005). In the following, we will provide a brief illustration of these studies to show what kinds of interactional features were analyzed in role-play data and how they were analyzed.

One study by Fukuya and Hill (2006) examined the effects of one implicit form of corrective feedback, recasts, on English learners' production of requests. Twenty Chinese learners of English were divided into either a treatment or control group. The learners completed open role plays of request situations. Each scenario contained a different combination of three variables: power, social distance, and imposition. The power variable represents the difference in relative power between the learner and the recipient of their request where +Power indicates the recipient has more power than the learner in the given scenario and −Power indicates the learner makes a request from someone of lesser or equal power. The social distance variable indicates whether or not the recipient of the request is known (−Distance) or unknown (+Distance) to the requester. The imposition variable indicates whether the request was significant (+Imposition) or inconsequential (−Imposition). The researchers used these variables to categorize role-play scenarios and determine which pragmatic conventions would be most appropriate (for example, in a low imposition, low distance scenario, the request could be more direct "*Could you x?*" while in higher imposition scenario, or in a situation where the recipient has more power or greater social distances from the request-maker, a more indirect convention such as "*Would it be possible to x?*" was deemed appropriate).

Examples of Open Role-play Scenarios

−Power, +distance, +imposition scenario: You are revising your thesis to submit to your university. Your advisor has already provided several rounds of revisions and has suggested you ask an additional professor, Dr. Garcia, from the department to provide more feedback. Although you do not know Dr. Garcia well, you must ask her to provide edits quickly. The deadline to submit your thesis is only two days away. You go to Dr. Garcia's office.

+Power, −distance, −imposition scenario: You are collecting data for your thesis using your department's lab. The deadline to complete your data collection is fast approaching and you notice your friend, a fellow student, has booked all the lab time-slots for the next few weeks. You need to ask your friend to swap time slots with you so that you can finish your data collection in time. You approach him at the library.

In the experimental group, the learners performing the role play received recasts on their request forms from the instructor (see examples below). The control group did not receive feedback on their requests. Pragmatic development was measured with pre-/post-discourse completion tests (DCTs). Results from the pre-/post-tests indicated that learners in the recast group outperformed learners in the control group (d=0.87) on both measures of grammatical accuracy and pragmatic appropriateness of their requests.

Example of Implicit and Explicit Pragmatic Feedback

Implicit feedback (recast)

Student: Would you please edit my thesis for me?
Teacher: I was wondering if you would help edit my thesis.

Explicit feedback (metalinguistic)

Student: Can you edit my thesis please?
Teacher: In this scenario, you are talking with a professor, so you should be less direct and more polite in your request. You could say, I'd be very grateful if you took the time to help my edit my thesis.

Fukuya and Hill's (2006) study was one of the first to extend findings about the effectiveness of corrective feedback for linguistic forms to the domain of pragmatics. However, the researchers only investigated one (implicit) form of corrective feedback, recasts. In a later study by Guo (2013), the effects of two forms of corrective feedback on English language learners' acquisition of request forms were compared. The study design was similar to that of Fukuya and Hill's, but it included three groups: a recast (implicit) feedback group, a metalinguistic (explicit feedback) group, and a control group. Forty-one English language learners participated in the study, again performing role plays and completing DCTs as pre-, post-, and delayed post-tests. The study revealed that the metalinguistic feedback group outperformed the recast and control groups in that they produced bi-clausal forms (most indirect form of requests) most frequently. However, these differences were not durable at delayed post-testing. This study bolsters previous findings that pragmatic knowledge can be affected by corrective feedback, but also points to a need for finer-grained study of which types of corrective feedback are most beneficial to pragmatic conventions. These studies all also examine one particular type of pragmatic convention – requests. There is clearly a need for more studies to compare previous findings on requests with other types of pragmatic skills and speech acts.

> **Points to remember**
> - Most studies under the interaction approach to SLA have examined only a select number of pragmatic conventions with the majority focusing on requests.
> - More research is needed to understand the effects of different forms of instruction and corrective feedback (either implicit or explicit) on the wide range of speech acts and pragmatic forms that learners acquire.

7.3 Conversation Analytic Approaches to Role-play Data

Conversation Analysis-informed Assessment of Open Role-play Data

In tune with the shift toward more emic approaches in pragmatics generally discussed in Section 6.1, more recent L2 pragmatics literature has explicitly advocated discursive pragmatics as an approach to examining pragmatic acts in situated interactions (Kasper, 2006). Following this trend, there is a growing body of studies that have applied CA to study action, meaning, and context. These studies have collected audio- or videotaped interactions and transcribed them using CA-specific conventions to provide micro-genetic analyses of L2 pragmatic interaction (e.g., Dippold, 2011; González-Lloret, 2010, 2016; Huth, 2006; Pekarek Doehler & Berger, 2017; Taleghani-Nikazm & Huth, 2010). In another line of research, CA has been used in assessing pragmatic competence (e.g., Al-Gahtani & Roever, 2012, 2014a, 2014b; Kasper & Ross, 2007; Walters, 2007; Youn, 2015).

In the context of L2 acquisition, CA views L2 development not only as the development of linguistic forms, but also as learners' developing use of a range of semiotic resources (e.g., gaze, embodied actions, and turn-taking) to communicate meaning. As Markee (2008) states, L2 learning involves using "these intersubjective resources to co-construct with their interlocutors locally enacted, progressively more accurate, fluent, and complex interactional repertoires in the L2" (p. 406). In this perspective, pragmatics learning is also situated within social practice. Learners draw on both linguistic and semiotic resources, and collaboratively construct a pragmatic act with their interlocutors. From the CA point of view, the limitation of the utterance-level analyses of role-play data (or one-turn response in DCT data) in L2 pragmatics research is that they do not allow for the concept of sequential organization in data. Instead, those analyses elicit responses relative to a pre-determined, intuition-based taxonomy of behavior, which makes inferences of real-world pragmatic interactions difficult.

> **Points to remember**
> - CA views L2 development not only as the development of linguistic forms, but also as learners' developing use of a range of semiotic resources (e.g., gaze, embodied actions, and turn-taking) to communicate meaning.

Recent CA-oriented studies in L2 pragmatics have attempted to account for this limitation by attending to the interactive, dynamic nature of a conversation in which a communicative act is jointly constructed between participants and negotiated over multiple turns. For instance, using open role play, Walters's (2007) study assessed the validity of CA-informed testing (CAIT) with 42 non-native speakers of English. In the CAIT, one native-English speaking tester and a non-native speaker examinee engaged in a directed open role-play task. They were instructed to ask questions to each other on topics related to the university community. During role play, the tester provided three pragmatic prompts – an assessment, a compliment, and a pre-sequence – as part of larger topic discussions.

The unique feature of the CAIT is that the tester and the examinee were "playing themselves" (p. 165). Although the author calls the task a "directed role play," participants were not instructed to take any imagined roles; instead, they engaged in a conversation as members of the same university community. In addition, the pragmatic prompts were delivered in a spontaneous manner and thus were unexpected to the examinees. For instance, when talking about adjustment problems to the university, the tester provided an assessment related to the topic (e.g., "Speaking another language is hard."). The examinee was expected to respond to this assessment spontaneously, either with agreement, disagreement, or a combination of these. The quality of the examinee's response to the prompt was evaluated.

As briefly noted in Section 6.3, an adjacency pair is a basic unit of sequence involving two utterances constituting a conversational exchange. For example, when the speaker asks a question, the listener is expected to provide a response to the question. Because the second-pair part is conditioned by the first-pair part, learners' ability to formulate sequentially relevant response to the first pair part is an indication of their interactional competence. Pragmatic prompts used in the CAIT can help reveal this ability.

Two CA-trained raters (native and non-native) transcribed role-play interactions using CA conventions and assessed examinees' performance using rubrics. In the sample below, examinees' ability to control their assessment responses was rated on a four-point scale (p. 168).

4 = evidence of control of assessment responses
3 = more evidence of control than evidence of no control of assessment responses
2 = more evidence of no control than of control of assessment responses
1 = no evidence of control of assessment responses

There was evidence that the raters were applying the CA-perspective to assessment, as found in their discussion about their rating discrepancies. See Transcript 3 for illustration. T refers to the tester, and E the examinee.

Transcript 3 (by investigator)
[Examinee 11 ASR; female, Chinese; score: NS 3, NNS 4]

1   T: This town really has a l- lot of good entertainment here.
2   E: uh:m. I don't like bars? (0.2) so,
3   T: oh you don't like bars.
4   E: and I seldom (0.2) uh watch a movie here because I like a Chi-
5   a Chinese movie.

(p. 172)

In line 1, the tester delivers an assessment (there is a lot of good entertainment in the town), which was followed by the examinee's responses in lines 2, 4, and 5. The native speaker gave a score of three, saying that these responses do not directly address the assessment about the town: these are just a few examples of entertainment in the town. However, the non-native speaker rater gave a perfect score of four, because he attended to the segment before this assessment sequence. Prior to line 1, the examinee commented on the small size of the town and provided her assessment saying that the town is boring. Hence, the examinee's response to the tester's assessment (lines 2, 4, and 5) is indeed an elaboration of her own assessment of the town in the preceding discourse by providing examples of entertainment available in the town (e.g., bars, movies). As shown here, when the examinee's assessment is analyzed in conjunction with what went on in the previous discourse, her response is appropriate, deserving a full score of four. These analyses reinforce that the single assessment response should not be the focus of analysis; the response needs to be situated in a broader exchange because it is contingent upon preceding turns.

In summary, the CAIT successfully demonstrated that pragmatic prompts embedded in the context of a loosely directed role play could simulate a naturalistic conversation, eliciting multiple turns and adjacency pairs. The CAIT is different from other methods that use focused elicitation of a pragmatic target in a tightly controlled environment. While benefits are notable, the CAIT also presents several challenges in terms of practicality. Each role play took 10 to 15 minutes to administer. Transcription and rating of pragmatic prompts took an additional 15 to 20 minutes. A total time of 25 to 35 minutes per participant to assess only three pragmatic responses may not be feasible in a large-scale assessment setting. In addition, although the three pragmatic prompts used in this study (assessment, compliment, and pre-sequence) might be delivered relatively easily during a conversation, it is questionable whether other prompts such as complaints, apologies, and promises can be implemented naturally with similar ease. Finally, to ensure comparability of data across participants and test situations, the delivery of the first-pair part (prompt) needs to be consistent across examinees. However, this consistency in turn could undermine the principle of CA, which intends to reveal how interlocutors orient to each other's utterance and mutually construct meaning. Because a pragmatic act is considered to "emerge" naturally through sequences of talk, contingent upon preceding discourse, consistency in the delivery of a prompt on the tester's part may work to artificially constrain these sequences.

> **Points to remember**
>
> - CA-informed testing (CAIT) is a powerful tool for assessing pragmatic competence, as pragmatic prompts embedded in the context of a loosely directed role play could simulate a naturalistic conversation, eliciting multiple turns and adjacency pairs.
> - Some drawbacks of CAIT (Walters, 2007) include the extensive time it takes to analyze a small number of pragmatic responses, the difficulty of naturally eliciting prompts such as complaints, apologies, and promises, and the difficulty of ensuring comparability of data across participants and test situations.

Applied Conversation Analysis for Analyzing Open Role-play Data

More recently, Al-Gahtani and Roever's (2012) study used "applied CA" as opposed to "pure CA" to analyze open role-play data and make inferences of L2 pragmatic development. "Pure CA" refers to traditional CA in which recordings of naturally occurring conversations are analyzed to uncover the tacit organizational principles that participants follow in co-constructing actions turn-by-turn (Atkinson & Heritage, 1984; Jacoby & Ochs, 1995; Schegloff & Sacks, 1973). According to Al-Gahtani and Roever, their study is in line with "applied CA" (ten Have, 2007), which takes the setting and participants into consideration to reveal how interactions differ across contexts, and does not require that the conversations be strictly "naturally-occurring." The authors investigated how 26 Saudi ESL learners co-produced request sequences with their interlocutor in English. There were three request situations (e.g., asking a housemate to buy bread, asking a professor for lecture notes). ESL learners role played each situation with a native Saudi interlocutor in English. During role play, the interlocutor was told not to accept hints as requests or make offers so learners can actually produce valid requests for analysis.

> • "Applied CA" as opposed to "pure CA" can be used to analyze open role-play data and make inferences of L2 pragmatic development (Al-Gahtani & Roever, 2012). Unlike pure CA, applied CA does not require that conversations be naturally occurring to constitute a unit of analysis.

Points to remember

This study documented sequential organizations of requests across four proficiency levels of learners. The authors found that upper-level learners frequently produced pre-expansions, namely sequences preceding the request such as greetings (e.g., "How are you?") and "preliminaries to preliminaries" (e.g., "Can you do me a favor?") (Schegloff, 2007). However, lower-level learners rarely used pre-expansions.

> • Pre-expansions refer to sequences preceding a request, such as greetings (e.g., "How are you?") and "preliminaries to preliminaries" (e.g., "Can you do me a favor?") (Schegloff, 2007). Based on Al-Gahtani and Roever's findings, these could be rarely used by low-level learners but produced very frequently by upper-level learners.

Points to remember

The excerpts below illustrate the contrast between low-level and upper-level learners in role-play data. In Excerpt 1, the beginning-level participant (P) produces a greeting in line 1, but then he proceeds to the request in line 3 without any pre-expansion for his interlocutor (I).

Excerpt 1: Bread, Beginner
1. P: ↑Excuse me::
2. I: yes
3. P: I (.) want bread
4. I: Ok
5. P: Yea::h
6. I: So:: you want bread?
7. P: Yes:: (.) it is enough in the ( )
8. I: .hhh (.) >you mean< there is nothing: in the fridge?
9. P: Yes

10. I: So: (.) you <u>wa</u>::nt me to go:: to the superma::rket and get some bread for <u>you</u>.

11. P: <u>Y</u>es

12. I: Ok (.) I'll go ↑now and get it for <u>you</u>

(Al-Ghatani & Roever, 2012, p. 50)

In sharp contrast, Excerpt 3 from an upper-intermediate participant involves a greeting sequence (lines 1–2), followed by the participant's pre-expansion in line 3 ("I wanna ask you something?") in order to prepare the interlocutor for the upcoming request. Following this, the participant provides another pre-expansion, a reason for his request.

Excerpt 3: Bread, Upper intermediate

1. P: hi ((name))
2. I: hi ((name))
3. P: .hhh >actually< I wanna ask <u>you</u> something?
4. I: <u>Su</u>::re.
5. P: → .hhh today I have <u>too</u> <u>many</u> (.) assignments to do=
6. I: =Yeah
7. P: → ↑so I have <u>no</u>:: more time (.1) to do <u>my</u> shopp[ing
8. I: [.hh
9. P: → for today (.) a::nd I'm running out (.) the <u>bread</u> so <u>could</u> you (.3) buy
10. some <u>bread</u> for me?
11. I: su::re (.) yeah (.) but >you know< right now I'm <u>wa</u>:tching this match so (.)
12. do you <u>wa</u>::nt it at the moment (.) or:: I can <u>buy</u> it later on?

(Al-Gahtani & Roever, 2012, pp. 51–52)

Some people may equate the pre-expansion with the supportive move of "preparator" in traditional DCT-based speech act studies (e.g., Blum-Kulka, House, & Kasper, 1989a). However, the difference is that the CA-based analysis focuses on the location of the pre-expansion in a sequential organization, rather than the presence or absence of the pre-expansion. As Al-Gahtani and Roever explain, in Excerpt 3, the learner produces the pre-expansion to check the interlocutor's availability for the request. In the following turn (line 4), the interlocutor provides a "go-ahead" cue ("Sure."). Acknowledging this, in the subsequent turns, the learner gives a reason for his request as another pre-expansion. The interlocutor's backchannels during his accounts (e.g., "Yeah") also function as "go-ahead" cues. Hence, the learner's pre-expansions occur in sequences along with the interlocutor's acknowledgment tokens. By attending to these cues coming from the interlocutor, the learner can interactively assess the likelihood of his request being accepted. Since the prospect is positive, the learner launches the request with a conventional form of "could you" in lines 9 to 10.

What these analyses reveal (which traditional utterance-level analyses cannot reveal) is the contingency of the learner's speech act. The request and various pre-expansions prior to the request are contingent upon the interlocutor's reactions and thus are embedded in the sequential organization of talk. Learners' ability to steer interaction by using these conversational moves is a reflection of their ability to construct a speech act collaboratively with their interlocutor. This ability was less prominent among lower proficiency learners, because they often produced the request upfront and relied on the interlocutor to elaborate on the reasons (see Excerpt 1). Hence, the interlocutor took the initiative in interaction in the lower proficiency group.

This study clearly shows strengths of open role play and CA for examining pragmatics in interaction. As illustrated above, open role plays can elicit extended discourse in which a speech act is co-constructed among participants through turns. CA is fitting for analyzing open role-play data because the method provides specific structures of a conversation as analytical focus (e.g., adjacency pairs, pre-expansions, and repair). These structures are useful in revealing how a pragmatic act is situated in a larger discourse and is contingent upon preceding turns. The CA-derived concept of sequential organization also helps us understand the importance of analyzing the interlocutor's contributions, which is often neglected in traditional speech act analyses. As Al-Gahtani and Roever contend, by incorporating the interlocutor's role into analysis, we can examine "how learners' proficiency-dependent deployment of interactive resources affected the interlocutor and thereby the overall structure of the talk" (2012, p. 60). This type of analysis offers new insight into proficiency effect on L2 pragmatics – how proficiency affects sequential organization of interaction.

Although the methodological advancement in this study is notable, we should also be mindful about the authors' point that this study used "applied CA," not "pure CA" (Al-Gahtani & Roever, 2012, p. 46), to reveal how interactions differ across contexts (ten Have, 2007). Because the study used data elicited from role

FIGURE 7.1 Sun skeptical of applied CA

play, the method is not compatible with "pure CA" (and would attract the attitude suggested in Figure 7.1 from a purist!). The authors claim that the study used CA to describe how learners of different proficiency levels perform request sequences differently by using linguistic and interactional resources available to them. Hence, this study pursued a "compromise" position (p. 46) and applied conversation analytic methods to unveil principles underlying in L2 role-play interaction.

In terms of practicality and feasibility, open role plays function well for assessment purposes because they provide a certain degree of control and standardization. Researchers can pre-determine target pragmatic features and manipulate contextual variables in situational scenarios. This standardization enables researchers to collect data systematically from different populations on a variable of interest (e.g., general proficiency, learning environment, and L1 background), and compare data across participant groups and time points. In Al-Gahtani and Roever's (2012) study, specific conversational structures that participants used to co-construct a request (e.g., pre-expansions) were able to distinguish proficiency levels in a reliable manner. Although their study did not use any assessment rubrics, these structures could be incorporated into rating descriptors so they serve as criteria for assessing pragmatic development.

Interaction-sensitive, Conversation Analysis-driven Rating Criteria for Assessing Open Role-play Data

Youn (2015) developed such CA-heuristic rating scales to assess ESL learners' role-play performances. See Box 7.2 for the summary of the study. This study employed the sequential mixed methods approach (Tashakkori & Teddlie, 2003). For the qualitative analysis, a subset of learners' role-play performances were analyzed using CA to identify linguistic and interactional resources used to accomplish a pragmatic act (e.g., request, agreement) collaboratively with their interlocutor. Then, in the quantitative part, those features were incorporated into rating rubrics to assess ESL learners' role-play performances.

The interaction-sensitive, data-driven rating criteria involved five aspects that successfully distinguished across proficiency levels: (1) contents delivery; (2) language use; (3) sensitivity to situation; (4) engaging in interaction; and (5) turn organization. The category of "language use" assessed pragmalinguistic aspects of speech acts, while sociopragmatic aspects were observed in the category of "sensitivity to situation," as indicated in participants' acknowledgment of situational factors. The "contents delivery" category addressed participants' turn-taking ability (e.g., delays and false starts). The "turn organization" category, on the other hand, addressed the ability to implement normative turn structures (e.g., adjacency pairs and preference organizations). The "engaging with interaction" category measured participants' ability to establish a shared understanding with the interlocutor. Use of acknowledgment tokens and discourse markers, as well as the delivery of sequentially relevant turn, were featured in this category. See the sample rating scale for the category of "engaging with interaction."

Score

3   A next turn shows understandings of a previous turn throughout the interaction. Evidence of engaging with conversation exists (e.g., clarification questions, backchannel, acknowledgement tokens).

2   Some evidence of engaging with the conversation, but not consistent. A next turn sometimes doesn't show understandings of previous turns.

1   Noticeable absence of discourse markers. Evidence of not achieving a shared understanding.

(Youn, 2015, pp. 223–224)

Results (see Box 7.2) indicate that these five categories work in tandem to characterize learners' pragmatic performance. The CA-based analysis of role-play data was able to reveal concrete resources (both linguistic and interactional) that typify an interaction and how they occur as participants co-construct a pragmatic act. Those resources go beyond the traditional aspects of pragmalinguistics and sociopragmatics in the kinds of way we discussed in Chapter 6. They extend to interactional features of turn-taking and turn organization, interactional engagement, and discourse features such as response tokens and discourse markers used to achieve mutual understanding. Youn's study further reinforces the idea that a pragmatic act is a product of interaction. Knowledge of forms and understanding of contextual factors alone does not guarantee a successful pragmatic performance. Learners' ability to implement the knowledge in the unfolding course of interaction is critical for a successful communicative act. Because the study found that learners of different proficiency levels used these resources differently, these resources, once incorporated into rating rubrics, help discern levels of interactional pragmatics. Using these rubrics, researchers can gain insights about the nature and development of pragmatic competence in interaction.

Future research could follow this lead and examine a wider range of pragmatic constructs. Youn's study examined task-essential pragmatic acts encoded in the role-play scenarios (e.g., request, agreement/disagreement, refusal). This particular paper referred to participants' performances in a high-imposition request to illustrate the five categories of evaluation, but it is uncertain whether these categories apply universally to other pragmatic acts. The descriptors encoded in each rating band may exhibit different features depending on the type of communicative act under study. For instance, turn organization is different between a preferred and dispreferred act, as well as between different situations. Pre-expansions such as "preliminaries to preliminaries" (e.g., May I ask you a favor?) might feature a high-imposition request of asking a professor for a recommendation letter, but the structure is probably less common in a low-imposition request such as asking a friend for a pen, which is usually conveyed using a simple, formulaic expression. Hence, validation of rubrics across pragmatic targets and situations is necessary.

BOX 7.2 Youn, S. J. (2015). Validity argument for assessing L2 pragmatics in interaction using mixed methods. *Language Testing, 32,* 199–225.

Research questions: (1) To what extent do the open role plays ensure authenticity and standardization? (2) Do the data-driven rating criteria reflect the construct definition and stably assess L2 pragmatics in interaction? (3) Do raters reliably assess the role-play pragmatic performances using the data driven rating criteria?

Participants: One hundred and two adult ESL learners in US colleges and 12 raters (native speakers, bilinguals, and advanced-level speakers of English).

Instrument: Two open role plays were used. Performances were tape-recorded and evaluated on five aspects: contents delivery, language use, sensitivity to situation, engaging in interaction, and turn organization. These aspects emerged from CA-based analysis of select performances.

Data analysis: Rasch measurement with four facets (examinee, rater, role-play task, and rating criteria) was conducted to assess the functionality of the role-play task and rating criteria in assessing examinees' performances. The raters' severity in assessment was also analyzed.

Results: FACET analysis revealed that the open role plays reliably distinguished across 102 participants' abilities. The raters showed different levels of severity when assessing examinees' performances, but internal consistency reliability was acceptable. The situations involving an interaction with a professor were more difficult than those with a classmate. The "language use" category was the most difficult and the "engaging with interaction" category the least.

In conclusion, this section has surveyed open role play methods for eliciting extended discourse and CA-informed analysis for revealing the co-construction of a pragmatic act in role-play interactions. As we have noted throughout our discussion, open role play has both advantages and disadvantages. Open role play can elicit interactive discourse over a number of turns and still provides a certain degree of standardization and control, so researchers can compare data across L2 groups, time points, and replication studies. Although open role play can simulate a naturalistic conversation, data obtained is not completely natural, as no real-life consequences are involved in the outcome of interactions. Although authentic discourse is motivated by participants' goals, role-play interaction is motivated by the researcher's goals. Participants act out roles specified in scenarios without genuine communicative motivations. As such, role plays are often considered lacking in rich interactions and negotiations that are likely to be present in authentic communication.

Similarly, the use of CA has both strengths and limitations. CA provides methods to conduct a sequential analysis of extended discourse and thus provides a means to analyze data from an interaction focus. However, if the interaction is not authentic to begin with, it is questionable whether the tacit organizational principles of interaction revealed using CA are actual representations of principles in naturalistic data. To account for these challenges of open role plays, in the next section, we will describe methods for recording authentic and semi-authentic data for interactional analysis.

7.4 Authentic/Semi-authentic Data for Pragmatic Interaction

Elicited Conversation

An elicited conversation refers to "any conversation staged for the purpose of data collection" (Kasper & Rose, 2002, p. 84). Unlike DCTs or role plays, participants do not assume specific roles assigned by the researcher. Instead, they are instructed to engage in a conversation based on a topic or task assigned by the researcher. For instance, they might be instructed to have an informal conversation on routine topics to get to know each other (e.g., Taguchi, 2015a). They might be asked to have a discussion on controversial topics (e.g., Dippold, 2011; Salsbury & Bardovi-Harlig, 2000) or perform certain communicative tasks (e.g., Al-Gahtani & Roever, 2014a, 2014b; Nguyen, 2008). Elicited conversation is different from a naturalistic conversation because it is a conversation for research purposes. Hence, the researcher has a certain degree of control on the type of data to be collected (e.g., topic, setting). Elicited conversation is also different from interviews because all participants assume equal responsibility and participation in a conversation.

> **Points to remember**
> • Unlike DCTs and role plays, participants are not assigned specific roles in elicited conversations. Additionally, unlike interviews, participants in elicited conversations assume equal participation.

While Al-Gahtani and Roever's (2012) study discussed in the previous section used open role plays to examine request sequences in L2 English, more recent studies by these authors used an elicited conversation task to examine request sequences among L2 learners of Arabic (Al-Gahtani & Roever, 2014a, 2014b). The task was implemented at an institutional-level in an Arabic language program in Riyadh. Data was collected twice during a period of the semester to gain developmental insights. At the beginning of the semester, the researchers intentionally introduced a schedule conflict with one of the classes in the program. Students were encouraged to talk to the program administrator to request a schedule change. At the end of the semester, a similar schedule conflict was introduced but this time during final exams. Students were again informed that they could ask the administrator to change the final exam schedule. In both cases, students went to the administrator's office to make a request. The administrator was told that his interactions with the students were being recorded for evaluation purposes. However, the students were not informed about the recording, which added authenticity to their interactions. Data was tape-recorded and transcribed using CA conventions.

Combining a cross-sectional and longitudinal investigation, Al-Gahtani and Roever (2014b) revealed how learners at different proficiency levels managed a preference structure in request sequences and how their use of the structure changed over a five-month period. Data revealed that, as their proficiency increased, learners used more pre-expansions (e.g., providing explanations) to preface a dispreferred act of request. In contrast, low proficiency learners rarely used prefacing but instead moved straight to their request, which often led to repair initiated by the interlocutor. However, learners' ability to incorporate pre-expansions prior to requests improved over time. Excerpt 2 (p. 12) illustrates a beginning-level learner's request sequences at the end of the semester. The learner (BEG) first introduces himself (line 3) and presents a reason for his visit (lines 6 and 7). After the interlocutor's go-ahead cue in line 8 ("yes"), the learner launches his request in line 9 with a "want" statement. Here, the learner demonstrates a typical preference structure of a request: he delayed his request by using preliminary moves.

1. BEG: *as-salaam-u 'alaykum.*
    peace upon you
    "Peace be upon you (hello)"

2. ADM: *wa: 'alaykum-u as-salaam*
    and upon you peace
    "Peace be upon you, too (hello)"

3. BEG: *ána (0.3)* ↑*a:lib fii al-mustawa (.) al-áw-wal*
    I (0.3) student in the level (.) one
    "I'm (0.3) a student in level (.) one"

4. ADM: *áhlan*
    welcome
    "Welcome"

5. (0.4)

6. BEG: *ána:: (.) ána jét-u élayk-a (0.2) bi-xušuuš,*
    I (.) I came to you (0.2) regarding
    "I (.) came to you (0.2) regarding
    émtiħaa:n (0,2) al-qawaa'id. wa al-qiraaáh=
    exam (0.2) Grammar and Reading
    the Grammar and Reading (0.2) exams"

7. ADM: *=na'am*
    yes
    "Yes"

8. BEG: *nuriid-u fii kul-i yawm (.) maadah* ↑*waaħidah*
    We want in each day (.) subject one
    "We want one subject in each day"

9. ADM: *tayyb (.) ma: ésmuk?*
    Okay (.) what your name
    "Okay (.) what's your name?"

Other studies have used the elicited conversation method in a range of formats to collect interaction data. Dippold (2011) examined L2 German learners' disagreement sequences. She developed a task instruction card containing a discussion question about a specific problem (e.g., binge drinking) and four options to address the problem. Participants were asked to rank order the options and discuss their ranking with their partner. Using CA, the author identified linguistic and interactional resources that the learners drew on to mitigate their disagreements and co-construct politeness with their interlocutor. For instance, advanced-level learners expanded the disagreement sequence by relating their turn to the interlocutor's preceding turn. They also produced partial agreement to the interlocutor's turn as a preface to disagreement. A similar rank order task was used in Flores-Ferrán and Lovejoy's (2015) study to elicit academic discussions among L2 Spanish learners. Salsbury and Bardovi-Harlig's (2000) study also used a peer discussion task to examine the nature of oppositional talk. Taguchi (2015a) used a three-way conversation task involving two L2 Japanese learners and the native speaker researcher conversing on routine topics. Data was analyzed for the instances of style shifting between the polite and plain form as a way of signaling discourse boundaries. Several learners showed sensitivity to changing participant membership, shifting from the plain form when conversing with their peer to the polite form when conversing with the researcher.

As illustrated above, elicited conversation tasks are useful in gathering data of extended discourse. Elicited conversations can reveal discourse-level features such as conversational organization and management, co-construction of a communicative act, conversation moves, and narrative structures. Because conversation data is "elicited" using specific task instructions, researchers can collect a sizable pool of interactions in one setting with relative ease. However, elicited conversations have a limitation because they do not allow researchers to manipulate participants' roles and settings as role plays do. Therefore, they may not be feasible for examining how contextual factors affect a communicative act during a conversation. As a result, the sorts of pragmatic acts that can be investigated using elicited conversation are limited.

Points to remember

- Elicited conversations are useful for gathering extended discourse, but they may not be the best choice for looking at how contextual factors affect communicative acts.

Confederate Scripting

Conversation partners may not always be who they seem to be. A technique called confederate scripting utilizes a conversation partner who, unbeknownst to the study participant, is actually a confederate or accomplice of the researcher, brought into the conversation with the purpose of controlling or staging the dialogue of their side of the conversation. Participants might be told they are interacting with a computer when in fact they are speaking with a live person, or they may be told they are having a natural, spontaneous conversation with another language learner, who is actually responding with pre-determined utterances. Confederate scripting may come in many forms and be used for a variety of purposes in eliciting conversation data that is not completely naturalistic data.

> **Points to remember**
> - Confederate scripting is a conversational data elicitation technique in which the participant of the study unknowingly interacts with an accomplice – confederate – of the researcher.

Confederate scripting has been utilized in the social psychology field for many years where a confederate's scripted or prescribed behavior is controlled to trigger a response in the study participant. While much can be gained from observing language data as it occurs in natural conversation (see the following section), uncontrolled dialogue often contains too wide an array of linguistic variation to effectively target the variable of interest. For example, researchers might be interested in learners' use of apology speech acts in their day-to-day interactions only to find that the participants hardly ever utilize the speech act in any of their recorded conversations. Recorded conversations do not allow for online probing for speaker intentions. For this reason, researchers utilize tasks in controlled situations to elicit specific data, sometimes using the strategies discussed in this chapter (role plays, etc.).

> **Points to remember**
> - Confederate scripting can be used in situations where targeted data is to be elicited in natural conversation.
> - Confederate scripting can assist researchers in collecting data more efficiently, help increase the frequency of relatively rare forms while reducing unnecessary forms, and increasing validity concerns for subsequent statistical testing.

In studies where conversations need to be held consistent across subjects or other variables, utilizing a confederate conversation partner may be the only way to achieve validity. The behaviors of the confederate can then be treated as a constant variable, much like pre-/post-testing instruments. Conversations with too much variation might inhibit subsequent statistical analyses in quantitative studies. Confederate behaviors can range from carefully scripted or spontaneous behavior depending on the nature of the experiment and research questions.

Kuhlen and Brennan (2013) describe a variety of ways in which confederates might be employed in conversational data collection. The confederate might be simply motivational in nature, present in the conversation to create the social context of a dialogue. In this role, the confederate is passive, and in extreme situations, simply a prop for the participant to speak with. On the other hand, the confederate could take the role of collaborative conversation partner. In this context, the confederate takes a more traditional conversation partner role while keeping the subject on a pre-defined conversational trajectory. In the collaborative conversation partner role, the confederate can adapt to the needs of the conversation and respond to the participant as necessary to keep the conversation moving. In contrast, the confederate could also be an egocentric partner that does converse but does not adapt to the perspectives or requests of the participant in conversation. The confederate might interrupt the participant to continue with planned utterances. The final role of the confederate might be to respond in a particular way to the participants' utterances through interactive alignment. For example, to test priming effects, the confederate might repeat certain structures along with the participant to see if the participant will begin to utilize those structures with more fluency.

As with most elicitation tools, confederate scripting involves limitations and drawbacks that should be taken into consideration when choosing this technique for a pragmatic study (Box 7.3). Concerns such as what to do if a participant becomes aware or suspecting of the confederate, or if a participant refuses to adjust the conversation to remain in line with the confederate, need to be addressed prior to conducting any study of pragmatic production or comprehension. For example, a researcher may decide to ask participants upon the conclusion of the study if they knew the purpose of the procedure and discard data from those who correctly identify their conversation partner as a confederate. A classic concern about the use of confederates in language studies is if the confederate becomes biased over the course of the study (Rosenthal, 1966). To avoid this, Kuhlen and Brennan (2013) suggest confederates also be kept blind to the study design and naive about the purposes of the study.

Points to remember

- When using confederate scripting in a study, confederates should be kept naive to the study design and purposes of the study to avoid unintentionally biasing the data collection.

BOX 7.3   Example of Confederate Scripting in a Language Study

McDonough, K., & Mackey, A. (2008). Syntactic priming and ESL question development. *Studies in Second Language Acquisition, 30,* **31–47.**

The researchers of this study utilized confederates to understand how a speaker's tendency to produce a previously spoken or heard structure (syntactic priming) occurred during interaction.

Research questions: Is there a relationship between syntactic priming and ESL question development?

Participants and data: Over two experiments, 46 intermediate-level Thai learners of English completed multiple communicative tasks with a confederate. The learners were told the confederate was a student at the same university who was participating in a class project. The confederate was told to speak first so that the learners can hear developmentally more advanced questions before they form any questions.

Data analysis: The researchers classified the participants' questions into the developmental sequence for ESL question formation. An independent rater coded a subset of the data.

Results: Results showed that L2 learners who evidenced high levels of syntactic priming tended to move to a developmentally higher question formation stage. This study has implications for teaching question structures to L2 learners through the use of priming techniques.

Another issue is confederates who let on that they know more about the research than they should (who Kuhlen and Brennan term "know-it all confederates"). If the confederates create a mismatch in expectations between their current role in the conversation or task and their behavior (perhaps from repeated exposure to the task or conversation), they might influence the participants in ways unintended for the purposes of the study. Confederates should be explicitly and carefully trained prior to data collection to avoid these pitfalls. In the case of scripted confederates who must remember the exact wording they are to use during the conversation, their delivery might seem unnatural and violate pragmatic principles alerting the participant that the conversation is not natural. If scripting is being used in a study, the script could be made to include naturally occurring language such as deliberate errors, pauses, or repairs.

Confederate scripting can be a useful way to elicit specific pragmatic features in dialogues without creating inauthentic scenarios or roles for participants to play. Confederates can either follow a detailed script for the conversation or act as more natural conversation partners that only subtly shape the conversation. Care should be used in employing confederates so that they do not unintentionally bias the data and so that study participants are kept unaware that they are in fact interacting with a researcher.

Naturalistic Conversation

In Chapter 3, we reviewed various methods for collecting naturalistic data (i.e., audio/video-recording of naturalistic language use, diaries, and field notes). We discussed these methods in light of pragmatic production by illustrating how they enable researchers to collect discrete tokens of pragmatic features under study. The studies reviewed in Chapter 3 recorded and analyzed specific pragmalinguistic forms in context, but the analysis largely focused on the forms themselves and did not address the interactional features that contributed to the emergence of the forms. In other words, those studies did not observe how linguistic forms occur over conversational sequences and serve as resources for participants to jointly construct a communicative act. In this section, we will turn to the studies that precisely addressed these neglected aspects of interaction in naturalistic data.

A number of studies have recorded and analyzed naturalistic conversations to reveal instances of L2 humor (e.g., Bell, 2005, 2007, 2011; Bell & Attardo, 2010; Shively, 2013). The ability to produce and comprehend humor is part of advanced pragmatic competence because humor draws on linguistic knowledge (see Figure 7.2), as well as culture-specific knowledge, genres, and creative language use. At the same time, this ability is part of interactional competence because humor takes place in a social interaction. Humorous exchanges are grounded in participants' mutual understandings and shared perspectives during interaction. Hence, L2 humor can be best examined in an extended, naturalistic interaction in which participants orient themselves toward the mutual goal of meaning co-construction.

Naturalistic, interactional data is critical for the investigation of humor because the hearer's reaction has to be part of the analysis in order to determine whether humor is successful or failed. Attempted humor gains legitimacy as humor when the listener recognizes the speaker's intended meaning and his/her communicative goal of being amusing and entertaining. In addition, interaction data is critical because humor is often co-constructed among participants. This means that comprehension of humor is not a solely individual, internal process; participants' understanding and appreciation of humor are situated in context and jointly constructed.

This interactive, socially situated view of humor has been adopted in Bell's (2007) analysis of interactive construction of humor. The author highlighted cases of two international students in a US university who tape-recorded their

FIGURE 7.2   Comic moment in the mind of a learner of L2 Spanish

interactions with native English speakers over a period of one to two years. In the excerpt below, one of the international students, Pum, is conversing with her boyfriend, Jake. In lines 1 to 12, Jake tells Pum how he tricked his nephew into eating fried calamari by telling him that it was an onion ring. Pum contributes to this story telling by adding laugher. From line 17 to the end, this amusing illustration of Jake's nephew eating calamari is co-constructed by Jake and Pum. In line 20, Pum collaborates in the telling by providing a continuation of Jake's narrative ("you eat that"). Overlapping with Pum's utterance, in line 20, Jake confirms that his nephew actually ate the calamari. He uses humorous revoicing (Pomerantz & Bell, 2011) by repeating his nephew's speech ("oh no, it's a squid!").

1	Jake:	We tricked my nephew on (3)
2		on Saturday
3		my little nephew
4	Pum:	mm-hm
5	Jake:	we had calamari (. . .)
6		it looks like onion rings
7		so we told him we said
8		(("eat this
9		it's an onion riHHng!"))

10	Pum:	heh uhuh
11	Jake:	said "oh no!
12		you ate a squid!"
13	Pum:	eheh
14		how old is she?
15	Jake:	I think he's uh
16		he's eight
17		(5) I said
18		"eat this it's a onion ring"
19		hhhuh huh
20	Pum:	and you eat [thaHHt
21	Jake:	[and he ate it
22		and he ate it
23		it's like
24		"oh no it's a squid!"
25	Pum:	(27) it's cold!

(Bell, 2007, pp. 378–379)

This excerpt illustrates how humor is interactively constructed among participants. Bell also interprets this excerpt from the perspective of humor appreciation. Although Pum recognized and understood the joke, she did not seem to have appreciated it completely, as seen in her minimum laugher and topic shift (in line 14, when she asked about the nephew's age). These analyses reiterate that humor is situated in a social context and negotiated in discourse. Naturalistic data is requisite to revealing this socially constructed nature of humor.

Naturalistic interaction was also analyzed in Shively's (2013) study, which examined humor by an L2 Spanish learner in a study abroad program. She analyzed audio-recordings of naturalistic conversations between the learner and his host family members and friend. Instances of humor were coded as either successful or failed. Successful humor occurred when the hearer perceived the humor to be funny by laughing or supporting the humor, whereas failed humor was identified when the humor was not perceived by the hearer to be amusing. Among various other categories, the author coded humorous utterances for functions (e.g., amusement, bonding, and identity display), as well as for contextualization cues such as laughter and intonation. These coding categories reinforce the argument that interaction data is indispensable for the analysis of humor. Interaction data can reveal whether humor is accepted by the hearer; what interpersonal functions that humor serves; and how humor is contextualized in discourse.

A major strength of natural discourse is that it offers authentic data, which is not attenuated by researchers or research purposes. On the other hand, it is difficult to systematically incorporate variables of interest (e.g., situational factors in interaction, individual learners' characteristics, learning environments) or control the amount of data to collect.

> **Points to remember**
> - Naturalistic data is authentic and enables researchers to examine constructs such as L2 humor.

Computer-mediated Communication

Although the studies described above analyzed audio-recorded face-to-face conversations, more recent studies have used digital technology as a tool to record and analyze interaction data. Particularly notable in this trend is the increasing number of studies collecting data in computer-mediated communication (CMC) through venues such as social networking, online gaming, blogging, and video conferencing. CMC has proliferated as a promising tool for data collection since the 1990s. More recently, CMC has advanced to a new level by Web 2.0 applications (Thomas & Peterson, 2014). According to Levy and Stockwell (2006), CMC tools, unlike stand-alone software programs, can facilitate interaction using the language produced by the users themselves, rather than the language provided by the computer. The primary advantage of CMC tools is that researchers can examine learners' naturalistic communication across physical distance with other users of the target language. CMC tools also allow researchers to collect data from multiple angles including text, sound, and visual sources. The process of data recording is also relatively automatic and uncomplicated. In the case of text-based CMC, researchers do not have to transcribe data.

> **Points to remember**
> - CMC allows researchers to easily collect data from different angles and does not require transcription.

Taking advantage of these features, a growing number of studies have analyzed synchronous and asynchronous CMC for pragmatic interaction. Belz and Kinginger's (2003) study is one of the early studies in this trend. They analyzed L2 German learners' development in the use of address forms through rich descriptions of asynchronous dyads between learners and their native speaker peers via emails and chat. They found that modeling and explicit feedback on

German address forms coming from peers were salient characteristics of CMC that promoted learners' noticing of the forms. More recently, the study of Gonzales (2013) examined how *Livemocha*, a social networking site for language learners, serves as space for pragmatic interaction by documenting a Spanish learner's use of politeness strategies in conversation closings. Kim and Brown's (2014) study examined the use of Korean address terms and honorifics. Learners of Korean interacted with multiple Korean speakers via email, Skype, and Kakao Talk over a three-month period. Interaction data revealed the situated use of the address forms and how it helped learners to establish personal relationships with Korean speakers. Tsai and Kinginger (2015) analyzed advice giving and receiving sequences occurring in CMC-based peer review sessions. They showed that the asymmetrical relationship between the advice giver and receiver was compromised through the use of various face-saving strategies and co-construction of politeness (see Box 7.4).

BOX 7.4 Tsai, M-H., & Kinginger, C. (2015). Giving and receiving advice in computer-mediated peer response activities. *CALICO, 32,* 82–112.

Research questions: How did advice givers and recipients manage the asymmetrical participant roles inherent in L2 peer response?

Participants and data: Participants were 14 students in a university-level ESL writing class.

Data were 21 online transcripts of students' peer review sessions collected in the writing class. Students worked in dyads. They read their peers' essays and provided comments online.

Data analysis: Data was analyzed for the instances in which advice recipients and advice givers managed power asymmetry (i.e., advice recipients requesting for advice and advice givers providing advice). Using CA, three focal episodes were analyzed turn-by-turn at a micro-level.

Results: Analysis revealed how the advice giver and recipient oriented to their roles, and at the same time tried to sustain rapport and interpersonal relationships by using face-saving strategies (e.g., complimenting, hedging). Politeness and face-saving were mutually constructed between the advice giver and receiver. For instance, an advice seeker asked for advice, but an advice giver avoided offering negative evaluations and instead opted for complimenting.

While CMC has been proven to be a useful venue to collect authentic interaction data, CMC has also expanded the option of analytical framework for interactional pragmatics. Rather than limiting analysis to textual features and conversational sequences, recent studies have incorporated CMC-specific features as analytical foci. González-Lloret (2016) is one such study that analyzed the use of emoticons. This study collected text-based synchronous CMC data between L2 Spanish learners and expert Spanish speakers via Yahoo Messenger and WhatsApp. There were numerous instances where participants co-constructed emotion using a range of linguistic and typographical resources such as emoticons, laughter, and elongated words.

See the excerpt below between a learner of Spanish (Kid) and a native Spanish speaker (Reme). In lines 144 and 145, Kid expresses his desire ("I want to go with you") and produces a sad emoticon. Reme responds to it by telling Kid to come to her place, but they both know that this is not possible because they live too far apart. Kid responds in line 147 by changing his sad face to a crying face in order to upgrade his emotional stance. However, Reme does not accept this emoticon as Kid's display of sadness. Instead, she attends to the playfulness of Kid's expression and responds with á token of laughter. Following this, she promises that she will drink for Kid. Kid accepts Reme's promise as a solution to his sadness by changing his sad emoticon to a happy face and using the exclamation mark (ok!) in line 150.

144. Kid (11:25:07 AM):   *quiero ir contigo*
"I want to go with you"

145. Kid (11:25:13 AM):

146. Reme (11:25:13 AM):   *pues ven!!*
"then come!!"

147. Kid (11:25:17 AM):

148.   Reme (11:25:20 AM):   *jajaja*
"hahaha"

149.   Reme (11:25:35 AM):   *no te preocupes, yo me*
tomare una copa a vuestra
salud!!
"don't worry, I will have a
drink to your health!!"

150.   Kid (11:25:40 AM):   *ok!* 😊
"ok!"

This excerpt reveals how this learner capably displays his changing emotion turn-by-turn by deploying multiple emoticons. The learner uses these emoticons in order to respond to his interlocutor's reaction, indicating that emotions are social constructs; they are negotiated and co-constructed sequentially among participants during the course of interaction. Multiple elements are at work collectively regarding the display of emotion.

As illustrated above, CMC has established itself as a useful context for the analysis of pragmatics in interaction. CMC technologies have generated places for context-embedded, socially consequential interaction to occur. Like in face-to-face communication, an extended, naturalistic discourse occurring in CMC helps direct researchers' attention to turn-taking and sequential organization of talk in their pragmatic analyses. As previous studies have indicated, various pragmatic features examined in CMC, for example, speech act strategies, address terms, honorifics, conversation closings, and expressions of emotions, are situated within broader analytical lenses of discursive pragmatics and interactional pragmatics, in which a pragmatic act is negotiated over turns and jointly accomplished among participants.

Features of CMC are considered similar to those characterizing face-to-face communication. Communication strategies such as clarification requests, confirmation checks, and topic management are ubiquitous in both CMC and face-to-face interaction (e.g., Smith, 2004). Sotillo (2000) also found that, similar to face-to-face communication, synchronous communication involves features of fluency and functional language use. Payne and Whitney (2002) also show that the synchronous online chat offers many opportunities for negotiation of meaning, which is a feature of naturalistic interaction.

However, CMC also exhibits unique features in terms of the format of participants' contributions and turn-taking. For instance, because of the lack of visual and auditory cues in a text-based chat, participants often use unique graphical representations of expressions (e.g., emoticons), as well as unconventional orthography for expressing prosody (e.g., repetitions of a letter such as "I'm sooooooo happy"). Furthermore, turn-taking in CMC usually involves a greater number of overlaps than face-to-face conversations because multiple parallel threads come in simultaneously (Smith, 2004). These overlaps may disrupt the sequential organization in CMC, but, in turn, they encourage researchers to analyze adjacency pairs in a larger stretch of discourse. Instead of strictly focusing on adjacency pairs, researchers may have to look at how individual turns are virtually related to other turns during interaction. Similarly, turn transition relevance places (TRP) (Sacks, Schegloff, & Jefferson, 1974) may require a different analytical focus, because in CMC, participants may not be monitoring TRP through verbal and non-verbal cues (Schönfeldt & Golato, 2003). Instead, each message posting can be regarded as a turn. In short, a face-to-face conversation and a CMC-based conversation are both suitable for analyzing the sequential, interactive nature of a pragmatic act, but they require different analytical frameworks and procedures depending on the type of interaction.

Corpus Approaches

While many approaches to studying pragmatic development offer windows, or snap-shots, of conversations or interactions, less have closely followed learner development longitudinally. One methodology that has fruitfully examined learner productions over time is learner corpus approaches. Learner corpora have been utilized in the field of applied linguistics for decades (see Nesselhauf, 2004) to examine the development of specific features in language learners by collecting a wide range of utterances and compiling them in a searchable, electronic database. Data collected for a learner corpus can take a variety of forms from naturalistically occurring data (e.g. the Louvain International Database of Spoken English Interlanguage, LINDSEI) to structured classroom interactions (University of Savoie's PAROLE corpus). Corpora of language learners can range from natural conversations, monologues, task-based interactions, and narrative story-telling. The type of corpus to utilize or develop depends on the research questions that are under investigation.

> Points to remember
> • Learner corpora are collections of learner utterances, either spoken or written, that are compiled into a searchable electronic database.

Learner corpora have been utilized to describe and investigate the development of L2 pragmatic competence in a small number of previous studies (Belz & Vyatkina, 2005, 2008; Polat, 2011; Vyatkina & Belz, 2006). Corpora of interactions or spoken language are much more difficult and time consuming to create due to the hours of manual transcription necessary. Furthermore, as previous sections and chapters have described, particular pragmatic features can be difficult to examine without specific elicitation, as they might be too rare in the data collection. These reasons, along with others, may account for the dearth of studies of pragmatic development utilizing corpus techniques available in the applied linguistics literature to date.

In one study, Vyatkina and Belz (2006) utilized a bilingual learner corpus "The Telecollaborative Learner corpus of English and German (TELEKORP)" to investigate the acquisition of German modal particles as English L1 speakers interacted telecollaboratively with German L1 speakers over a six-year period. The English L1 students were US university students, while their German L1 peers were enrolled in an English teacher education program in Germany. The learners chatted with each other online as part of their course work at their respective universities. The learners also received interventions on the target forms as part of the coursework. The researchers counted the number of modal particles used by both the NSs and the learners pre- and post-instruction, as well as how accurately the particles were used. Results indicated that learners produced modal particles patterning similarly to those they encountered throughout their interactions with their NS peers. This is an example of a corpus that utilized CMC text data as its basis rather than spoken data. In another study, Polat (2011) utilized oral data to investigate the acquisition of discourse markers in a learner corpus (see Box 7.5).

Learner corpora offer a window in the longitudinal development of language that is difficult to effectively examine without the use of a searchable corpus. Statistical analyses can be utilized to examine what areas are most problematic for learners at what stages of their pragmatic development. Learner corpora may also help to shed light on the developmental sequences that may or may not occur in L2 pragmatics.

In summary, this section has described elicited and naturalistic conversation as sources of data for L2 pragmatic interactions. Naturalistic data does not allow a systematic comparison because researchers cannot easily control variables (e.g., participant background and context of learning). In addition, researchers cannot control situational variables such as setting, interlocutors' relationships, content of talk, and goals of interaction. Since a pragmatic act is sensitive to those contextual features, without controlling the variables, systematic comparison of learners' pragmatic performances becomes challenging.

7.5 Conclusions

The field of L2 pragmatics in SLA research has benefited from the use of a wide array of innovative methodological techniques. From role plays to confederate

BOX 7.5   Polat, B. (2011). Investigating acquisition of discourse markers through a developmental learner corpus. *Journal of Pragmatics, 43,* 3745–3756.

Research aim: This study utilizes a learner corpus to investigate the development of three discourse markers (*you know, like,* and *well*) in an adult language learner over the course of one year.

Participants and data: The study employed a case study design with one participant. The focal participant was an L1 Turkish speaker and a recent immigrant to the US. Data was collected from the participant every two weeks for one year and took the form of recordings of informal conversations with the researcher. The 24 conversations resulted in a corpus of 104,041 words.

Data analysis: The corpus was analyzed to isolate the focal discourse markers "you know," "like," and "well," and each instance was coded for pragmatic appropriateness. A native speaker corpus (the Santa Barbara Corpus of Spoken American English) was utilized as a comparison corpus.

Results: The corpus data indicated that the participant overused the marker "you know" compared with native speakers but his use of "you know" decreased by 50% over the course of the year of data collection. The use of "like" increased from zero usage to 2,300 occurrences per 100,000 words by mid-year and then decreased again by the end of the year of data collection. The study demonstrates the usefulness of using a learner corpus as a tool for studying pragmatic acquisition by language learners.

scripting to corpus approaches, researchers interested in pragmatic development and acquisition have a wide selection at their disposal when choosing a methodology that will benefit their studies. However, despite the range of methods outlined in this chapter, the majority of studies in L2 pragmatics have used only a selection of methods including DCTs and questionnaires, and only thoroughly investigated a handful of speech acts such as requests. DCTs and questionnaires, for example, do not allow researchers to examine discourse-level factors shaping the structure of a communicative act. For example, Bardovi-Harlig's (2010) synthesis reviewed 152 studies published since the 1980s that examined pragmatic production. Among these studies, fewer than 30% used authentic language samples (e.g., institutional talk, classroom discourse). Only about 50% of these studies examined interaction, and the rest used written instruments or monologue tasks to examine features of spoken production. The number of studies that analyzed a two-way interaction based on conversational sequences and turn-taking was even smaller. Bardovi-Harlig (2010) points this out in her recommendation:

> In order to meet the explicitly stated goals of studying use, interaction, and effect of speakers' contributions on other speakers, samples of authentic and consequential language use should be collected whenever possible. Given the focus of pragmatics research, this should be the default design for studies of production. Authentic and consequential data best reveal language use and where two-way communication occurs, interaction and effect on participants as well.
>
> *(p. 242)*

This chapter illustrates how this recommendation can be followed up in L2 pragmatics so that researchers can address pragmatics in interaction. The field of L2 pragmatics will profit from researchers who utilize innovative techniques and a range of pragmatic targets to answer the important questions concerning pragmatic development and acquisition. Researchers should also employ mixed methods combining quantitative approaches to understanding pragmatic development with qualitative approaches such as rich conversation analyses and interview methods. By combining the methods outlined in the current chapter, researchers will be able to paint a fuller picture of the acquisition of L2 pragmatic features.

Discussion Questions

1. What are some of the benefits and drawbacks to utilizing more structured forms of pragmatic data collection such as role plays instead of naturalistic data? Find a study that utilized naturalistic data and ask yourself what more could have been examined if the data had been structured. Find a study of highly structured role play and ask what is lacking that would have been present in naturalistic interactions.
2. The chapter described some common forms of data collection that have been used in a variety of L2 pragmatics studies. What are some of the challenges of collecting data for pragmatic forms that are less problematic for phonology (sounds) or morphosyntax (structure)? Why do you think these common data collection techniques are among the most utilized in the field?
3. Confederate scripting can be a useful method for avoiding collecting data that does not include the pragmatic features under investigation. Design a protocol that you would use to train a confederate in a pragmatic study. Would you want the confederate to be highly scripted or more natural? Why? What are some potential benefits and drawbacks to a highly scripted confederate?
4. Analyzing CMC data offers some unique insights into language development that cannot be easily identified in face-to-face communication. How does CMC enable researchers to analyze turn-taking and pragmatics language use in interaction?

8

CONCLUSIONS

Initially, the methods involved in the study of L2 pragmatics emerged from the combination of questions prompted by theories and studies of second language acquisition (SLA) in the context of L1 pragmatics research. In this book, we have described how current L2 pragmatics research is expanding from its initial base, and drawing from a wider range of sources, ranging from education to psychology to computational, and cognitive. Concomitantly, elicitation methods and practices developed within L2 pragmatics research are now also helpfully filtering through to other areas, enriching general SLA research and beginning to inform theory construction.

In most theories of how second languages are learned, the development of pragmatic ability is part of the data the theory seeks to explain. Having said that, it is surprising that the focus of most of the theories and the empirical research they generate in the field of SLA has been primarily on L2 grammar until relatively recently. Pragmatic knowledge is obviously a key part of what it means to know and use a language well.

For L2 pragmatics researchers, there are various theoretical options that can be used to drive research and explain data. For example, Schmidt's noticing hypothesis focuses on the important role of attention in second language learning – notice it, and you might learn it. Likewise, the interaction approach highlights the role of corrective feedback and its role in focusing attention in the process of L2 development. Skill acquisition theories hold that repeated practice drives the consolidation of L2 knowledge. Collaborative dialogue and sociocultural theory consider verbalization a means for bringing about understanding of language and then learning. In the language socialization paradigm, L2 knowledge becomes consolidated through participation in routine social activities with more skilled interlocutors, while dynamic systems theory provides insightful information on the way cognitive, social, and environmental factors interact with each other and shape L2 development. These theories have a wide range of associated and sometimes overlapping data collection and analysis methodologies, ranging from a prompted response/production to a multimodal analysis of naturalistic interaction, and the field of L2 pragmatics is increasingly informed by many of them.

Aside from improving understandings of pragmatic theory that underpin L2 pragmatics, a key feature of this book is that we set out both to cure L2 pragmatics of its theoretical sclerosis as far as pragmatics is concerned, and to show the potential of pragmatic theories and phenomena that have been ignored or underplayed in L2 pragmatics. A case in point is the plethora of L2 pragmatic studies that have uncritically used the categorization of directness strategies devised by Shoshana Blum-Kulka and her colleagues for the analysis of requests. This categorization is neither consistent with Searle's original theory of indirectness (see Section 2.4), nor cognizant of the other issues that feed into indirectness and call for a different approach (see Sections 2.4 and 6.3). This is not to say that Blum-Kulka's approach is without value. However, L2 pragmatics research in this area to date includes results that are an artifact of decisions concerning the theoretical framework and thus are not easy to interpret, and at worst, are erroneously interpreted. There are also phenomena in the data that simply are not accounted for.

We have argued that communication is a dynamic process that involves constant collaboration and negotiation in order to reach mutual understanding among speakers of different languages and socio-cultural backgrounds. We focused on how speakers convey messages to hearers. We believe that the range of participants in communicative events, the ways in which they can participate, and the dynamic nature of those events, are broader than simple categories of speaker and hearer. For example, observers are neither speaker nor hearer, but they can still be parties to conversations and affect the nature of the input. We noted a bias in speech act theory toward focusing only on the speaker. This is important because it has impacted empirical research carried out in the field. Hearers have been underplayed or overlooked in pragmatics research. This is particularly important in L2 pragmatics, where listening as well as speaking is essential to our understanding of how a second language is learned. In this book, we have tried to redress this imbalance by focusing equally on speaker and hearer as interactants. We have pointed out that the focus in L2 pragmatics needs to be on both understanding and producing in terms of pragmatic knowledge, and the methods needed to reflect this joint emphasis.

We have interpreted what it means to learn L2 pragmatic knowledge as an understanding of sociopragmatics, concerned with the contextual features of pragmatics, and pragmalinguistics, that is concerned with the linguistic structure of pragmatics. These two types of knowledge together enable speakers to decide when to, and how to, use language appropriately and effectively in social contexts. A great deal of early L2 pragmatic research focused on speech acts and politeness. These are concerned with the function of individual utterances and how polite speech is compelled by a mutual goal to mitigate face threats. Previous research and meta-analyses in L2 pragmatics instruction have shown that explicit teaching, especially when combined with metapragmatic information, is generally more effective than implicit teaching, although more research is clearly needed to confirm this viewpoint for various languages, learner profiles, and L2 pragmatic constructs. We have called for more longitudinal research (research conducted over a period of time as opposed to "one shot" research) in L2 pragmatics, designed to answer questions such as: What mechanisms drive pragmatic development? How are learners pushed from their current state to a higher level of pragmatic competence? What type of developmental patterns do language learners follow for various pragmatic constructs?

We have described a number of methods traditionally used within L2 pragmatics research, and talked about how they are being driven forward by insights from different areas, starting, for example, with *discourse completion tasks* (DCTs), which have frequently been used to elicit speech acts such as requests, apologies, and refusals. DCTs allow for manipulation of contextual factors, such as power, social distance, and degree of imposition, and make it possible to compare speech act expressions across cultures. However, DCTs do not easily elicit typical conversational features such as turn-taking, sequential organization of talk, speaker-hearer collaboration, features of speech (e.g., hesitation, repetition), and non-verbal features (e.g., intonation, gestures). DCTs can be spoken or written, and they can make use of audio-visual enhancement, animation, and audio and video clips thanks to technological advancements. DCTs can be researcher generated or student generated, and they can be resolved individually or collaboratively. We described new updates to DCTs, such as their use with concurrent and retrospective verbal reports in order to gain an understanding of a learner's cognitive processes and thoughts.

We have also looked at *role plays*, both as they have traditionally been used, and with some new and interesting features so that they can elicit more interesting data. Role plays can be open or closed, spontaneous or structured. One advantage of role plays over DCTs is that they are closer to simulating real-life communicative encounters. Role plays can be done face-to-face, via chat, by phone or video, and most recently, have been done via virtual reality and role-playing software and computer programs. Updates include stimulated recalls, which can be carried out after role play in order to gain an understanding of learners' thought processes. We noted that role plays are constrained by the fact that they fail to collect naturalistic data. Indeed, all forced-elicitation techniques like DCTs and role plays present a limitation for L2 pragmatics research because pragmatics is about language use in context.

In language teaching, task-based language teaching (TBLT) highlights the importance of authentic tasks that allow learners to do real things with language.

Authentic data collected through real-life simulated tasks can reveal spontaneous, non-contrived language use. *Diaries and field notes* present alternative ways of gathering authentic language data and can be used in L2 pragmatics research too. Diaries, journals, and blogs can also serve as tools for revealing metapragmatic awareness and result in rich qualitative data that can illustrate how metapragmatic awareness has occurred in a specific moment and developed over time. However, at the same time, the participant-directed nature of diaries can mean that the resulting data are heavily subjective.

We have described how *multiple-choice tests* have several advantages over other methods when assessing comprehension of implicature and recognition of speech act strategies. Like DCTs, they serve as quick, convenient, and controlled ways of gathering large amounts of data in a short time period. With multiple choice tests, replication and comparison of data is easier. Like all methods, multiple-choice tests also have several disadvantages, including potential inauthenticity, a time-consuming development process, and sometimes low reliability due to the subjective nature of responses and chance factor that comes with the test format. Updates to multiple choice tests include the use of response time data when responding to multiple choice questions, which can provide an indirect reflection of the ease or difficulty of processing the stimuli, as well as the relative amount of linguistic, cognitive, and affective resources required for processing pragmatic input. Scaled-response questionnaires can also help researchers gain insights about how learners evaluate the contextual parameters in a communicative act (e.g., interlocutor relationship, social distance) and how they assess linguistic realizations of the act in terms of appropriateness, politeness, and formality.

Verbal response data also arguably gets closer to authentic contexts. Such data includes metapragmatic discussions, interviews, and verbal protocols, all of which can tap into learners' L2 pragmatic awareness. In all cases, concerns about the validity and reliability of verbal data can be mitigated by collecting verbal protocols immediately after the performance task; replaying participants' performances to them to assist their memory and recall; giving participants explicit instructions for the reporting or recall process; and offering participants the option of speaking in whichever language they prefer. Even so, when using verbal reports, the potential for reactivity and memory loss to occur are high.

Some of the newer-to-our-field techniques we described can be used with a range of traditional methods. For example, *confederate scripting* is a conversational data elicitation technique in which a participant in the study unknowingly interacts with an accomplice – confederate – of the researcher, while assuming the confederate is actually a peer participant. Confederate scripting can be used in situations where targeted data is to be elicited in natural conversation. Confederate scripting can assist researchers in collecting data more efficiently, helping to increase the frequency of relatively rare forms while reducing unnecessary forms, and increasing validity concerns for subsequent statistical testing. When using confederate scripting in a study, confederates should be kept naive to the study design and purposes of the study to avoid unintentionally biasing the data collection.

Naturalistic data is authentic and enables researchers to examine constructs such as L2 humor. For example, computer-mediated communication (CMC) allows researchers to easily collect data from different angles and does not require transcription. Learner corpora are collections of learner utterances, either spoken or written, that are compiled into a searchable electronic database. Corpora methods are constantly developing, with the advent of big data and more sophisticated algorithms, and we described how this impacts L2 pragmatics research and can be used for generalization and L2 pragmatic assessment purposes.

We have focused particularly on methods that bring the speaker and the hearer together in the interactive process that comprises the production and comprehension of meaning. We see interactional pragmatics as an alternative way of looking at pragmatics, one that emphasizes the indeterminacy of meaning, as well as its dynamic construction. We focused on three core areas in interactional pragmatics, including: *contexts*, where the relationship between language and contexts is dynamic and reflexive; *co-acts*, how meaning emerges in the flow of interaction, and how placement within a sequence lends meaning; and *activities*, where constellations of communicative contributions combine to form activity types, how they play a role in shaping and being shaped by context, and how they influence meaning.

We conclude by emphasizing that employing mixed methods combining quantitative approaches to understanding pragmatic development with qualitative, data-driven approaches might allow a more complete picture of the acquisition of L2 pragmatic features. A mixed methods approach can also encourage researchers to carry out more longitudinal research to reveal patterns of pragmatic development over time and influences on development. This sort of a methodological approach is consistent with the recent shift to more inclusive approaches to pragmatics generally, such as integrative pragmatics (Culpeper & Haugh, 2014), approaches that are not restricted by old dichotomies such as emic versus etic. Finally, keeping an open mind about how to collect rich and exciting data will allow us to benefit from the use of methodologies and innovative data collection tools that develop in other fields, as well as this one.

GLOSSARY

Appropriateness: Social oughts concerning what should happen according to authoritative standards of behavior *and/or* common social habits in a particular context.

Associative processes: Inferencing mechanisms that enable interactants to make meaning on the basis of knowledge about things that tend to go together (i.e., contiguities).

Blog: See *Diary method.*

Closed role play: A type of data elicitation practice where role play participants interact according to a specific goal and/or predetermined instructions. Typically, a close role play elicits a limited number of turns.

Co-acts: Acts, speech acts or discoursal acts, that orientate in some way to each other, and draw at least part of their meaning from their mutual interaction.

Commissive: A type of speech act such as promising or threatening by which the speaker commits to doing something in the future.

Communicative acts: Utterances or behaviors that perform a specific communicative function.

Communicative competence: A speaker's ability to use grammatical, textual, and sociocultural knowledge in order to produce effective, socially appropriate communication in context.

Computer-mediated communication (CMC): Communication that is facilitated by technology, for example, an internet chat program or application.

Confederate scripting: Using an individual unknown to a study participant to help elicit a target communication from the participant.

Conventional expressions: See *Formulaic language.*

Conventional implicature: Implicature that is determined by the linguistic meaning of the lexical items (e.g., "but," as for example in "He was 80, but leapt over the wall," implies a contrast between the information before it and after it).

Conversation analysis (CA): The study of social human interaction, especially the practices by which talk works in sequences of interaction (how it is produced, responded to, how interpretations are displayed, and so on).

Conversational implicature: Implicature that people generate based on the maxims of conversation and context.

Conversational maxims: A term proposed by Grice for the rational principles or guidelines that are observed at some level to achieve the exchange of information in conversation. There are four maxims: quality, quantity, relation, and manner.

Cooperative Principle: The idea that successful communication of information occurs because participants follow, at some level, maxims of conversation, which Grice termed as the maxims of quantity, quality, relation, and manner.

Corpus linguistics: A field in which researchers analyze language use in systematically collected large amounts of authentic computer-readable language data (i.e., corpora).

Corpus pragmatics: An emerging research field in pragmatics that makes use of large systematic computer-readable collections of authentic language data, for example, the British National Corpus (BNC) or the Michigan Corpus of Academic Spoken English (MICASE) amongst many others.

Corpus/Corpora: A systematic computer-readable collection of large amounts of spoken or written text.

Corrective feedback: A type of feedback provided to second language learners on their language use. Corrective feedback can be explicit or implicit.

Cross-cultural pragmatics: A subfield of pragmatics that studies the differences and similarities of language use and understanding of people of different language, dialectic, cultural, or other backgrounds (including intersectionality).

Cross-Cultural Speech Act Realization Project (CCSARP): A large-scale investigation that examined variations in speech act strategies across situations and languages (Blum-Kulka, House, & Kasper).

Declaration: A type of a speech act that brings immediate change to the context when it is uttered or performed (Searle).

Declarative: A sentence that is a statement. Not to be confused with declaration.

Deictic expressions/Deixis: Referring expressions (e.g., words, phrases) whose meaning cannot be fully understood without contextual information. Typically, they "point" to the time or place relating to the speaker. Example: "here," "there," "you," "me," "now," "then," and so on.

Diary method: A means of data collection in which participants make written, recorded, or internet-based journal entries typically regarding their own impressions and language learning experiences, involving specific pragmatic input, interpretation of pragmatic behaviors that he/she observed, and reflection on their own understandings of pragmatic acts.

Direct speech acts: A type of speech act in which the illocutionary force and the sentence syntax correspond with each other, so there is little need for inference.

Direction of fit: The way in which the words of an utterance orient to the world (Searle).

Directive: A type of speech act that makes the hearer do something.

Directness: The degree of match between the utterance form and its underlying meaning.

Disambiguation: The process of clarifying the sense of an unclear or ambiguous word or utterance by considering its context.

Discourse Completion Task (DCT): A data collection tool that typically presents a learner with a scenario, followed by a blank space that elicits a targeted speech act utterance. They may be spoken, technology-enhanced, reversed DCT, or collaborative.

Discourse markers: Linguistic expressions such as particles, words, or phrases that signal speaker attitudes, indicate how hearers might "take" an utterance, and/or contribute to the coherence/flow of the discourse. Example: "but," "well," "you know."

Discourse: Communication through language use.

Ecological validity: Refers to the applicability of research findings to real-life contexts.

English as a foreign language (EFL): English language learners who learn a language in an environment where English is not spoken as a native language.

English as a second language (ESL): English language learners who learn a language in an environment where English is natively spoken by the majority.

English as Lingua Franca (ELF): Use of English among non-native speakers of English, and between native and non-native speakers of English.

Ethical Review: A committee or board that assesses the risks of research to participants, and ensures they have fully consented to take part and that they understand the risks.

Expressive: A type of speech act that conveys the speaker's emotions and the psychological world of the speaker (Searle).

Face-Threatening Act (FTA): A type of communication or action that typically threatens the face of the hearer (Brown and Levinson).

Face: A speaker's public self-image as mediated in social interactions (Goffman).

Felicity conditions: Contextual elements and circumstances that are required for a successful speech act (Austin).

Field notes: Data collected by a researcher who writes or records observations on behaviors, activities, and events in a context to help understand the phenomenon being investigated.

Flouting a maxim: The blatant non-observance of a conversational maxim by a speaker, which generates implicature.

Forced elicitation techniques: A data collection method that compels a participant to produce a target utterance through use of various prompts in given contexts.

Foreign language (FL): Frequently used to refer to a second or additional language studied outside the context of where the target language is spoken.

Form-focused instruction: A type of instructional activity that directs language learners' attention to a particular linguistic form. Form-focused instruction can be focus-on-form (FoF) or focus-on-forms (FoFs) oriented.

Formulaic language: Words and expressions that carry the conventionalized pragmatic meanings of their associated contexts. For example, "Ladies and Gentlemen" has the conventionalized meaning of requesting attention and opening an address on a formal occasion.

Generalized implicature: Implicature that requires no particular (or very minimal) contextual information to be understood.

Grice's Maxims: See *Cooperative Principle*.

Heritage learners: Second language learners who study a language to which they have a cultural connection, often via their family language background.

Illocutionary act: The act or function the speaker intends to achieve through producing an utterance or expression. Example: "Can we close the window?" conveys the illocutionary act of a request to close the window. Often taken to be synonymous with "speech act."

Imperative: A verb in the imperative mood or a sentence containing such a verb that expresses a command or exhortation.

Implicature: What the speaker means beyond the literal meanings of the words they say (associated with flouts of the Cooperative Principle) (Grice).

Imply: The speaker generates some meaning beyond the semantic or literal meaning of the words. See also *Implicature*.

Indeterminacy: The idea that meanings are not simply matched to language forms on a one-to-one basis by decoding words, but are inherently indeterminate. Probable meanings, including implications and inferences, have to be worked out in context. (Occasionally, utterances remain indeterminate, i.e., they give rise to a range of equally strong implicatures.)

Indirect criticism: Utterance in which a speaker veils a direct negative comment by using implicature to avoid making it indirectly.

Indirect speech acts: A type of speech act in which the illocutionary force and the sentence syntax do not correspond with each other, so the hearer may infer a speech act without it being stated explicitly. Traditionally, conceived of as one speech act produced to achieve another (Searle). Example: *Can you speak louder?* is a question (about ability) performing a request (an indirect request to speak louder).

Infer: The hearer derives meaning beyond the semantics or literal meaning of the words. See also *Inference*.

Inference: The meaning, beyond the literal meaning of the words, derived by the hearer through reasoning or cognitive processes, which may or may not be the same as the speaker's intended meaning.

Infringing a maxim: Inadvertent failure to observe a maxim due to lack of linguistic competency or other impairment.

Input: Target language that is available to the language learner.

Interactional competence: Ability to use various linguistic and interactional resources for successful interactions in social contexts (Young).

Interactional pragmatics: An approach to pragmatics that examines the co-construction of meaning between participants through pragmatic acts during interaction.

Interactionist approach: A theory that posits second language development is fostered through meaningful interaction in the target language, including feedback and modified output.

Intercultural pragmatics: The study of communication among speakers of different first languages, dialects, or varieties (or the intersection of these).

Interlanguage pragmatics: Second language learners' pragmatic knowledge and performance.

Interrogative: A word or sentence that has the grammatical form of a question.

Interview: A type of data collection tool that aims to elicit information by asking questions to the participants. Researcher-directed or facilitated data collection that aims at revealing learners' understanding of pragmatic acts, usually with open-ended questions.

Introspective methods: A type of research method that enables participants to reflect on and self-report or self-evaluate an aspect of their language learning experience. Interviews, journals, and diaries are some examples.

Irony: Traditionally, a type of speech in which the speaker means the opposite of what the utterance literally says.

Journal: See *Diary method*.

L2 pragmatics: A field of study that investigates how learners come to comprehend and produce language accurately and appropriately in a social context in a second or additional language.

L2: See *Second language*.

Language socialization theory: A theory that holds that novices learn to become competent members in a society through interaction with expert members of a society (Ochs & Schieffelin).

Locutionary act: The actual utterance of phonetic, syntactic, and semantic features that produce something meaningful (Austin).

Longitudinal design: Research in which observations of the phenomena under investigation are made at periodic intervals for an extended period of time.

Meta-: A prefix used to denote something that the item to which it is affixed is about.

Metapragmatic discussions: Data collection technique in which participants are engaged in a dialogue about pragmalinguistic forms, sociopragmatic factors, and the connection between them to develop a joint understanding of the underlying principles.

Metapragmatic expressions: Types of expressions and comments that are about pragmatic notions and acts.

Metapragmatic knowledge: A type of knowledge that refers to what language learners know about pragmatic acts.

Metapragmatics (explicit): The study of expressions that are about some pragmatic aspect of the communication in hand (e.g., all speech act labels are explicit metapragmatic expressions).

Metapragmatics (implicit): The study of indicators that interlocutors are aware of their pragmatics, namely that they are articulating beliefs and understandings about language use in language. Often, it is focused on an awareness of the relationships between linguistic forms and situated contexts.

Multimedia Elicitation Task (MET): A discourse completion task using audio-visual enhancement.

Multiple-choice test: A questionnaire with fixed closed-response answers that allows researchers to collect a large amount of data in one setting.

Naturalistic language: Data consisting of tokens of linguistic features collected through audio/video-recording of authentic interactions or digital media sources.

Negative face: The desire to be unimpeded in one's actions (Brown & Levinson).

Negative feedback: See *Corrective feedback*.

Non-native speaker (NNS): A speaker of a language who did not learn or speak it as their first language.

Non-verbal cues: Communicating through cues such as gestures, intonation, body language, and so on.

Noticing hypothesis: The claim that L2 learners' attention to form-function-context associations is a necessary condition for development (Schmidt).

Open role play: A type of data elicitation activity in which participants simulate interaction based on a prompt or a situation without being limited by the pre-determined goals or instructions. Typically, an open role play elicits a number of turns and longer interaction.

Paralinguistic competence: A part of language competence that is concerned with the ability to convey meaning through non-verbal cues (e.g., intonation, volume).

Participant observation: A technique in which the researcher learns about the perspectives of participants under study by observing and participating in routine activities in context.

Performatives: Utterances that effect a change in the world; they do not merely describe it. Example: "I hereby sentence you to life imprisonment" (Austin).

Perlocutionary act: A speech act that produces certain effects ("perlocutionary effects") on the hearer's feelings, thoughts, and actions (Austin).

Politeness: One of the main areas of study in pragmatics, which focuses on how harmony is maintained or enhanced in social interaction, despite actions (e.g., face threats) that might upset it.

Pope implicature: Classic example of a conventionalized implicature, in which a speaker views something in the context as obvious information (the Pope is Catholic).

Positive face: One's desire to be liked and approved by others (Brown and Levinson).

Positive politeness: The use of strategies designed to address the hearer's positive face wants. They can also reinforce solidarity.

Power: A social dimension involving the ability to control someone else. In Politeness Theory, this concept refers to the power dynamics between the interlocutors. Interlocutors can have equal, more, or less power depending on the social context.

Pragmalinguistic competence: A person's ability to use and understand pragmalinguistic resources.

Pragmalinguistic failure: Pragmatic failure caused by differences in beliefs about the linguistic encoding of pragmatic force.

Pragmalinguistics: The area of pragmatics that concerns the linguistic resources available to speakers, such as grammar and vocabulary, which are used to convey pragmatic meanings.

Pragmatic ambiguity: Utterances that have multiple interpretations, particularly multiple pragmatic interpretations (e.g., one utterance could be interpreted as several different speech acts).

Pragmatic competence: The ability to use language both effectively in conveying intended meanings and appropriately in various social contexts, and to understand other speakers' messages in context.

Pragmatic conventionalization: The process by which forms become associated with their pragmatic contexts.

Pragmatic explicitness: The transparency of the illocutionary point, target (often the addressee) and semantic content of the utterance (Culpeper and Haugh). A broader notion than directness.

Pragmatic failure: Inability to convey or comprehend intended and/or appropriate meanings in context.

Pragmatic frames: Schema-like clusters that are constructed out of the contextual (typically situational) features that regularly accompany particular speech acts.

Pragmatic reflexive awareness: An awareness of the pragmatic features that participants and their interactants use, and the potential meanings they have in context.

Pragmatics: A branch of linguistics that focuses on meanings that arise from the use of communicative resources in context, and in particular, the meanings implied by speakers, inferred by hearers, and negotiated between them in interaction.

Pre-expansion: A type of utterance that appears before adjacency pairs.

Productive pragmatic knowledge: The ability to convey pragmatic meaning accurately and appropriately.

Rank of imposition: In Politeness Theory, the rank of imposition refers to an act's position on a theoretical ranking running from highly imposing (e.g., a request to borrow a car) to minimally imposing (e.g., a request to borrow a pen) (Brown & Levinson).

Receptive pragmatic knowledge: The ability to comprehend pragmatic meaning accurately.

Relevance theory: A communicative-cognitive theory that proposes that a communicative act carries a guarantee of relevance, namely, that you will be able to derive sufficient information from it to counterbalance the effort you expend in doing so (Sperber & Wilson).

Representative: A type of speech act in which the words reflect or fit the world.

Rogative: A type of speech act such as questioning or asking in which the hearer is responsible for supplying information to fit what the speaker is missing

Role play: Interaction played out by two or more people as given characters in response to situations provided by a researcher. They may be open or closed, spontaneous or structured.

Routines: Fixed linguistic forms or chunks that are systematic and conventionalized according to a particular context. See also *Formulaic language*.

Sarcasm: A negative remark conveyed indirectly by saying something that is obviously insincere (often takes the form of mock politeness, politeness that is obviously insincere).

Scaled response: In L2 pragmatics, a questionnaire on which participants evaluate the degree of appropriateness of target pragmalinguistic expressions on a multiple-point scale.

Scenario: This refers to social situations that require using certain specific speech acts (see also *Pragmatic frames*). Scenarios are often used in L2 pragmatics research to elicit pragmatic data.

Second language (L2): Frequently used to refer to a second or additional language acquired after one's native language.

Second language (SL): A term that is frequently used to refer to a second or any additional language acquired in the context where the target language is spoken.

Second language acquisition (SLA): Frequently used to refer to the field of research concerning the acquisition/learning of second or additional languages.

Semantics: A field of linguistics that is concerned with the abstract meaning of words and sentences in the language.

Sequence implicature: An implicature derived from a certain order of events assumed from an utterance.

Service encounters: These are interactions that occur between a service provider (e.g., clerk, sales associate, travel agent) and a customer.

Social distance: In Politeness Theory, this refers to the observed distance between the interlocutors, and is usually considered in terms of their familiarity with each other and/or the extent to which they share commonalities.

Sociocognitive approach: The sociocognitive approach in pragmatics is based on two key claims: (1) the speaker and hearer are equal participants in the communicative process; and (2) communication is a dynamic process in which individuals are constrained by societal conditions but also shape them at the same time (Kecskes).

Sociolinguistic competence: A person's ability to use and understand communication appropriate to context (i.e., sociopragmatics).

Sociopragmatic failure: Pragmatic failure caused by differences in beliefs about the social context (e.g., degree of politeness required, rights and obligations, costs/benefits).

Sociopragmatics: The area of pragmatics that concerns the specific contextual phenomena that shape pragmatic meanings on a particular occasion of use.

Speech act: An utterance that performs a communicative action, such as a refusal, request, or promise.

Stimulated recall: A technique in which a researcher plays a recording or video or shows other illustrative data of an individual's language learning or use and asks the individual to reflect on and describe what their thought processes were during the experience.

Target Language Use domain (TLU): The degree of correspondence between contexts in which learners will use their target language in test tasks and real life (Bachman).

Task-based Language Teaching (TBLT): An instructional approach that emphasizes use of authentic language that learners need to successfully resolve tasks and do things with a target language in the real world.

Think-aloud: A type of research method in which participants speak about their thoughts while completing a task.

Turn-taking: The organization of turns-at-talk that constitute a conversation.

Uptake: What the second language learner learns from the available input. (Not to be confused with the abbreviated version of "perlocutionary uptake.")

Utterance: A unit of speech that carries a specific meaning depending on its context.

Validity: The extent to which a research tool accurately measures the construct it is attempting to measure, as opposed to measuring something else.

Verbal reports/protocols: A type of interview that takes place during or immediately after completion of a task.

Violating a maxim: Cases where there is no intention to generate an implicature, but there is usually an intention to surreptitiously mislead a hearer.

REFERENCES

Aijmer, K. (1996). *Conversational routines in English: Convention and creativity*. London: Routledge.

Al-Gahtani, S., & Roever, C. (2012). Proficiency and sequential organization of L2 requests. *Applied Linguistics*, *33*, 42–65.

Al-Gahtani, S., & Roever, C. (2014a). Insert and post-expansion in L2 Arabic requests. *System*, *42*, 189–206.

Al-Gahtani, S., & Roever, C. (2014b). Preference structure in L2 Arabic requests. *Intercultural Pragmatics*, *11*, 619–643.

Alcón-Soler, E. (2013). Teachability and bilingual effects on third language knowledge of refusals. *Intercultural Pragmatics*, *9*, 511–541.

Alcón-Soler, E. (2015). Pragmatic learning and study abroad: Effects of instruction and length of stay. *System*, *48*, 62–74.

Archer, D., & Ackert, R. M. (1977). Words and everything else: Verbal and nonverbal cues in social interpretation. *Journal of Personality and Social Psychology*, *35*, 443–449.

Arndt, H., & Janney, R. W. (1987). *Intergrammar: Toward an integrative model of verbal, prosodic and kinesic choices in speech*. Berlin: De Gruyter.

Arundale, R. B. (1999). An alternative model and ideology of communication for an alternative to politeness theory. *Pragmatics*, *9*, 119–153.

Arundale, R. B. (2006). Face as relational and interactional: A communication framework for research on face, facework, and politeness. *Journal of Politeness Research: Language, Behaviour, Culture*, *2*, 193–217.

Atkinson, J., & Heritage, J. (1984). *Structures of social action: Studies in conversation analysis*. Cambridge: Cambridge University Press.

Austin, J. L. (1962). *How to do things with words*. Cambridge, MA: Harvard University Press.

Austin, J. L. (1975). *How to do things with words (William James lectures)*, J. O. Urmson & Marina Sbisà (Eds.). Oxford: Oxford University Press.

Bachman, L. F. (1990). *Fundamental considerations in language testing*. Oxford: Oxford University Press.

Bachman, L. F., & Palmer, A. S. (1996). *Language testing in practice: Designing and developing useful language tests*. Oxford: Oxford University Press.

Bachman, L. F., & Palmer, A. S. (2010). *Language assessment in practice: Developing language assessments and justifying their use in the real world*. Oxford: Oxford University Press.

Badjadi, N. E. I. (2016). A meta-analysis of the effects of instructional tasks on L2 pragmatics comprehension and production. In S.F. Tang & L. Logonnathan (Eds.), *Assessment for learning within and beyond the classroom* (pp. 241–268). Singapore: Springer.

Bardovi-Harlig, K. (1999). The interlanguage of interlanguage pragmatics: A research agenda for acquisitional pragmatics. *Language Learning, 49*, 677–713.

Bardovi-Harlig, K. (2009). Conventional expressions as a pragmalinguistic resource: Recognition and production of conventional expressions in L2 pragmatics. *Language Learning, 59*, 755–795.

Bardovi-Harlig, K. (2010). Exploring the pragmatics of interlanguage pragmatics: Definition by design. In A. Trosborg (Ed.), *Handbook of pragmatics* (pp. 219–260). Berlin: Mouton de Gruyter.

Bardovi-Harlig, K. (2012). Formulas, routines, and conventional expressions in pragmatics research. *Annual Review of Applied Linguistics, 32*, 206–227.

Bardovi-Harlig, K. (2013). Developing L2 pragmatics. *Language Learning, 63*(Suppl. 1), 68–86.

Bardovi-Harlig, K. (2015). Operationalizing conversation in studies of instructional effect in L2 pragmatics. *System, 48*, 21–34.

Bardovi-Harlig, K., & Bastos, M. T. (2011). Proficiency, length of stay, and intensity of interaction and the acquisition of conventional expressions in L2 pragmatics. *Intercultural Pragmatics, 8*, 347–384.

Bardovi-Harlig, K., & Dörnyei, Z. (1998). Do language learners recognize pragmatic violations? Pragmatic versus grammatical awareness in instructed L2 learning. *TESOL Quarterly, 32*, 233–259.

Bardovi-Harlig, K., & Hartford, B. S. (1993). Learning the rules of academic talk: A longitudinal study of pragmatic change. *Studies in Second Language Acquisition, 15*, 279–304.

Bardovi-Harlig, K., & Hartford, S. (Eds.). (2005). *Interlanguage pragmatics: Exploring institutional talk*. Mahwah, NJ: Erlbaum.

Bardovi-Harlig, K., & Shin, S.-Y. (2014). Expanding traditional testing measures with tasks from L2 pragmatics research. *Iranian Journal of Language Testing, 4*, 26–49.

Barron, A. (2003). *Acquisition in interlanguage pragmatics: Learning how to do things with words in a study abroad context* (Vol. 108). Amsterdam: John Benjamins Publishing.

Baxter, L. A. (1984). An investigation of compliance-gaining as politeness. *Human Communication Research, 10*, 427–456.

Beebe, L. M., & Cummings, M. C. (1996). Natural speech act data versus written questionnaire data: How data collection method affects speech act performance. In S. Gass & J. Neu (Eds.), *Speech acts across cultures: Challenges to communication in a second language* (Vol. 11, pp. 65–86). Berlin: Mouton de Gruyter.

Bell, N. D. (2005). Exploring L2 language play as an aid to SLL: A case study of humor in NS–NNS interaction. *Applied Linguistics, 26*, 192–218.

Bell, N. D. (2007). Humor comprehension: Lessons learned from cross-cultural communication. *Humor, 20–4*, 367–387.

Bell, N. D. (2011). Humor scholarship and TESOL: Applying findings and establishing a research agenda. *TESOL Quarterly, 45*, 134–159.

Bell, N. D., & Attardo, S. (2010). Failed humor: Issues in nonnative speakers' appreciation and understanding of humor. *Intercultural Pragmatics, 7*, 423–447.

Beltrán-Palanques, V. (2013). *Exploring research methods in interlanguage pragmatics: A study based on apologies.* Saarbrücken: LAP LAMBERT Academic Publishing.

Belz, J., & Kinginger, C. (2003). Discourse options and the development pragmatic competence by classroom learners of German: The case of address forms. *Language Learning, 53,* 591–647.

Belz, J. A., & Vyatkina, N. (2005). Learner corpus analysis and the development of L2 pragmatic competence in networked inter-cultural language study: The case of German modal particles. *Canadian Modern Language Review, 62,* 17–48.

Belz, J. A., & Vyatkina, N. (2008). The pedagogical mediation of a developmental learner corpus for classroom-based language instruction, *Language Learning and Technology, 12,* 33–52.

Biber, D., Conrad, S., & Cortes, V. (2004). If you look at…: Lexical bundles in university teaching and textbooks. *Applied Linguistics, 25,* 371–405.

Biber, D., Conrad, S., Reppen, R., Byrd, P., & Helt, M. (2002). Speaking and writing in the university: A multidimensional comparison. *TESOL Quarterly, 36,* 9–48.

Billmyer, K., & Varghese, M. (2000). Investigating instrument-based pragmatic variability: Effects of enhancing discourse completion tests. *Applied Linguistics, 21,* 517–552.

Bloom, B. S. (1954). The thought process of students in discussion. *Accent on Teaching: Experiments in General Education, 1,* 23–46.

Blum-Kulka, S. (1982). Learning to say what you mean in a second language: A study of the speech act performance of learners of Hebrew as a second language. *Applied Linguistics, 3,* 29.

Blum-Kulka, S. (1985). The language of requesting in Israeli society. In J. Forgas (Ed.), *Language and social situations* (pp. 113–139). New York, NY: Springer-Verlag.

Blum-Kulka, S., & House, J. (1989). Cross-cultural and situational variation in requesting behaviour. In S. Blum-Kulka, J. House, & G. Kasper (Eds.), *Cross-cultural pragmatics: Requests and apologies* (pp. 123–154). Norwood, NJ: Ablex.

Blum-Kulka, S., House, J., & Kasper, G. (Eds.). (1989a). *Cross-cultural pragmatics: Requests and apologies.* Vol. XXXI Advances in discourse processes. Norwood, NJ: Ablex.

Blum-Kulka, S., House, J., & Kasper, G. (1989b). The CCSARP coding manual. In S. Blum-Kulka, J. House, & G. Kasper (Eds.), *Cross-cultural pragmatics: Requests and apologies* (pp. 273–294). Vol. XXXI Advances in discourse processes. Norwood, NJ: Ablex.

Bouton, L. F. (1992). The Interpretation of implicature in English by NNS: Does it come automatically – without being explicitly taught? *Pragmatics and Language Learning, 3,* 53–65.

Bouton, L. F. (1994). Conversational implicature in a second language: Learned slowly when not deliberately taught. *Journal of Pragmatics, 22,* 157–167.

Brown, J. D. (2014). The future of world Englishes in language testing. *Language Assessment Quarterly, 11,* 5–26.

Brown, D. (2016). The type and linguistic foci of oral corrective feedback in the L2 classroom: A meta-analysis. *Language Teaching Research, 20,* 436–458.

Brown, P., & Levinson, S. C. (1987). *Politeness: Some universals in language usage.* Cambridge: Cambridge University Press.

Brown, R., & Gilman, A. (1960). The pronouns of power and solidarity. In T. A. Sebeok (Ed.), *Style in language* (pp. 253–276). Cambridge, MA: MIT Press.

Brown, L., & Prieto, P. (2017). (Im)politeness: Prosody and gesture. In J. Culpeper, M. Haugh, & D. Kádár (Eds.), *The Palgrave handbook on linguistic (im)politeness* (pp. 357–379). London: Palgrave Macmillan.

Caffi, C. (1998). Metapragmatics. In J. Mey (Ed.), *Concise encyclopedia of pragmatics* (pp. 581–586). Amsterdam: Elsevier.

Caffi, C. (2006). Mitigation. In K. Brown (Ed.), *Encyclopedia of language and linguistics* (pp. 171–175). Oxford: Elsevier.

Canale, M., & Swain, M. (1980). Theoretical bases of communicative approaches to second language teaching and testing. *Applied Linguistics, 1*, 1–47.

Carrell, P. (1979). Indirect speech acts in ESL: Indirect answers. In C. Yorio, K. Perkins, & J. Schachter (Eds.), *On TESOL '79: The learner I focus* (pp. 297–307). Washington, DC: TESOL.

Celce-Murcia, M. (2007). Rethinking the role of communicative competence in language teaching. In E. Alcón-Soler & M. P. Safont Jordà (Eds.), *Intercultural language use and language learning* (pp. 7–22). Dordrecht: Springer.

Cheng, D. (2011). New insights on compliment responses: A comparison between native English speakers and Chinese L2 speakers. *Journal of Pragmatics, 43*, 2204–2214.

Clark, H. H. (1996). *Using language*. Cambridge: Cambridge University Press.

Cogo, A., & House, J. (2017). Intercultural pragmatics. In A. Barron, Y. Gu., & G. Steen (Eds.), *Routledge handbook of pragmatics* (pp. 168–183). London/New York, NY: Routledge.

Cohen, A. D. (1997). Developing pragmatic ability: Insights from the accelerated study of Japanese. *New Trends and Issues in Teaching Japanese Language and Culture, 15*, 133–159.

Cohen, A. D. (2004). *The interface between interlanguage pragmatics and assessment*. Proceedings of the 3rd Annual JALT Pan-SIG Conference, Tokyo, Japan.

Cohen, A. D. (2014). *Strategies in learning and using a second language* (2nd ed.). New York, NY: Harlow.

Cohen, A. D., & Ishihara, N. (2013). Pragmatics. In B. Tomlinson (Ed.), *Applied linguistics and materials development* (pp. 113–126). London/New York, NY: Bloomsbury.

Cohen, L., & Manion, L. (1994). *Research methods in education* (4th ed.). New York, NY: Routledge.

Cohen, A. D., & Olshtain, E. (1993). The production of speech acts by EFL learners. *TESOL Quarterly, 27*, 33–56.

Cohen, A. D., & Shively, R. L. (2007). Acquisition of requests and apologies in Spanish and French: Impact of study abroad and strategy building intervention. *The Modern Language Journal, 91*, 189–212.

Cook, H. (2008). *Socializing identities through speech style*. New York, NY: Multilingual Matters.

Coupland, N., & Jaworski, A. (2004). Sociolinguistic perspectives on metalanguage: Reflexivity, evaluation, and ideology. In A. Jaworski, N. Coupland, & D. Galasinski (Eds.), *Metalanguage: Social and ideological perspectives* (pp. 15–51). Berlin: Mouton de Gruyter.

Craig, R. T., Tracy, K., & Spisak, F. (1986). The discourse of requests: Assessment of a politeness approach. *Human Communication Research, 12*, 437–468.

Culpeper, J. (2011). *Impoliteness: Using language to cause offence*. Cambridge: Cambridge University Press.

Culpeper, J., & Haugh, M. (2014). *Pragmatics and the English language*. Basingstoke: Palgrave Macmillan.

Culpeper, J., & McIntyre, D. (2010). Activity types and characterisation in dramatic discourse. In J. Eder, F. Jannidis, & R. Schneider (Eds.), *Characters in fictional worlds: Understanding imaginary beings in literature, film and other media* (pp. 176–207). Berlin: De Gruyter.

Culpeper, J., Crawshaw, R., & Harrison, J. (2008). 'Activity types' and 'discourse types': Mediating 'advice' in interactions between foreign language assistants and their supervisors in schools in France and England. *Multilingua, 27*, 297–324.

Culpeper, J., Katamba, F., Kerswill, P., Wodak, R., & McEnery, T. (2009). *English language: Description, variation and context.* Basingstoke: Palgrave.

Davies, B. L. (2007). Grice's cooperative principle: Meaning and rationality. *Journal of Pragmatics, 39*, 2308–2331.

De Bot, K., Lowie, W., & Verspoor, M. (2007). A dynamic systems theory approach to second language acquisition. *Bilingualism: Language and Cognition, 10*, 7–21.

DeWalt, K. M., & DeWalt, B. R. (2002). *Participant observation: A guide for fieldworkers.* Walnut Creek, CA: AltaMira Press.

Diao, W. (2014). Peer socialization into gendered Mandarin practices in a study abroad context: Talk in the dorm. *Applied Linguistics, 37*, 599–620.

Diao, W. (2016). Peer socialization into gendered L2 Mandarin practices in a study abroad context: Talk in the dorm. *Applied Linguistics, 37*, 599–620.

Dippold, D. (2011). Argumentative discourse in L2 German: A sociocognitive perspective on the development of facework strategies. *Modern Language Journal, 95*, 171–187.

DuBois, J. W., Chafe, W. L, Meyer, C., & Thompson, S. A. (2000). *Santa Barbara Corpus of spoken American English—Part 1.* Philadelphia, PA: Linguistic Data Consortium.

Duranti, A., & Goodwin, C. (Eds.). (1992). *Rethinking context: Language as an interactive phenomenon.* Cambridge: Cambridge University Press.

Economidou-Kogetsidis, M. (2013). Strategies, modification and perspective in native speakers' requests: A comparison of WDCT and naturally occurring requests. *Journal of Pragmatics, 53*, 21–38.

Eelen, G. (2001). *A critique of politeness theories.* Manchester: St. Jerome Publishing.

Eisenstein, M., & Bodman, J. (1993). Expressing gratitude in American English. In G. Kasper & S. Blum-Kulka (Eds.), *Interlanguage pragmatics* (pp. 64–81). New York, NY: Oxford University Press.

Ericsson, K. A., & Simon, H. A. (1993). *Protocol analysis.* Cambridge, MA: MIT Press.

Ervin-Tripp, S. M., Strage, A., Lampert, M., & Bell, N. (1987). Understanding requests. *Linguistics, 25*, 107–144.

Félix-Brasdefer, J. C. (2004). Interlanguage refusals: Linguistic politeness and length of residence in the target community. *Language Learning, 54*, 587–653.

Félix-Brasdefer, J. C. (2007). Pragmatic development in the Spanish as a FL classroom: A cross-sectional study of learner requests. *Intercultural Pragmatics, 4*, 253–286.

Félix-Brasdefer, J. C. (2008). Perceptions of refusals to invitations: Exploring the minds of foreign language learners. *Language Awareness, 17*, 195–211.

Félix-Brasdefer, J. C. (2010). Data collection methods in speech act performance: DCTs, role-plays, and verbal reports. In A. Martínez-Flor & Usó-Juan, E. (Eds.), *Speech act performance: Theoretical, empirical and methodological issues* (pp. 41–56). Amsterdam: John Benjamins Publishing.

Félix-Brasdefer, J. C., & Hasler-Barker, M. (2015). Complimenting in Spanish in a short-term study abroad context. E. Alcon-Soler & L. Yates (Eds.), *Pragmatic learning across contexts.* Special issue. *System, 48*, 75–85.

Fiske, S. T., & Taylor, S. E. (1984). *Social cognition.* Reading, MA: Addison-Wesley.

Fiske, S. T., & Taylor, S. E. (1991). *Social cognition* (2nd ed.). New York, NY: McGraw-Hill.

Flores-Ferrán, N., & Lovejoy, K. (2015). An examination of mitigating devices in the argument interactions of L2 Spanish learners. *Journal of Pragmatics, 76*, 67–86.

Fordyce, K. (2014). The differential effects of explicit and Implicit Instruction on EFL learners' use of epistemic stance. *Applied Linguistics, 35*, 6–28.

Fox, K. (2004). *Watching the English: The hidden rules of English behaviour.* London: Hodder & Stoughton.

Fraser, B. (1990). Perspectives on politeness. *Journal of Pragmatics, 14*, 219–236.

Fukuya, Y. J., & Hill, Y. Z. (2006). The effects of recasting on the production of pragmalinguistic conventions of request by Chinese learners of English. *Issues in Applied Linguistics, 15*, 59–91.

Fukuya, Y., Reeve, M. G. J., & Christianson, M. (1998). *Does focus on form work for teaching sociopragmatics?* Paper presented at the 12th international conference on pragmatics and language learning, Urbana, IL.

Gal'perin, P. Y. (1989). Organization of mental activity and the effectiveness of learning. *Soviet Psychology, 27*, 65–82.

Garcia, P. (2004). *Meaning in academic contexts: A corpus-based study of pragmatic utterances* (Unpublished doctoral dissertation). Northern Arizona University, Flagstaff, AZ.

Garcia, P. (2007). Pragmatics in academic contexts: A spoken corpus study. In M. C. Campoy & M. J. Luzón (Eds.), *Spoken corpora in applied linguistics* (pp. 97–128). Bern: Peter Lang.

Gass, S. M., & Houck, N. (1999). *Interlanguage refusals.* Berlin: de Gruyter.

Gass, S. M., & Mackey, A. (2000). *Stimulated recall methodology in second language research.* New York, NY: Routledge.

Gass, S. M., & Mackey, A. (2006). Input, interaction and output: An overview. *AILA review, 19*, 3–17.

Gass, S. M., & Mackey, A. (2016). *Stimulated recall methodology in applied linguistics and L2 research.* New York, NY: Routledge.

Gibbs, R. W. (1981). Memory for requests in conversation. *Journal of Verbal Learning and Verbal Behavior, 20*, 630–640.

Goffman, E. (1961). *Encounters: Two studies in the sociology of interaction.* Indianapolis, IN: Bobbs-Merrill.

Goffman, E. (1967). *Interaction ritual: Essays on face-to-face behavior.* Garden City, NY: Anchor/Doubleday.

Goffman, E. (1972). The neglected situation. In P. P. Giglioli (Ed.), *Language and social context* (pp. 61–66). Harmondsworth: Penguin.

Golato, A. (2003). Studying compliment responses: A comparison of DCTs and recordings of naturally occurring talk. *Applied Linguistics, 24*, 90–121.

Gonzales, A. M. (2013). Development of politeness strategies in participatory online environments: A case study. In N. Taguchi & J. Sykes (Eds.), *Technology in interlanguage pragmatics research and teaching* (pp. 101–120). Philadelphia, PA: John Benjamins.

González-Lloret, M. (2010). Conversation analysis and speech act performance. In A. Martínez-Flor & E. Usó-Juan (Eds.), *Speech act performance: Theoretical, empirical and methodological issues* (pp. 57–74). Amsterdam: John Benjamins.

González-Lloret, M. (2016). The construction of emotion in multilingual computer-mediated interaction In M. Prior & G. Kasper (Eds.), *Emotion in multilingual interaction* (pp. 291–313). Amsterdam: John Benjamins.

Greenall, A. K. (2009). Towards a new theory of flouting. *Journal of Pragmatics, 41*, 2295–2311.

Grice, H. P. (1957). Meaning. *Philosophical Review, 66*, 377–388.

Grice, H. P. (1975/1989). *Studies in the way of words.* Cambridge, MA: Harvard University Press.

Grice, P. H. (1989). Logic and conversation. In P. Cole and J. Morgan (Eds.), *Syntax and semantics, volume 3, speech acts* (pp. 41–58). New York, NY: Academic Press.

Gu, Y. (1990). Politeness phenomena in modern Chinese. *Journal of Pragmatics, 14*, 237–257.

Gumperz, J. J. (1982). *Discourse strategies.* Cambridge: Cambridge University Press.

Gumperz, J. J. (1992). Interviewing in intercultural situations. In P. Drew & J. Heritage (Eds.), *Talk at work: Interaction in institutional settings* (pp. 307–327). Cambridge: Cambridge University Press.

Guo, L. (2013). *Effects of recasts and metalinguistic feedback on developing ESL learners' pragmatic competence* (Unpublished doctoral dissertation). University of Kansas, Lawrence, KS.

Halenko, N. (2013). *Using computer animation to assess and improve spoken language skills.* Conference proceedings: ICT for language learning (p. 286). Florence: Libreriauniversitaria.

Hall, J. K. (1993). The role of oral practices in the accomplishment of our everyday lives: The sociocultural dimension of interaction with implications for the learning of another language. *Applied Linguistics, 14*, 145–166.

Hall, J. K. (1995). "Aw, man, where you goin'?" Classroom interaction and the development of L2 interactional competence. *Issues in Applied Linguistics, 6*, 37–62.

Hall, J. K., Hellermann, J., & Doehler, S. P. (2011). *L2 interactional competence and development.* New York, NY: Multilingual Matters.

Harré, R. (1995). The necessity of personhood as embodied being. *Theory & Psychology, 5*, 369–373.

Harré, R., & Gillett, G. (1994). *The discursive mind.* Thousand Oaks, CA: Sage Publications.

Hartford, B. S., & Bardovi-Harlig, K. (1992). Closing the conversation: Evidence from the academic advising session. *Discourse Processes, 15*, 93–116.

Hassall, T. (2006). Learning to take leave in social conversations: A diary study. In M. DuFon & E. Churchill (Eds.), *Language learners in study abroad contexts* (pp. 31–58). Clevedon: Multilingual Matters.

Hassall, T. (2008). Pragmatic performance: What are learners thinking? In E. A. Soler & A. M. Flor (Eds.), *Investigating pragmatics in foreign language learning, teaching and testing* (pp. 72–93). Bristol: Multilingual Matters.

Hassall, T. (2015a). Individual variation in L2 study-abroad outcomes: A case study from Indonesian pragmatics. *Multilingua, 34*, 33–59.

Hassall, T. (2015b). Influence of fellow L2 learners on pragmatic development during study abroad. *Intercultural Pragmatics, 12*, 415–442.

Haugh, M. (2007a). Emic conceptualisations of (im)politeness and face in Japanese: Implications for the discursive negotiation of second language learner identities. *Journal of Pragmatics: An Interdisciplinary Journal of Language Studies, 39*, 657–680.

Haugh, M. (2007b). The co-constitution of politeness implicature in conversation. *Journal of Pragmatics, 39*, 84–110.

Heritage, J. (1984). *Garfinkel and ethnomethodology.* Cambridge: Polity Press.

Holmes, J. (2012). Politeness in intercultural discourse and communication. In C. B. Paulston, S. F. Kiesling, & E. S. Rangel (Eds.), *Handbook of intercultural discourse and communication* (pp. 205–228). Oxford: Blackwell.

Holtgraves, T. (1994). Communication in context: Effects of speaker status on the comprehension of indirect requests. *Journal of Experimental Psychology: Learning, Memory, and Cognition, 20*, 1205–1218.

Holtgraves, T. (2005). The production and perception of implicit performatives. *Journal of Pragmatics, 37*, 2024–2043.

Holtgraves, T. (2007). Second language learners and speech act comprehension. *Language Learning, 57*, 595–610.

Holtgraves, T., & Yang, J. (1990). Politeness as universal: Cross-cultural perceptions of request strategies and inferences based on their use. *Journal of Personality and Social Psychology, 59*, 719–729.

Houck, N., & Tatsuki, D. (2011). *Pragmatics from research to practice: New directions.* Alexandria, VA: TESOL.

House, J. (2010). The pragmatics of English as a lingua franca. In A. Trosborg (Ed.), *Handbook of pragmatics VII* (pp. 363–387). Berlin: Mouton de Gruyter.

Hübler, A. (2011). Metapragmatics. In W. Bublitz & N. R. Norrick (Eds.), *Foundations of pragmatics* (Vol. 1, pp. 107–136). Berlin: Mouton de Gruyter.

Hübler, A., & Bublitz, W. (Eds.). (2007). *Metapragmatics in use* (Vol. 165). Amsterdam: John Benjamins Publishing.

Hudson, T., Detmer, E., Brown, J. D. (1995). *Developing prototypic measures of cross-cultural pragmatics*. Honolulu, HI: University of Hawai'i Press.

Hutchby, I., & Wooffitt, R. (2008). *Conversation analysis* (2nd ed.). Malden, MA: Blackwell.

Huth, T. (2006). Negotiating structure and culture: L2 learners' realization of L2 compliment-response sequences in talk-in-interaction. *Journal of Pragmatics, 38,* 2025–2050.

Hymes, D. (1972a). Models of interaction of language and social life. In J. Gumperz & D. Hymes (Eds.), *Directions in sociolinguistics: Ethnography of communication* (pp. 35–75). New York, NY: Holt, Rinehart and Winston.

Hymes, D. (1972b). On communicative competence. In J. B. Pride & J. Holmes (Eds.), *Sociolinguistics: Selected readings* (pp. 269–293). Harmondsworth: Penguin.

Hymes, D. (1974). *Foundations in sociolinguistics: An ethnographic approach*. Philadelphia, PA: University of Pennsylvania Press.

Ishida, K. (2007). *Developing understanding of how the desu/masu and plain forms express one's stance*. Selected papers from the conference on pragmatics in the CJK classroom: The state of the art (pp. 181–202). Honolulu, HI: University of Hawaii.

Ishida, M. (2009). Development of interactional competence: Changes in the use of *ne* in L2 Japanese during study abroad. In H. T. Nguyen & G. Kasper (Eds.), *Talk-in-interaction: Multilingual perspectives* (pp. 351–385). Honolulu, HI: National Foreign Language Resource Center.

Ishihara, N. (2009). Teacher-based assessment for foreign language pragmatics. *TESOL Quarterly, 43,* 445–470.

Ishihara, N. (2010). Assessing learners' pragmatic ability in the classroom. In D. Tatsuki & N. Houck (Eds.), *Pragmatics: Teaching speech acts* (pp. 209–227). Alexandria, VA: Teachers of English to Speakers of Other Languages.

Ishihara, N., & Cohen, A. D. (2010). *Teaching and learning pragmatics: Where language and culture meet*. Harlow: Pearson Longman.

Jacoby, S., & Ochs, E. (1995). Co-construction: An introduction. *Research on Language and Social Interaction, 28,* 171–183.

Jakobson, R. (1960). Linguistics and poetics. In T. A. Sebeok (Ed.), *Style in language* (pp. 350–377). Cambridge, MA: MIT Press.

Jenkins, J. (2015). *Global Englishes* (3rd ed.). London: Routledge.

Jeon, E. H., & Kaya, T. (2006). Effects of L2 instruction on interlanguage pragmatic development: A meta-analysis. In J. M. Norris & L. Ortega (Eds.), *Synthesizing research on language learning and teaching* (pp. 165–211). Amsterdam: John Benjamins Publishing.

Jin, L. (2012). When in China, do as the Chinese do? Learning compliment responding in a study abroad program. *Chinese as a Second Language Research, 1,* 211–240.

Johnston, B., Kasper, G., & Ross, S. (1998). The effect of rejoinders in production question-naires. *Applied Linguistics, 19,* 157–182.

Jones, K. (2007). The development of pragmatic competence in children learning Japanese as a second language. In D. R. Yoshimi & H. Wang (Eds.), *Selected papers from pragmatics in the CJK classroom: The state of the art* (pp. 141–169). Honolulu, HI: National Foreign Language Center.

Kallen, J. L., & Kirk, J. M. (2012). *SPICE-Ireland: A user's guide*. Belfast: Cló Ollscoil na Banríona.

Kanagy, R. (1999). Interactional routines as a mechanism for L2 acquisition and socialization in an immersion context. *Journal of Pragmatics, 31*, 1467–1492.

Kanik, M. (2013). Reverse discourse completion task as an assessment tool for intercultural competence. *Studies in Second Language Learning and Teaching, 3*, 621–644.

Kasper, G. (Ed.). (1992a). *Pragmatics of Japanese as a native and target language*. Second Language Teaching and Curriculum Center Technical Report No. 3 (pp. 27–82). Honolulu, HI: University of Hawai'i Press.

Kasper, G. (1992b). Pragmatic transfer. *Second Language Research, 8*, 203–231.

Kasper, G. (2001). Four perspectives on L2 pragmatic development. *Applied Linguistics, 22*, 502–530.

Kasper, G. (2006). Speech acts in interaction: Towards discursive pragmatics. In K. Bardovi-Harlig, C. Félix-Brasdefer, & A. Omar (Eds.), *Pragmatics and language learning* (Vol. 11, pp. 281–314). Honolulu, HI: University of Hawai'i, National Foreign Language Resource Center.

Kasper, G. (2008). Data collection in pragmatics research. In H. Spencer-Oatey (Ed.), *Culturally speaking: Culture, communication and politeness theory* (2nd ed., pp. 279–303). London: Continuum.

Kasper, G., & Dahl, M. (1991). Research methods in interlanguage pragmatics. *Studies in Second Language Acquisition, 13*, 215–247.

Kasper, G., & Rose, K.R. (1999). Pragmatics and SLA. *Annual Review of Applied Linguistics, 19*, 81–104.

Kasper, G., & Rose, K. R. (2002). *Pragmatic development in a second language*. Oxford: Blackwell.

Kasper, G., & Ross, S. (2007). Multiple questions in oral proficiency interviews. *Journal of Pragmatics, 39*, 2045–2070.

Kasper, G., & Schmidt, R. (1996). Developmental issues in ILP. *Studies in Second Language Acquisition, 18*, 149–169.

Kawulich, B. B. (2005). Participant observation as a data collection method. *Forum: Qualitative Social Research, 6*, Art. 43.

Kecskes, I. (2014). *Intercultural pragmatics*. New York, NY: Oxford University Press.

Kim, E.Y., & Brown, L. (2014). Negotiating pragmatic competence in computer mediated communication: The case of Korean address terms. *CALICO, 31*, 264–284.

Kinginger, C. (2008). Language learning in study abroad: Case studies of Americans in France. *Modern Language Journal, 92*(s1), 1–124.

Kinginger, C., & Blattner, C. (2008). Histories of engagement and sociolinguistic awareness in study abroad: Colloquial French. In L. Ortega & H. Byrnes (Eds.), *The longitudinal study of advanced L2 capacities* (pp. 223–246). New York, NY: Routledge.

Kipper, D. A. (1988). The differential effect of role-playing conditions on the accuracy of self-evaluation. *Journal of Group Psychotherapy, Psychodrama & Sociometry, 41*, 30–35.

Koike, D. A., & Pearson, L. (2005). The effect of instruction and feedback in the development of pragmatic competence. *System, 33*, 481–501.

Koven, M. (2006). Feeling in two languages: A comparative analysis of a bilingual's affective displays in French and Portuguese. In A. Pavlenko (Ed.), *Bilingual minds: Emotional experience, expression, and representation* (pp. 84–117). Clevedon: Multilingual Matters.

Kramsch, C. (2014). Teaching foreign languages in an era of globalization: Introduction. *Modern Language Journal, 98*, 296–311.

Kuha, M. (1999). *The influence of interaction and instructions on speech act data* (Unpublished doctoral dissertation). Indiana University, Bloomington, IN.

Kuhlen, A. K., & Brennan, S. E. (2013). Language in dialogue: when confederates might be hazardous to your data. *Psychonomic Bulletin and Review, 20*, 54–72.

Labov, W. (1972). *Language in the inner city: Studies in the black English vernacular.* Philadelphia, PA: University of Pennsylvania Press.

Lakoff, R. T. (1973). *The logic of politeness, or minding your p's and q's.* Papers from the ninth regional meeting of the Chicago Linguistic Society, 292–305.

Larsen-Freeman, D., & Cameron, L. (2008). *Complex systems and applied linguistics.* Oxford/ New York, NY: Oxford University Press.

Leech, G. N. (1983). *Principles of pragmatics.* London: Longman.

Leech, G. N. (2014). *The pragmatics of politeness.* New York, NY: Oxford University Press.

Levinson, S. C. (1979) Activity types and language. *Linguistics, 17*, 365–399.

Levinson, S. C. (1983). *Pragmatics.* Cambridge: Cambridge University Press.

Levinson, S. C. (1992). Activity types and language. In P. Drew & J. Heritage (Eds.), *Talk at work* (pp. 66–100). Cambridge: Cambridge University Press.

Levy, M., & Stockwell, G. (2006). *CALL dimensions: Options and issues in computer-assisted language learning.* Mahwah, NJ: Erlbaum.

Li, D. (2000). The pragmatics of making requests in the L2 workplace: A case study of language socialization. *Canadian Modern Language Review, 57*, 58–87.

Li, Q. (2016). Variations in developmental patterns across pragmatic features. *Studies in Second Language Acquisition, 6*, 587–617.

Li, S. (2010). The effectiveness of corrective feedback in SLA: A meta-analysis. *Language Learning, 60*, 309–365.

Li, S. (2012). The effects of input-based practice on pragmatic development of requests in L2 Chinese. *Language Learning, 62*, 403–438.

Li, S., & Taguchi, N. (2014). The effect of practice modality on the development of pragmatic performance in L2 Chinese. *Modern Language Journal, 98*, 794–812.

Liddicoat, A. J., & Crozet, C. (2001). Acquiring French interactional norms through instruction. In K. R. Rose & G. Kasper (Eds.), *Pragmatic development in instructional contexts* (pp. 125–144). Cambridge: Cambridge University Press.

Lim, T. S., & Bowers, J. W. (1991). Facework solidarity, approbation, and tact. *Human Communication Research, 17*, 415–450.

Linell, P. (1998). *Approaching dialogue: Talk, interaction and contexts in dialogical perspectives.* Amsterdam: John Benjamins Publishing.

Liu, J. (2007). Developing a pragmatics test for Chinese EFL learners. *Language Testing, 24*, 391–415.

LoCastro, V. (2003). *An introduction to pragmatics: Social action for language teachers.* Ann Arbor, MI: University of Michigan Press.

Locher, M. A. (2006). Polite behaviour within relational work: The discursive approach to politeness. *Multilingua, 25*, 249–267.

Locher, M, A., & Watts, R. J. (2005). Politeness theory and relational work. *Journal of Politeness Research: Language, Behaviour, Culture, 1*, 9–33.

Long, M. H. (1996). The role of the linguistic environment in second language acquisition. In W. Ritchie & T. Bhatia (Eds.), *Handbook of language acquisition: Vol. 2. Second language acquisition* (pp. 413–468). San Diego, CA: Academic Press.

Long, M. H. (2016). In defense of tasks and TBLT: Nonissues and real issues. *Annual Review of Applied Linguistics, 36*, 5–33.

Lucy, J. A. (Ed.). (1993). *Reflexive language: Reported speech and metapragmatics.* Cambridge: Cambridge University Press.

Lyster, R., & Saito, K. (2010). Oral feedback in classroom SLA: A meta-analysis. *Studies in Second Language Acquisition, 32*, 265–302.

Mackey, A., & Gass, S. M. (2015). *Second language research: Methodology and design.* New York, NY: Routledge.

Mackey, A., Gass, S., & McDonough, K. (2000). How do learners perceive interactional feedback? *Studies in Second Language Acquisition, 22*, 471–497.

Mackey, A., & Goo, J. (2007) Interaction research in SLA: A meta-analysis and research synthesis. In: *Conversational interaction in second language acquisition: a series of empirical studies. Oxford applied linguistics* (pp. 407–453). Oxford: Oxford University Press.

MacSwan, J. (2017). A multilingual perspective on translanguaging. *American Educational Research Journal, 54*, 167–201.

Maeshiba, N., Yoshinaga, N. K., Kasper, G. G., & Ross, S. (1996). Transfer and proficiency in interlanguage apologizing. In S. Gass & J. Neu (Eds.), *Speech acts across cultures: Challenges to communication in a second language* (pp. 155–187). Berlin: Mouton de Gruyter.

Manes, J., & Wolfson, N. (1981). The compliment formula. In F. Coulmas (Ed.), *Conversational routine: Explorations in standardized communication situations and prepatterned speech* (pp. 115–132). The Hague: Mouton Publishers.

Mao, L. R. (1994). Beyond politeness theory: 'Face' revisited and renewed. *Journal of Pragmatics, 21*, 451–486.

Mackey, A. (2012). *Input, interaction, and corrective feedback in L2 learning.* Oxford: Oxford University Press.

Markee, N. (2008). Toward a learning behavior tracking methodology for CA-for-SLA. *Applied Linguistics, 29*, 404–427.

Marmaridou, S. (2011). Pragmalinguistics and sociopragmatics. In W. Bublitz & N. R. Norrick (Eds.), *Foundations of pragmatics* (pp. 77–106). Berlin: De Gruyter Mouton.

Martínez-Flor, A. (2006). The effectiveness of explicit and implicit treatments on EFL learners' confidence in recognizing appropriate suggestions. *Pragmatics and Language Learning, 11*, 199–225.

Martínez-Flor, A. (2008). Analysing request modification devices in films: Implications for pragmatic learning in instructed foreign language contexts. In E. Alcón Soler & M. Pilar Safont Jordà (Eds.), *Intercultural language use and language learning* (pp. 245–280). Dordrecht: Springer.

Martínez-Flor, A., & Usó-Juan, E. (2006). A comprehensive pedagogical framework to develop pragmatics in the foreign language classroom: The 6Rs approach. *Applied Language Learning 16*, 39–64.

Matsumoto, Y. (1988). Reexamination of the universality of face: Politeness phenomena in Japanese. *Journal of Pragmatics, 12*, 403–426.

Mazzone, M. (2011). Schemata and associative processes in pragmatics. *Journal of Pragmatics, 43*, 2148–2159.

Meier, A. J. (1995). Passages of politeness. *Journal of Pragmatics, 24*, 381–392.

McLean, T. (2005). "Why no tip?" Student-generated DCTs in the ESL classroom. In D. Tatsuki (Ed.), *Pragmatics in language learning, theory and practice* (pp. 150–156). Tokyo: JALT Pragmatics SIG.

McMeekin, A. (2014). Japanese learners' indexical uses of the da style in a study abroad setting. *Japanese Language and Literature 48*, 1–38.

Melissa. (2004, December 26). 25 Thoughts on "Christmas and New Year 2005" [A comment made in response to a blog by Boris Johnson, a UK government minister]. Retrieved from www.boris-johnson.com/2004/12/24/christmas-and-new-year-2005/.

Mills, S. (2003). *Gender and politeness.* Cambridge: Cambridge University Press.

Moody, S. J. (2014). Should we teach rules for pragmatics? Explicit instruction and emergent awareness of Japanese plain and polite forms. *Japanese Language and Literature, 1*(48), 39–69.

Morgan, J. (1978). Two types of convention in speech acts. In P. Cole (Ed.), *Syntax and Semantics* (Vol. 9: Pragmatics) (pp. 261–280). New York, NY: Academic Press.

Mori, J. (2006). The workings of the Japanese token *hee* in informing sequences: An analysis of sequential context, turn shape, and prosody. *Journal of Pragmatics, 38,* 1175–1205.

Mori, J. (2009). The social turn in second language acquisition and Japanese pragmatics research: Reflection on ideologies, methodologies and instructional implications. In N. Taguchi (Ed.), *Pragmatic competence* (pp. 335–338). New York, NY: Mouton de Gruyter.

Morris, C.W. (1938). Foundations of the theory of signs. In O. Neurath, R. Carnap, & C. Morris (Eds.), *International encyclopedia of unified science* (Vol. 1, pp. 1–59). Chicago, IL: University of Chicago Press.

Myers, G. (1991). Politeness and certainty: The language of collaboration in an AI project. *Social Studies of Science, 21,* 37–73.

Nadeau, J., & Barlow, J. (2003). *Sixty million Frenchmen can't be wrong: Why we love France but not the French.* Naperville, IL: Sourcebooks.

Nesselhauf, N. (2004). Learner corpora and their potential for language teaching. *How to Use Corpora in Language Teaching, 12,* 125–156.

Nguyen, T. T. M. (2008). Modifying L2 criticism: How learners do it? *Journal of Pragmatics, 40,* 768–791.

Nguyen, T.T. M. (2013). Instructional effects on the acquisition of modifiers in constructive criticisms by EFL learners. *Language Awareness, 22,* 76–94.

Nikula, T. (2008). Learning pragmatics in content-based classrooms. In E. Alcón Soler & A. Martínez-Flor (Eds.), *Investigating pragmatics in foreign language learning, teaching and testing* (pp. 94–113). Bristol: Multilingual Matters.

Nisbett, R. E., & Wilson, T. D. (1977). Telling more than we can know: Verbal reports on mental processes. *Psychological Review, 84,* 231–259.

Nwoye, O. G. (1992). Linguistic politeness and socio-cultural variations of the notion of face. *Journal of Pragmatics, 18,* 309–328.

Ohta, A. (2001). *Second language acquisition processes in the classroom: Learning Japanese.* Mahwah, NJ: Lawrence Erlbaum.

O'Keeffe, A., Clancy, B., & Adolphs, S. (2011). *Introducing pragmatics in use.* London: Routledge.

Opp, K. D. (1982). The evolutionary emergence of norms. *British Journal of Social Psychology, 21,* 139–149.

Pekarek Doehler, S., & Berger, E. (2017). L2 interactional competence as increased ability for context-sensitive conduct: A longitudinal study of story-openings. *Applied Linguistics,* http://dx.doi.org/10.1093/applin/amw021.

Park, E. (2006). Grandparents, grandchildren, and heritage language use in Korean. In K. Kondo-Brown (Ed.), *Heritage language development: Focus on East Asian immigrants* (pp. 57–87). Amsterdam: John Benjamins.

Payne, J. S., & Whitney, P. J. (2002). Developing L2 oral proficiency through synchronous CMC: Output, working memory, and interlanguage development. *CALICO Journal, 20,* 7–32.

Peccei, J. S. (1999). *Pragmatics.* London: Routledge.

Piirainen-Marsh, A. (2005). Managing adversarial questions in broadcast interviews. *Journal of Politeness Research: Language, Behaviour, Culture, 1,* 193–217.

Pike, K. (1967). Etic and emic standpoints for the description of behavior. In D. C. Hildum (Ed.), *Language and thought: An enduring problem in psychology* (pp. 32–39). Princeton, NJ: D. Van Norstrand Company.

Pinto, D., & Raschio, R. (2008). Oye, ¿qué onda con mi dinero? An analysis of heritage speaker complaints. *Sociolinguistic Studies, 2,* 221–249.

Plonsky, L., & Zhuang, J. (forthcoming). A meta-analysis of second language pragmatics instruction. In N. Taguchi (Ed.), *Routledge handbook of SLA and pragmatics.* New York, NY: Routledge.

Polat, B. (2011). Investigating acquisition of discourse markers through a developmental learner corpus. *Journal of Pragmatics, 43,* 3745–3756.

Pomerantz, A. (1984). Agreeing and disagreeing with assessments: Some features of preferred/dispreferred turn shapes. In J. M. Atkinson & J. Heritage (Eds.), *Structures of social action: Studies in Conversation Analysis* (pp. 57–101). New York, NY: Cambridge University Press.

Pomerantz, A., & Bell, N. D. (2011). Humor as safe house in the foreign language classroom. *Modern Language Journal, 95,* 148–161.

Psathas, G. (1995). *Conversation analysis: The study of talk-in-interaction.* Thousand Oaks, CA: Sage.

Quirk, R., Greenbaum, S., Leech, G., & Svartvik, J. (1985). *A comprehensive grammar of the English language.* London: Longman.

Recanati, F. (2004). *Literal meaning.* Cambridge: Cambridge University Press.

Ren, W. (2012). Pragmatic development in Chinese speakers' L2 English refusals. *EUROSLA Yearbook, 12,* 63–87.

Ren, W. (2014). A longitudinal investigation into L2 learners' cognitive processes during study abroad. *Applied Linguistics, 35,* 575–594.

Robinson, M. A. (1992). Introspective methodology in interlanguage pragmatics research. In G. Kasper (Ed.), *Pragmatics of Japanese as native and target language* (Technical Report No. 3, pp. 27–82). Honolulu, HI: University of Hawai'i at Manoa, Second Language Teaching and Curriculum Center.

Roever, C. (2005). *Testing ESL pragmatics.* Frankfurt: Peter Lang.

Roever, C. (2011). Tests of second language pragmatics: Past and future. *Language Testing, 28,* 463–481.

Roever, C., Fraser, C., & Elder, C. (2014). *Testing ESL sociopragmatics: Development and validation of a web-based test battery.* Frankfurt: Peter Lang.

Roever, C., Wang, S., & Brophy, S. (2014). Learner background factors and learning of second language pragmatics. *International Review of Applied Linguistics, 52,* 377–401.

Rogerson-Revell, P. (2007). Using English for international business: A European case study. *English for Specific Purposes, 26,* 103–120.

Rosa, E. E., & Leow, R. P. (2004). Awareness, different learning conditions, and L2 development. *Applied Psycholinguistics, 25,* 269–292.

Rose, K. R., & Ng, C. K. (2001). Inductive and deductive teaching of compliments and compliment responses. In K. Rose & G. Kasper (Eds.), *Pragmatics in language teaching* (pp. 145–170). Cambridge: Cambridge University Press.

Rosenthal, R. (1966). *Experimenter effects in behavioral research.* East Norwalk, CT: Appleton-Century-Crofts.

Rumelhart, D. E. (1984). Schemata and cognitive systems. In R. S. Wyer & T. K. Srull (Eds.), *Handbook of social cognition* (Vol. 2, pp. 161–188). Hillsdale, NJ: Erlbaum.

Russo, J. E., Johnson, E. J., & Stephens, D. L. (1989). The validity of verbal protocols. *Memory & Cognition, 17,* 759–769.

224 References

Sacks, H., Schegloff, E., & Jefferson, G. (1974). A simplest systematics for the organization of turn-taking for conversation. *Language, 50,* 696–735.

Sadanobu, T. (2004). A natural history of Japanese pressed voice. *Journal of the Phonetic Society of Japan, 8,* 29–44.

Salsbury, T., & Bardovi-Harlig, K. (2000). Oppositional talk and the acquisition of modality in L2 English. In B. Swierzbin, F. Morris, M. E. Anderson, C. A. Klee, & E. Tarone (Eds.), *Social and cognitive factors in second language acquisition: Selected proceedings of the 1999 Second Language Research Forum* (pp. 57–76). Somerville, MA: Cascadilla Press.

Sarangi, S. (2000). Activity types, discourse types and interactional hybridity: The case of genetic counselling. In S. Sarangi & M. Coulthard (Eds.), *Discourse and social life* (pp. 1–27). Harlow: Longman.

Sasaki, M. (1998). Investigating EFL students' production of speech acts: A comparison of production questionnaires and role plays. *Journal of Pragmatics, 30,* 457–484.

Schank, R. C., & Abelson, R. P. (1977). *Scripts, plans, goals, and understanding: An inquiry into human knowledge structures.* Hillsdale, NJ: L. Erlbaum Associates.

Schauer, G. (2007). Finding the right words in the study abroad context: The development of German learners' use of external modifiers in English. *Intercultural Pragmatics, 4,* 193–220.

Schegloff, E. A. (1984). On some questions and ambiguities in conversation. In J. M. Atkinson & J. Heritage (Eds.), *Structures of social action* (pp. 28–52). Cambridge: Cambridge University Press.

Schegloff, E. A. (1996). Turn organization: One intersection of grammar and interaction. In E. Ochs, E. A. Schegloff, & S. Thompson (Eds.), *Interaction and grammar* (pp. 52–133). Cambridge: Cambridge University Press.

Schegloff, E. A. (2007). *Sequence organization in interaction.* Cambridge: Cambridge University Press.

Schegloff, E. A., & Sacks, H. (1973). Opening up closings. *Semiotica, 7,* 289–327.

Schensul, S. L., Schensul, J. J., & LeCompte, M. D. (1999). *Essential ethnographic methods: Observations, interviews, and questionnaires* (Vol. 2). Walnut Creek, CA: Rowman Altamira.

Schieffelin, B. B., & Ochs, E. (1986). *Language socialization across cultures.* Cambridge: Cambridge University Press.

Schmidt, R. (1983). Interaction, acculturation, and the acquisition of communicative competence: A case study of an adult. In N. Wolfson & E. Judd (Eds.), *Sociolinguistics and language acquisition* (pp. 137–174). Rowley, MA: Newbury House.

Schmidt, R. (1993). Consciousness, learning and interlanguage pragmatics. In G. Kasper, & S. Blum-Kulka (Eds.), *Interlanguage pragmatics* (pp. 21–42). Oxford: Oxford University Press.

Schmidt, R. (2001). Attention. In P. Robinson (Ed.), *Cognition and second language instruction* (pp. 3–32). Cambridge: Cambridge University Press.

Schneider, K. P., & Barron, A. (Eds.). (2008). *Variational pragmatics: A focus on regional varieties in pluricentric languages* (Vol. 178). Amsterdam: John Benjamins Publishing.

Schönfeldt, J., & Golato, A. (2003). Repair in chats: A conversation analytic approach. *Research on Language and Social Interaction, 36,* 241–284.

Scollon, R., & Scollon, S. W. (1981). *Narrative, literacy and face in interethnic communication* (Vol. 7). Norwood, NJ: Ablex Publishing.

Searle, J. R. (1969). *Speech acts: An essay in the philosophy of language.* Cambridge: Cambridge University Press.

Searle, J. R. (1985). *Expression and meaning: Studies in theory of speech acts.* Cambridge: Cambridge University Press.

Seidlhofer, B. (2011). *Understanding English as a lingua franca*. Oxford: Oxford University Press.

Shimanoff, S. B. (1977). Investigating politeness. In E. O. Keenan & T. L. Bennett (Eds.), *Discourse across time and space, Southern California Occasional Papers in Linguistics, 5*, 213–241.

Shively, R. (2011). L2 pragmatic development in study abroad: A longitudinal study of Spanish service encounters. *Journal of Pragmatics, 43*, 1818–1835.

Shively, R. (2013). Learning to be funny in Spanish study abroad: L2 humor development. *Modern Language Journal, 97*, 939–946.

Shively, R. L. (forthcoming). Naturalistic data in L2 pragmatics research: Challenges and opportunities. In A. Gudmestad & A. Edmonds (Eds.), *Critical reflections on data in second language acquisition*. Amsterdam: John Benjamins.

Shochi, T., Auberge, V., & Rilliard, A. (2007). *Cross-listening of Japanese, English and French social affect: About universals, false friends and unknown attitudes*. Proceedings from 16th Congress of Phonetic Sciences. Saarbrücken, Germany. Retrieved from www.icphs2007.de/conference/session16.html.

Silverstein, M. (1993). Metapragmatic discourse and metapragmatic function. In J. A. Lucy (Ed.), *Reflexive language: Reported speech and metapragmatics* (pp. 33–58). Cambridge: Cambridge University Press.

Silverstein, M. (1998). The uses and utility of ideology: A commentary. In B. Schieffelin, K. Woolard, & P. V. Kroskrity (Eds.), *Language ideologies: Practice and theory* (pp. 123–145). Oxford: Oxford University Press.

Silverstein, M. (2003). Indexical order and the dialectics of sociolinguistic life. *Language & Communication, 23*, 193–229.

Smith, B. (2004). Computer-mediated negotiated interaction and lexical acquisition. *Studies in Second Language Acquisition, 26*, 365–398.

Someren, M. W. V., Barnard, Y. F., & Sandberg, J. (1994). *The think aloud method: A practical guide to modelling cognitive processes*. San Diego, CA: Academic Press.

Sotillo, S. (2000). Discourse functions and syntactic complexity in synchronous and asynchronous communication. *Language Learning and Technology, 4*, 82–119.

Spencer-Oatey, H. (1996). Reconsidering power and social distance. *Journal of Pragmatics, 26*, 1–24.

Spencer-Oatey, H., & Franklin, P. (2009). *Intercultural interaction*. New York, NY: Palgrave MacMillan.

Sperber, D., & Wilson, D. (1986). *Relevance: Communication and cognition*. Oxford: Blackwell.

Sperber, D., & Wilson, D. (1995). *Relevance: Communication and cognition* (2nd ed.). Cambridge, MA: Oxford.

Spurrier, P. (2005). Paul Spurrier talks Thailand, ghosts, and P. Retrieved from https://screenanarchy.com/2005/04/paul-spurrier-talks-thailand-ghosts-and-p.html.

Staples, S. (2015). *The discourse of nurse-patient interactions: Contrasting the communicative styles of U.S. and international nurses*. Amsterdam: John Benjamins Publishing Company.

Swain, M. (2006). Verbal protocols: What does it mean for research to use speaking as a data collection tool? In M. Chalhoub-Deville, C. A. Chapelle, & P. A. Duff (Eds.), *Inference and generalizability in applied linguistics: Multiple perspectives* (pp. 97–114). Amsterdam: John Benjamins Publishing.

Swain, M., & Lapkin, S. (1998). Interaction and second language learning: Two adolescent French immersion students working together. *Modern Language Journal, 82*, 320–337.

Sydorenko, T. (2015). The use of computer-delivered structured tasks in pragmatic instruction: An exploratory study. *Intercultural Pragmatics, 12*, 333–362.

Sykes, I. M. (2013). Multiuser virtual environments: Learner apologies in Spanish. In N. Taguchi & J. M. Sykes (Eds.), *Technology in interlanguage pragmatics research and teaching* (pp. 71–100). Amsterdam: John Benjamins Publishing.

Taguchi, N. (2002). An application of relevance theory to the analysis of L2 interpretation processes: The comprehension of indirect replies. *International Review of Applied Linguistics, 40,* 151–176.

Taguchi, N. (2005). Comprehension of implied meaning in English as a second language. *Modern Language Journal, 89,* 543–562.

Taguchi, N. (2006). Analysis of appropriateness in a speech act of request in L2 English. *Pragmatics: Quarterly Publication of the International Pragmatics Association, 16,* 513–533.

Taguchi, N. (2007). Development of speed and accuracy in pragmatic comprehension in English as a foreign language. *TESOL Quarterly, 42,* 313–338.

Taguchi, N. (2008). The role of learning environment in the development of pragmatic comprehension: A comparison of gains between ESL and EFL learners. *Studies in Second Language Acquisition, 30,* 423–452.

Taguchi, N. (2010). Longitudinal studies in interlanguage pragmatics. In A. Trosborg (Ed.), *Handbook of pragmatics* (Vol. 7: Pragmatics across languages and cultures) (pp. 333–361). Berlin: Mouton de Gruyter.

Taguchi, N. (2011a). Do proficiency and study-abroad experience affect speech act production? Analysis of appropriateness, accuracy, and fluency. *International Review of Applied Linguistics, 49,* 265–293.

Taguchi, N. (2011b). The effect of L2 proficiency and study-abroad experience in pragmatic comprehension. *Language Learning, 61,* 904–939.

Taguchi, N. (2012). *Context, individual differences, and pragmatic competence.* Bristol: Multilingual Matters.

Taguchi, N. (2015a). *Developing interactional competence in a Japanese study abroad context.* New York, NY: Multilingual Matters.

Taguchi, N. (2015b). Instructed pragmatics at a glance: Where instructional studies were, are, and should be going. *Language Teaching, 48,* 1–50.

Taguchi, N., Gomez-Laich, P. M., & Arrufat-Marqués, M. J. (2016). Comprehension of indirect meaning in Spanish as a foreign language. *Foreign Language Annals, 49,* 677–698.

Taguchi, N., & Kim, Y. (2016). Collaborative dialogue in learning pragmatics: Pragmatics-related episodes as an opportunity for learning request-making. *Applied Linguistics, 37,* 416–437.

Taguchi, N., Li, S., & Liu, Y. (2013). Comprehension of conversational implicature in L2 Chinese. *Pragmatics & Cognition, 21,* 139–157.

Taguchi, N., Li, Q., & Tang, X. (2017). Learning Chinese formulaic expressions in a scenario-based interactive environment. *Foreign Language Annals, 50,* 641–660.

Taguchi, N., Li, S., & Xiao, F. (2013). Production of formulaic expressions in L2 Chinese: A developmental investigation in a study abroad context. *Chinese as a Second Language Research Journal, 2,* 23–58.

Taguchi, N., & Roever, C. (2017). *Second language pragmatics.* Oxford: Oxford University Press.

Taguchi, N., Xiao, F., & Li, S. (2016). Development of pragmatic knowledge in L2 Chinese: Effects of intercultural competence and social contact on speech act production in a study abroad context. *Modern Language Journal, 100,* 775–796.

Takahashi, S. (2001). The role of input enhancement in developing pragmatic competence. In G. Kasper & K. R. Rose (Eds.), *Pragmatics in language teaching* (pp. 171–199). Cambridge: Cambridge University Press.

Takahashi, S. (2010). The effect of pragmatic instruction on speech act performance. In A. Martinez-Flor & E. Uso-Juan (Eds.), *Speech act performance: Theoretical, empirical and methodological issues* (pp. 127–144). Amsterdam: John Benjamins.

Takamiya, Y., & Ishihara, N. (2013). Blogging: cross-cultural interaction for pragmatic development. In N. Taguchi & J. M. Sykes (Eds.), *Technology in interlanguage pragmatics research and teaching* (pp. 185–214). Amsterdam: John Benjamins Publishing.

Takimoto, M. (2009). Exploring the effects of input-based treatment and test on the development of learners' pragmatic proficiency. *Journal of Pragmatics, 41*, 1029–1046.

Taleghani-Nikazm, C., & Huth, T. (2010). L2 requests: Preference structure in talk-in-interaction. *Multilingua, 29*, 185–202.

Tan, K. H., & Farashaiyan, A. (2012). The effectiveness of teaching formulaic politeness strategies in making request to undergraduates in an ESL classroom. *Asian Social Science, 8*, 189.

Tannen, D. (1984). *Conversational style: Analyzing talk among friends.* Oxford: Oxford University Press.

Tannen, D. (2005). *Conversational style: Analyzing talk among friends* (Revised ed.). New York, NY: Oxford University Press.

Tarone, E. (2013). Applied linguists without borders. *Language Teaching: Surveys and Studies, 46*, 355–364.

Tashakkori, A., & Teddlie, C. (2003). *Handbook of mixed methods in social and behavior research.* Thousand Oaks, CA: Sage.

ten Have, P. (2007). *Doing conversation analysis: A practical guide.* Los Angeles, CA: Sage.

Terkourafi, M. (2001). *Politeness in Cypriot Greek: A frame-based approach* (Unpublished doctoral dissertation). Cambridge: University of Cambridge.

Terkourafi, M. (2002). Politeness and formulaicity: Evidence from Cypriot Greek. *Journal of Greek Linguistics, 3*, 179–201.

Terkourafi, M. (2003). Generalised and particularised implicatures of politeness. In P. Kühnlein, H. Rieser, & H. Zeevat (Eds.), *Perspectives on dialogue in the new millennium* (pp. 151–166). Amsterdam: John Benjamins.

Terkourafi, M. (2005a). Beyond the micro-level in politeness research. *Journal of Politeness Research, 1*, 237–262.

Terkourafi, M. (2005b). Pragmatic correlates of frequency of use: The case for a notion of "minimal context." In S. Marmaridou, K. Nikiforidou, & E. Antonopoulou (Eds.), *Reviewing linguistic thought: Converging trends for the 21st century* (pp. 209–233). Berlin: Mouton de Gruyter.

Thomas, J. A. (1981). *Pragmatic failure* (Unpublished master's thesis). University of Lancaster, Lancaster.

Thomas, J. A. (1983). Cross-cultural pragmatic failure. *Applied Linguistics, 4*, 91–112.

Thomas, J. A. (1995). *Meaning in interaction: An introduction to pragmatics.* London: Longman.

Thomas, M., & Peterson, M. (2014). Web 2.0 and language learning. Special issue. *CALICO, 31*, i–iii.

Tracy, K. (1990). The many faces of facework. In H. Giles & W. P. Robinson (Eds.), *Handbook of language and social psychology* (pp. 209–226). Chichester: Wiley.

Trosborg, A. (1995). *Interlanguage pragmatics: Requests, complaints, and apologies* (Vol. 7). Berlin: Mouton de Gruyter.

Tsai, M.-H., & Kinginger, C. (2015). Giving and receiving advice in computer-mediated peer response activities. *CALICO, 32*, 82–112.

Turnbull, W. (2001). An appraisal of pragmatic elicitation techniques for the social psychological study of talk: The case of request refusals. *Pragmatics, 11*, 31–61.

van Compernolle, R. A., & Henery, A. (2014). Instructed concept appropriation and L2 pragmatic development in the classroom. *Language Learning, 64*, 549–578.

van der Bom, I., & Mills, S. (2015). A discursive approach to the analysis of politeness data. *Journal of Politeness Research, 11*, 179–206.

Verschueren, J. (1999). *Understanding pragmatics*. Oxford: Oxford University Press.

Verschueren, J. (2000). Notes on the role of metapragmatic awareness in language use. *Pragmatics: Quarterly Publication of the International Pragmatics Association (IPrA), 10*, 439–456.

Vilar-Beltrán, E., & Melchor-Couto, S. (2013). Refusing in second life. *Utrecht studies in language and communication, 25*, 23–40.

Vyatkina, N., & Belz, J. A. (2006). A learner corpus-driven intervention for the development of L2 pragmatic competence. In K. Bardovi-Harlig, C. Félix-Brasdefer, & A. S. Omar (Eds.), *Pragmatics and language learning* (pp. 315–357). Honolulu: University of Hawai'i, National Foreign Language Resource Center.

Walker, T., Drew, P., & Local, J. (2011). Responding indirectly. *Journal of Pragmatics, 43*, 2434–2451.

Walters, F. S. (2007). A conversation-analytic hermeneutic rating protocol to assess L2 oral pragmatic competence. *Language Testing, 27*, 155–183.

Walters, F. S. (2009). A conversation analysis—informed test of L2 aural pragmatic comprehension. *TESOL Quarterly, 43*, 29–54.

Watts, R. J. (2003). *Politeness*. Cambridge: Cambridge University Press.

Watts, R. J., Ide, S., & Ehlich, K. (Eds.). (2005). *Politeness in language: Studies in its history, theory and practice* (2nd ed.). Berlin: Mouton de Gruyter.

Wharton, T. (2009). *Pragmatics and non-verbal communication*. Cambridge: Cambridge University Press.

Wierzbicka, A. (1991/2003). *Cross-cultural pragmatics: The semantics of human interaction*. Berlin: De Gruyter Mouton.

Wilson, D., & Sperber, D. (2012). *Meaning and relevance*. Cambridge: Cambridge University Press.

Winke, P., & Teng, C. (2010). Using task-based pragmatics tutorials while studying abroad in China. *Intercultural Pragmatics, 7*, 363–399.

Wood, D. (2006). Uses and functions of formulaic sequences in second language speech: An exploration of the foundations of fluency. *Canadian Modern Language Review, 63*, 13–33.

Woodfield, H. (2008). Interlanguage requests: A contrastive study. In M. Pütz & J. Neff-van Aertselaer (Eds.), *Developing contrastive pragmatics: Interlanguage and cross-cultural perspectives* (pp. 231–264). Berlin: Mouton de Gruyter.

Woodfield, H. (2010). What lies beneath? Verbal report in interlanguage requests in English. *Multilingua: Journal of Cross-Cultural and Interlanguage Communication, 29*, 1–27.

Woodfield, H. (2012). "I think maybe I want to lend the notes from you:" Development of request modification in graduate learners. In M. Economidou-Kogetsidis & H. Woodfield (Eds.), *Interlanguage request modification* (pp. 9–49). Amsterdam: John Benjamins Publishing.

Wray, A. (2002). Formulaic language in computer-supported communication: Theory meets reality. *Language Awareness, 11*, 114–131.

Yamanaka, J. E. (2003). Effects of proficiency and length of residence on the pragmatic comprehension of Japanese ESL. *University of Hawai'i Second Langauge Studies Paper, 22*(1), 107–175.

Yamashita, S. O. (1996). *Six measures of JSL pragmatics* (Vol. 3, Technical Report #14). Honolulu, HI: University of Hawai'i at Manoa, Second Language Teaching and Curriculum Centre.

Yang, H. C., & Zapata-Rivera, D. (2009). An exploratory study into interlanguage pragmatics of requests: A game of persuasion. *ETS Research Report Series, 2009*(1), 1–28.

Youn, S. J. (2015). Validity argument for assessing L2 pragmatics in interaction using mixed methods. *Language Testing, 32,* 199–225.

Young, R. (2008a) *Discursive practices in language learning and teaching.* Malden, MA: Wiley-Blackwell.

Young, R. F. (2008b). *Language and interaction: An advanced resource book.* London: Routledge.

Young, R. (2011a). Interactional competence in language learning, teaching, and testing. In H. Hinkel (Ed.), *Handbook of research in language learning and teaching* (pp. 426–443). New York, NY: Routledge.

Young, R. F. (2011b). Interactional competence in language learning, teaching, and testing. In E. Hinkel (Ed.), *Handbook of research in second language teaching and learning* (Vol. 2, pp. 426–443). London: Routledge.

Yuan, Y. (2001). An inquiry into empirical pragmatics data-gathering methods: Written DCTs, oral DCTs, field notes, and natural conversations. *Journal of Pragmatics, 33,* 271–292.

INDEX

当代国外语言学与应用语言学文库（升级版）
已出版书目

——**Applied Linguistics 应用语言学**

Qualitative Research in Applied Linguistics: A Practical Introduction
《应用语言学中的质性研究实践导论》
　Juanita Heigham & Robert A. Croker

——**Cognitive Linguistics 认知语言学**

Cognitive Linguistics and Language Teaching
《认知语言学和语言教学》
　Randal Holme

An Introduction to Cognitive Linguistics (Second Edition)
《认知语言学入门（第二版）》
　F. Ungerer & H.-J. Schmid

Multimodality and Cognitive Linguistics
《多模态与认知语言学》
　María Jesús Pinar Sanz

Women, Fire, and Dangerous Things: What Categories Reveal about the Mind
《女人、火与危险事物：范畴所揭示的心智》
　George Lakoff

——**Cognitive Poetics 认知诗学**

Kinesic Humor: Literature, Embodied Cognition, and the Dynamics of Gesture
《身势幽默：文学、具身认知以及身势语动力学》
　Guillemette Bolens

Reading Beyond the Code: Literature and Relevance Theory
《阅读"码"外之意：文学与关联理论》
　Terence Cave & Deirdre Wilson

——Computational Linguistics 计算语言学

Natural Language Processing and Computational Linguistics 1: Speech, Morphology and Syntax
《计算语言学概论（第一卷）：语音、词法、句法》
　　Mohamed Zakaria Kurdi

Natural Language Processing and Computational Linguistics 2: Semantics, Discourse and Applications
《计算语言学概论（第二卷）：语义、篇章、应用》
　　Mohamed Zakaria Kurdi

——Corpus Linguistics 语料库语言学

Introduction to Corpus Linguistics
《语料库语言学导论》
　　Sandrine Zufferey

——Curriculum Design 课程设计

Curriculum Development in Language Teaching (Second Edition)
《语言教学中的课程设计（第二版）》
　　Jack C. Richards

Developing the Curriculum: Improved Outcomes Through Systems Approaches (Ninth Edition)
《课程建设：系统论方法与教学成效提升（第九版）》
　　William R. Gordon II, Rosemarye T. Taylor & Peter F. Oliva

——Ecolinguistics 生态语言学

The Ecolinguistics Reader: Language, Ecology and Environment
《生态语言学手册：语言、生态与环境》
　　Alwin Fill & Peter Mühlhäusler

——First Language Acquisition 第一语言习得

An Introduction to Child Language Development
《儿童语言发展引论》
　　Susan H. Foster-Cohen

——Functional Linguistics 功能语言学

The Functional Analysis of English: A Hallidayan Approach (Third Edition)
《英语的功能分析：韩礼德模式（第三版）》
　　Thomas Bloor & Meriel Bloor

Genre Relations: Mapping Culture
《语类关系与文化映射》
   J. R. Martin & David Rose

Introducing Functional Grammar (Third Edition)
《功能语法入门（第三版）》
   Geoff Thompson

An Introduction to Functional Grammar (Third Edition)
《功能语法导论（第三版）》
   M. A. K. Halliday, Revised by Christian Matthiessen

——General Linguistics 普通语言学

Course in General Linguistics
《普通语言学教程》
   F. de Saussure

General Linguistics (Fourth Edition)
《普通语言学概论（第四版）》
   R. H. Robins

An Introduction to Linguistics
《语言学入门》
   Stuart C. Poole

Language
《语言论》
   L. Bloomfield

Language: An Introduction to the Study of Speech
《语言论：言语研究导论》
   Edward Sapir

——History of Linguistics 语言学史

A Short History of Linguistics (Fourth Edition)
《语言学简史（第四版）》
   R. H. Robins

——Intercultural Communication 跨文化交际

Intercultural Communication: A Discourse Approach (Third Edition)
《跨文化交际：语篇分析法（第三版）》
   Ron Scollon, Suzanne Wong Scollon & Rodney H. Jones

Intercultural Interaction: A Multidisciplinary Approach to Intercultural Communication
《跨文化互动：跨文化交际的多学科研究》
 Helen Spencer-Oatey & Peter Franklin

——**Language Education 语言教育**
Approaches and Methods in Language Teaching (Third Edition)
《语言教学的流派（第三版）》
 Jack C. Richards & Theodore S. Rodgers
A Course in English Language Teaching (Second Edition)
《语言教学教程：实践与理论（第二版）》
 Penny Ur
Experiences of Second Language Teacher Education
《第二语言教师教育经验》
 Tony Wright & Mike Beaumont
Principles of Language Learning and Teaching (Sixth Edition)
《语言学习与语言教学的原则（第六版）》
 H. Douglas Brown
Teaching by Principles: An Interactive Approach to Language Pedagogy (Fourth Edition)
《根据原理教学：交互式语言教学（第四版）》
 H. Douglas Brown & Heekyeong Lee
Usage-inspired L2 Instruction: Researched Pedagogy
《使用驱动的二语教学：实证依据》
 Andrea E. Tyler, Lourdes Ortega, Mariko Uno & Hae In Park

——**Morphology 形态学**
Morphological Theory: An Introduction to Word Structure in Generative Grammar
《形态学理论：生成语法的词结构导论》
 Andrew Spencer

——**Neurolinguistics 神经语言学**
The Handbook of the Neuropsychology of Language (2 Volume Set)
《语言的神经心理学手册（第一卷、第二卷）》
 Miriam Faust
Introduction to Neurolinguistics
《神经语言学导论》
 Elisabeth Ahlsén

—— **Philosophy of Language** 语言哲学

How to Do Things with Words
《如何以言行事》
  J. L. Austin

—— **Phonetics and Phonology** 语音学与音系学

English Phonetics and Phonology: A Practical Course (Fourth Edition)
《英语语音学与音系学实用教程（第四版）》
  Peter Roach

—— **Pragmatics** 语用学

Meaning in Interaction: An Introduction to Pragmatics
《言谈互动中的意义：语用学引论》
  Jenny Thomas

Pragmatics: An Introduction (Second Edition)
《语用学引论（第二版）》
  Jacob L. Mey

Relevance: Communication and Cognition (Second Edition)
《关联性：交际与认知（第二版）》
  Dan Sperber & Deirdre Wilson

Second Language Pragmatics: From Theory to Research
《二语语用学：理论与研究》
  Jonathan Culpeper, Alison Mackey & Naoko Taguchi

—— **Psycholinguistics** 心理语言学

The Articulate Mammal: An Introduction to Psycholinguistics (Fourth Edition)
《会说话的哺乳动物：心理语言学入门（第四版）》
  Jean Aitchison

Research Methods in Psycholinguistics and the Neurobiology of Language: A Practical Guide
《心理语言学及语言的神经生物学研究方法实用指导》
  Annette M. B. de Groot & Peter Hagoort

—— **Research Method** 研究方法

Projects in Linguistics and Language Studies: A Practical Guide to Researching Language (Third Edition)
《语言学课题：语言研究实用指导（第三版）》
  Alison Wray & Aileen Bloomer

Research Perspectives on English for Academic Purposes
《学术英语的多维研究视角》
John Flowerdew & Matthew Peacock

—— Second Language Acquisition 第二语言习得

Fossilization in Adult Second Language Acquisition
《成人二语习得中的僵化现象》
韩照红（Zhaohong Han）

Innovative Research and Practices in Second Language Acquisition and Bilingualism
《二语习得与双语现象的创新研究及实践》
John W. Schwieter

Linguistics and Second Language Acquisition
《语言学和第二语言习得》
Vivian Cook

Second Language Learning and Language Teaching (Fifth Edition)
《第二语言学习与教学（第五版）》
Vivian Cook

Second Language Needs Analysis
《第二语言需求分析》
Michael H. Long

Strategies in Learning and Using a Second Language (Second Edition)
《学习和运用第二语言的策略（第二版）》
Andrew D. Cohen

Tasks in Second Language Learning
《第二语言学习中的任务》
Virginia Samuda & Martin Bygate

Working Memory in Second Language Acquisition and Processing
《工作记忆与二语习得及加工》
温植胜（Edward），Mailce Borges Mota & Arthur McNeill

—— Semantics 语义学

Analyzing Meaning: An Introduction to Semantics and Pragmatics (Second Edition)
《意义分析：语义学与语用学导论（第二版）》
Paul R. Kroeger

Meaning in Language: An Introduction to Semantics and Pragmatics (Third Edition)
《语言的意义：语义学与语用学导论（第三版）》
Alan Cruse

Semantics (Fourth Edition)
《语义学（第四版）》
　　John I. Saeed

——Sociolinguistics 社会语言学

The Handbook of Sociolinguistics
《社会语言学通览》
　　Florian Coulmas

An Introduction to Sociolinguistics (Seventh Edition)
《社会语言学引论（第七版）》
　　Ronald Wardhaugh & Janet M. Fuller

——Stylistics 文体学

The Bloomsbury Companion to Stylistics
《布鲁姆斯伯里文体学导论》
　　Violeta Sotirova

A Linguistic Guide to English Poetry
《英诗学习指南：语言学的分析方法》
　　Geoffrey N. Leech

Patterns in Language: Stylistics for Students of Language and Literature
《语言模式：文体学入门》
　　Joanna Thornborrow & Shân Wareing

Style in Fiction: A Linguistic Introduction to English Fictional Prose (Second Edition)
《小说文体论：英语小说的语言学入门（第二版）》
　　Geoffrey Leech & Mick Short

Stylistics: A Practical Coursebook
《实用文体学教程》
　　Laura Wright & Jonathan Hope

——Syntax 句法学

Chomsky's Universal Grammar: An Introduction (Third Edition)
《乔姆斯基的普遍语法教程（第三版）》
　　V. J. Cook & Mark Newson

Syntax: A Generative Introduction (Fourth Edition)
《句法学：生成语法导论（第四版）》
　　Andrew Carnie

——Testing 语言测试

Assessing the Language of Young Learners
《少儿和青少年的语言测评》
   Angela Hasselgreen & Gwendydd Caudwell

Designing Listening Tests: A Practical Approach
《英语听力测试设计指导》
   Rita Green

Language Testing and Validation: An Evidence-Based Approach
《语言测试与效度验证：基于证据的研究方法》
   Cyril J. Weir

Second Language Pronunciation Assessment: Interdisciplinary Perspectives
《二语语音评测：跨学科视角》
   Talia Isaacs & Pavel Trofimovich

Statistical Analyses for Language Assessment
《语言测评中的统计分析》
   Lyle F. Bachman & Antony J. Kunnan

Writing English Language Tests (Second Edition)
《英语测试（第二版）》
   J. B. Heaton

——Text Linguistics 语篇语言学

The Language of Evaluation: Appraisal in English
《评估语言：英语评价系统》
   J. R. Martin & P. R. R. White

Metadiscourse
《元话语》
   Ken Hyland

——Translatology 翻译学

Border Crossings: Translation Studies and Other Disciplines
《跨越边界：翻译的跨学科研究》
   Yves Gambier & Luc van Doorslaer

In Other Words: A Coursebook on Translation (Third Edition)
《换言之：翻译教程（第三版）》
   Mona Baker

The Neurocognition of Translation and Interpreting
《口笔译的认知神经科学研究》
   Adolfo M. García